Sunset

Home Remodeling

ILLUSTRATED

By the Editors of Sunset Books and Sunset Magazine

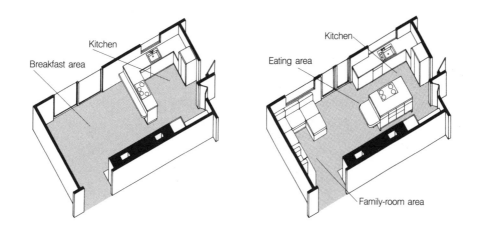

Sunset Publishing Corporation ■ **Menlo Park, California**

Book Editors
Scott Atkinson
Cynthia Overbeck Bix
Fran Feldman

Research & Text
Barbara J. Braasch
Pamela Evans
Steve Larson
Bill Roberts

Coordinating Editor
Suzanne Normand Mathison

Design
Joe di Chiarro

Illustrations
Bill Oetinger
Mark Pechenik
Rik Olson

Photo Stylist
JoAnn Masaoka

Photographers: **D. Gary Henry,** 39; **Jack McDowell,** 15 (top right), 34 (bottom); **Stephen Marley,** 10, 41, 42, 43, 44, 45, 46, 47, 48, 49, 50, 52, 53, 54, 55, 56, 57, 58, 59, 60, 61, 62, 63, 64, 65, 66, 67, 68, 69, 70, 71; **Tom Wyatt,** 15 (left and bottom right), 18, 23, 26, 31, 34 (top); **Tom Yee,** 72.

Cover: Knocking down several interior walls (garage, laundry room, bathroom, hallway, and kitchen) gave architect Victor Lee space to create this wide-open kitchen-dining arrangement—plus a family room, out of photo to left. Architect: Victor Lee. Cover design by Guild West Graphic Design. Photo styling by JoAnn Masaoka. Photographed by Stephen Marley.

Building Your Dream

Whether you've owned your house for years or for just weeks, no doubt you're well aware of the areas where it could stand improvement. Perhaps the closets are small and inadequate, or the traffic flows awkwardly from room to room. Maybe what your home needs is a spacious family room or a skylight that opens up the entry hall. Or it may be that you'd settle for an updated kitchen.

Remodeling can transform an ordinary house into your dream-come-true. Moreover, it offers the special advantage of tailoring your home improvements to suit your individual taste, needs, and budget.

But don't think that remodeling is an easy answer. It's a challenge to any homeowner. To help you through its complexities, we've prepared this manual. Whether you plan to do the work yourself or manage someone who will do it for you, this book will explain every step of the remodeling process.

To get your plans underway, we offer expert practical advice on design, as well as on how to work with professionals in the building field. We've also included a colorful gallery section of outstanding remodels to help you envision your remodeling dream. "Before" and "after" floor plans show at a glance how spatial reorganizations were achieved.

Further along, the book explains and illustrates in detail how to carry out such phases of remodeling as wiring for new light fixtures, installing a greenhouse window, putting up a partition wall, and much more.

For his technical assistance with this book, we are grateful to Geoff Alexander of Dovetail Systems. We also want to thank Kathy Oetinger for cutting color screens for the illustrations.

Editor, Sunset Books: Elizabeth L. Hogan

Second printing January 1991

Contents

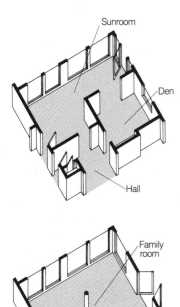

Planning & Design

Only a few years ago, people sold a house when they were tired of it or felt it no longer suited their life-style. Today, with the rising cost of land and construction, more people are taking a new look at their present house and planning how they can transform it into the home of their dreams. With a successful remodel, you can have a different house—without changing your address.

Reasons for remodeling are as individual as your life-style. At the top of the list are such needs as more space or more efficient use of existing space, an updated kitchen or bathroom, added storage, or more light.

Some houses become candidates for remodeling as the occupants' needs change: when children leave home, bedrooms may become settings for home offices or spaces to pursue new hobbies and interests.

Regardless of the reason or type of remodel, every renovation starts with careful planning. In this chapter, we'll show you how to evaluate the home you already have and analyze what you want. Next, we present detailed information on basic design elements, from different types of lighting to bathroom and kitchen layout and design. Finally, we spell out how to choose—and work with—professionals.

When you're ready to start work, turn to the how-to section beginning on page 82 for specific construction information.

4

Remodeling Approaches

Does your home no longer fit the life-style of your family? Is your bathroom or kitchen badly in need of a facelift? Do you yearn for additional storage space, more light, or larger rooms? The reasons for remodeling are as varied as the actual solutions themselves. But before you can determine the best course of action for you and your family, it's helpful to consider your options.

Updating existing space

One of the easiest—and most instantly gratifying—ways to improve your home is updating. Replacing the wallpaper in the kitchen, adding a new light fixture, and putting down a new, more durable floor covering, for example, can give a tired room a bright, fresh look, as well as make it more efficient.

Though it won't solve underlying problems with a basic floor plan or add to the available space, this type of remodel is the easiest for a novice and will often do as much for a dreary room as rearranging the walls—at half the cost.

Redefining space

In contrast to a simple update, reassigning interior space allows you to alter your home's floor plan to make the space you already have more efficient and usable.

Adding a wall to divide a large space, for example, gives you two separate living areas instead of one. Conversely, taking down a wall or opening up a ceiling brings in light and contributes a new feeling of spaciousness.

Another way to gain more space without pushing out any exterior walls is to add a bay or greenhouse window. Such a unit can often replace an existing window, or it can be installed where no opening existed before.

Room conversions

If an interior redesign doesn't solve your problem, try thinking about your house in a new way. Look up, down, and around—it's possible that at least some of the space you need already exists and can easily be converted to a new use.

Your home may be hiding usable space in areas already under ceiling or roof, some with walls and possibly even a floor. The three most obvious choices are the attic, basement, and garage. There may be others, too.

Hillside homes often have substantial crawlspaces beneath the floor, perhaps reaching minimum ceiling height as the grade falls away. Two other traditional—and valuable—sources of space are porches and carports.

Remodeling: Three Ways to Go

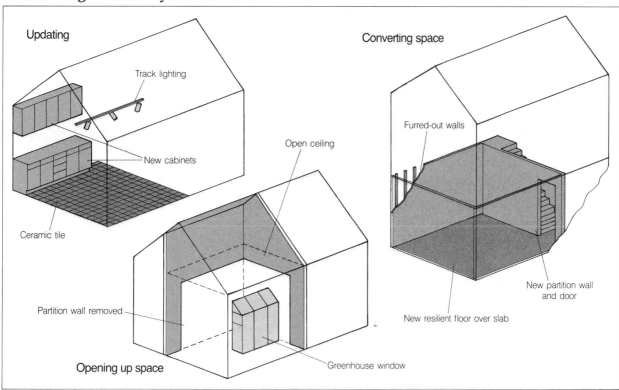

Fig. 1

Taking Stock

Well-planned and carefully carried through, remodeling a home can be a personally satisfying activity and can also prove to be a good investment. But more significantly, it can meet many of your most important living needs.

To plan an effective remodel, you'll need to become acquainted with your house in its present form—both its good points and its problems. Though making lists and drawing floor plans of your present structure may seem time-consuming, the knowledge you gain now will save you time and money later on.

Getting to know your house

How does your house work for you? Chances are, you've already made observations about your home, such as the need for more light in your living room or your desire for a more modern-looking bathroom. Often, however, you can't immediately recall all its shortcomings. Nor are you thoroughly familiar with where its pipes and wires are hidden, or where the floor and ceiling joists are located.

Whether you plan to do the work yourself or you need professional help, the following steps will help you evaluate your remodeling goals.

Your home's balance sheet. To make a permanent record of your home's assets and liabilities, keep a clipboard and paper in a convenient location, such as the kitchen. Use one side of the paper for things you like or would like to have, the other for things you don't like.

Each time you or another member of the family has a thought about the house, jot it down. Perhaps you dislike the way mail piles up on the kitchen counter, or you wish you had a permanent place to store the ironing board. Don't hesitate to list everything that comes to mind, no matter how small.

Don't try to be orderly about your impressions; just jot them down. You can worry later about the costs of accomplishing your objectives. At this point, it's not necessary to attempt to solve the negatives you list.

Keep your list for about a week; then set it aside for later use.

Mapping your house. By now you've probably been able to identify the areas of your home that are candidates for remodeling. The next step is to map those areas. Your goal is to produce a rough representation of the location of the walls and the rooms they enclose.

Using a tape measure, pencil, and ¼-inch-square graph paper (make each square represent a foot), draw the interior features of the areas you want to remodel. Include any plumbing or electrical fixtures, appliances, windows, and doors, as well as switches and receptacles. For an illustration of a typical floor plan, see **Fig. 2** (upper left).

It's not necessary to be too precise. Also, don't be concerned with exterior details unless they're extensions of interior space, such as a deck.

If all you plan to do is update a bathroom or add storage space to a bedroom, you probably won't need much more information than what you've just drawn. But if you're thinking of something more extensive, such as converting your attic to living space or opening up the ceiling in the living room, knowing the locations of such structural elements as bearing walls, floor and ceiling joists, electrical cables, and heating ducts may be crucial.

Beginning on page 73, you'll find a detailed look at how your house works. That information will help you identify the major structural components of your house.

If possible, climb into your attic to map the location of joists, wires, and pipes (see **Fig. 2,** center). Don overalls, arm yourself with a good flashlight, and bring a copy of your floor plan with you. You don't have to identify every wire and pipe; simply draw in those that are visible above the insulation.

If necessary, go into your basement or crawlspace and repeat the process on another copy of your floor plan to map floor joists and utility runs below the floor.

Identifying your goals

Often, compiling a list of what's good and bad about your house and how it could be better, then making specific notes about everything can help you pinpoint what you want to change; you can then address each concern as you plan your remodel. Even though your budget may preclude making every improvement, it's best to bring them all up at this time.

Room use. In the areas you want to remodel, analyze how each room is used. Take a few minutes each day for a full week to review the varied activities taking place there, both during the day and in the evening.

Note on a copy of your floor plan any conflicts that may have occurred between users of a certain space. Are the children doing their homework in the same room where the TV is in use? Are two cooks crowded into the kitchen at the same time? You may also want to identify any area that appears to be underutilized. (For an example of a room-use analysis, see **Fig. 2,** lower right.)

Traffic patterns. If circulation seems to be a problem in your home, record the bottlenecks on the same floor plan as room use. It's impossible to be completely accurate, but you may be able to get an idea of how efficiently rooms are connected and what rooms are used in conjunction with others. If hallways are too narrow, for example, or constant traffic through the kitchen is distracting, be sure to note it on your plan.

Other considerations. It's easy to overlook many factors that contribute to your comfort. Some of the categories that follow may already be on your list. If not, mark a floor plan with any reactions.

Light, both natural and artificial, has a tremendous influence on how you feel about a room, as well as how you feel *in* the room. Too little light is often a problem; too much light, such as a west-facing room in the path of the afternoon sun, can be just as unwelcome.

When you analyze lighting, keep in mind the type of activity that takes place in the room, the time of day it occurs, and what specific kind of lighting is required for each task. You may also want to note on the perimeter of your floor plan the position of the sun at various times of the day.

Ventilation can also be categorized as natural (windows, doors, and opening skylights) or artificial (range hoods and fans). Besides bathrooms and kitchens, don't forget to consider rooms that heat up during the day or a room used for hobbies.

Heating, plumbing, and electrical needs should be assessed. Likely candidates for improvement include rooms that are so far from the furnace that they never quite get warm

Mapping Your Remodel

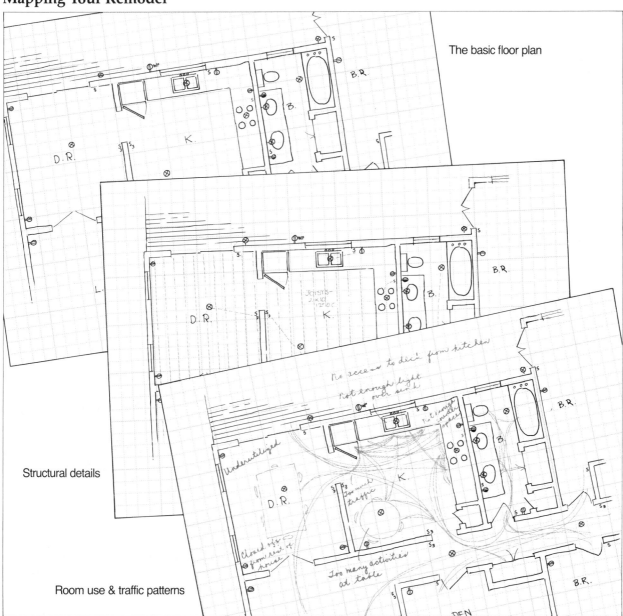

Fig. 2. A basic floor plan *(upper left) is a handy remodeling tool. Make several copies and use them to record such details as structural framing and wires (center) and room use and traffic patterns (lower right).*

... *taking stock*

in winter, light switches that are inconveniently located, and areas where a shortage of receptacles produces a viper pit of extension cords.

■ **Energy** concerns, such as a room that has no insulation or windows that are drafty or need curtains, shades, or shutters to block the sun, are important to note.

■ **Privacy** affects your feelings about a room. Think about areas where you feel invaded by sound or physical intrusion. These can range from wanting to close off a messy kitchen when company drops by to keeping stereo sound out of your home office.

■ **Aesthetic** considerations may already appear on your list. If not, note them on your floor plan. If, for example, your kitchen cabinets are in poor condition, your bathroom wallpaper is peeling, or you simply don't like the color of your old carpeting, record your comments.

Developing your design

Once you've recorded all your observations and identified the areas you want to remodel, you're ready to turn these statements into a positive course of action. This will give you a complete picture of desired improvements from which you can formulate a design.

Making a wish list. Using another copy of your floor plan, translate all your research into a "wish list."

If, for example, you've criticized your kitchen for having insufficient natural light, you may want to write "more natural light—add skylight or bigger windows" on your floor plan. If you feel isolated when you're preparing meals, perhaps you'd write "make a pass-through" or "enlarge doorway." Follow this procedure with each item on your list. **Fig. 3** shows how such a plan might look.

Don't be concerned if a solution isn't readily apparent or if all the elements don't seem to fit together; that comes later.

Looking ahead. Examine your wish list not only in light of your present life-style, but also in terms of whether it will meet your family's needs in the future. If the number of people living in the house is apt to increase or decrease over the next few years, your plans for certain rooms will be affected.

Even if numbers don't change, circumstances often do. Consider how your children's needs will evolve over the years. Also think about the adults in the family: if anyone joins the work force, retires from it, or shifts some or all of their working environment to your home, it can have a major impact on your living conditions.

Finally, remodel with the goal of meeting the needs of your family, not for some vague notion of improving your house for resale. Then, once the work is completed, you'll be able to enjoy the changes you've made.

Choosing design elements. Once you've finalized your wish list, you can begin thinking about specific design choices, such as types of flooring, colors and textures, window and door styles, and light fixtures. For valuable guidelines on all the basic design elements, plus specific suggestions for kitchens, baths, and attic, basement, and garage conversions, see pages 9–34.

You may also want to check out other sources for specific design and product ideas. Here are some suggestions.

■ **Home design books and magazines** provide the easiest way to become familiar with the widest display of decor. Start a file of pages clipped from magazines featuring colors, materials, fixtures, and appliances you like.

■ **Designer showrooms** and home improvement centers are good places to evaluate the latest styles.

■ **Open houses** often provide a wealth of remodeling and redecorating ideas, as do the homes of friends who have remodeled.

Compiling the Data

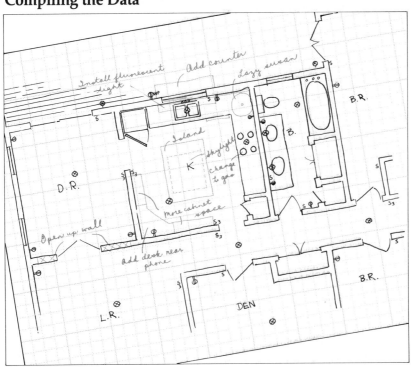

Fig. 3. The composite floor plan *is the end result of all the pluses and minuses you've recorded. Use this "wish list" to help you shop and plan.*

Lighting

The essential ingredient in planning lighting is simple common sense—determining where light is wanted and needed and then putting it there with economy and flair.

Usually, you can achieve a pleasing level and balance by bringing in natural light through windows, doors, and skylights and supplementing it with artificial light from fixed and movable light fixtures.

When you drew up your floor plan, you probably thought about how and where to bring in natural light and where to locate light fixtures. For specific information on window and skylight choices and placement, see pages 12–13. Below are general lighting principles, as well as design guidelines for choosing light fixtures.

Types of light

One kind of lighting eases visual tasks like reading or sewing. Another kind creates a soothing, relaxed environment. Still a different lighting is required for dramatic effects.

Task lighting. This type of lighting illuminates a particular area where a concentrated visual activity—such as reading or preparing food—takes place. Task lighting requires a greater degree of contrast, measured not only in intensity, but also in quality and direction. You can achieve task lighting with both natural and artificial light sources.

Ambient lighting. Ambient lighting is the less concentrated, less intense light required for watching television or navigating safely down a hallway. Lighting for such uses depends less on direct light than on reflected light from walls, ceiling, or mirrors. When the walls and ceiling—and skylight shaft, if you have one—are painted in a light, nonglossy color, they become sec-

ondary light sources that spread the light evenly over an area.

Accent lighting. This type consists largely of directional light. Primarily decorative, accent lighting focuses attention on artwork, highlights architectural features, or sets a mood.

Lighting design elements

The selection and placement of artificial light sources require planning. The type of activities carried on in each room, the light sources and features you want, and the general amount of light needed in each location are all factors in determining a lighting plan.

Lighting for active living. Along with design factors, the activities that take place in each living area play an important part in determining your lighting needs.

Some areas—including hallways, stairs, entries, closets, laundry areas, and workshops—host only one type of activity. These are the simplest to plan for; often, one level of light and one set of fixtures are sufficient.

Multiple-use areas, such as family rooms, living rooms, and combination kitchen-dining rooms, are more of a challenge. Today's family room may be the site of such diverse activities as television viewing, sewing, entertaining, and reading.

The light levels required for these activities range from very soft ambient light to strong directional task lighting. And just as all those activities aren't likely to be going on at the same time, you probably won't want to have all the room's specialized lights on at the same time. What you'll need is a variety of light levels, sources, and controls.

Light sources. Incandescent and fluorescent fixtures are the two main sources of artificial home lighting. Either can be used for both general and task lighting. Several factors may affect your choice: lumens, or light output; wattage, or the amount of energy used; life expectancy; and aesthetics.

Though incandescent lighting provides a warmer ambience, it also generates a lot of heat. Fluorescent lighting operates at a lower temperature and is more energy efficient.

If the "cold" look of most fluorescent lighting bothers you, look for "incandescent/fluorescent" tubes, designed to produce a much more pleasing tone.

How much light do you need?

Comfortable light levels are a matter of individual preference. Some people who work in brightly lighted offices grow accustomed to that kind of environment and want the same level of light in their homes. Others feel more relaxed in relatively low light levels, preferring to illuminate primarily the area in which they're reading or working.

With the present concern for energy conservation, the trend now is toward providing bright lighting in task areas, with surroundings more softly lit.

It's also a good idea to include dimmers and timers in your lighting plan. By reducing the electrical current consumed, solid-state dimmers save energy and extend the life of bulbs.

Light fixtures: types & styles

Once you've decided on the amount and location of the lighting you need, you're ready to look for fixtures that provide exactly what you want. All lighting systems include fixtures that give strong directional light, general diffused light, or a combination. Directional fixtures throw the light from the fixture to the task or display area. Diffused fixtures, on the other hand, spread light freely.

Keep in mind as you plan that installing light fixtures where none existed before may mean extending wires, adding new switches or receptacles, or perhaps even adding a new circuit.

Fixtures may be movable, surface-mounted, or recessed. Within each category there's a wide range of

Large gable window *and side-wall clerestories combine to balance the light in this remodeled living room. Light passing through the room brightens the roofed patio just outside the French doors. New raised ceiling made the clerestories possible—and necessary for illumination. Design: MLA/Architects.*

... *lighting*

styles available. **Fig. 4** shows some examples.

Movable. Table lamps, floor lamps, and such small specialty lamps as clip-ons, high-intensity lamps, and mini-reflector spotlights are easy to buy, easy to change, and easy to take along if you move. As decorative tools, they can add individuality and style to your room. The height of the shade and the height of the bulb within the shade affect the circle of light: light is spread farther when the bulb is set low in the shade.

Surface-mounted. Installed on walls or ceilings, surface-mounted fixtures are integral to most home lighting designs.

 Track lighting is versatile and easy to install. Available in varying lengths, tracks are really electrical lines extended from receptacles or hooked up directly to housing boxes. Because tracks can accommodate hanging lamps, fluorescent tubes, and special low-voltage spots in addition to theatrical, high-tech, and traditional-style fixtures, you can use them in a variety of lighting situations. For safety, avoid track lighting in wet areas.

■ **Chandeliers and pendant fixtures,** offering task and/or ambient light, add sparkle and style in high-ceilinged entries and above dining and game tables. If used over a table, the fixture should be at least 12 inches narrower than the width of the table to prevent collisions. Hanging it about 30 inches above the table surface helps avoid glare.

■ **Ceiling and wall fixtures** provide general illumination in traffic areas such as entries and hallways, where safety is a consideration. In kitchens, bathrooms, and workshops, combine ceiling fixtures with task lighting for best results.

Recessed ceiling fixtures. Two popular types are recessed downlights and recessed ceiling panels.

A Gallery of Light Fixtures

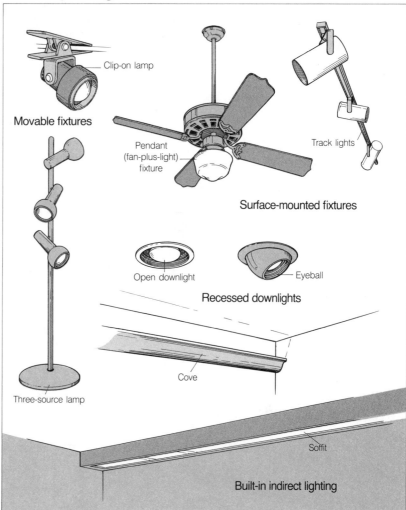

Fig. 4

Both offer illumination without the intrusion of a visible fixture.

Basically a dome with a light bulb inside, a recessed downlight is particularly effective in a room with a low ceiling and sleek lines.

When used over sinks and kitchen countertops, an open downlight with a glare-cutting baffle spreads a strong task light over work surfaces. Equipped as a wall-washer fixture, a recessed downlight throws light onto a nearby wall; a series of such fixtures can be used for even, balanced lighting of a wall of artwork or bookcases. An adjustable eyeball fixture highlights objects on a wall.

Recessed ceiling panels, designed to fit between ceiling joists, often stand in for surface-mounted fixtures in kitchens and home offices. Some take the place of panels or tiles in a suspended ceiling.

Built-in indirect lighting. Coves, cornices, valances, wall brackets, and soffits allow light to spill out around them. Coves direct light upward onto the ceiling; cornices spread light below. Used over windows, valances send light both up to the ceiling and down over draperies. Wall brackets spread light both up and down and can be used to highlight artwork or to provide ambient light in living areas. Soffits, used over work areas, throw a strong light directly below.

Windows & Skylights

Because they're such important sources of light and ventilation, windows and skylights are popular remodeling features. Without moving a wall or adding on any space, such an opening brings in natural light and makes your living area appear brighter, larger, and cheerier. The information below will help you choose windows and skylights.

Choosing windows

Windows provide light, view, and ventilation; they also can create a sense of space and act as passive solar devices. For a look at some different styles, see **Fig. 5.**

Basic window styles. At first glance, windows may look very different because of the variety of sizes, shapes, and muntin arrangements. But most windows fall into one of four basic categories—sliding, swinging, fixed, or rotary.

■ **Sliding** windows move either in horizontal or, as with the double-hung type, in vertical tracks. Since sliding sashes generally seal more tightly than swinging ones, they're good for harsh climates; but they're not as suitable for ventilation because only half the window can be opened at a time.

■ **Swinging** windows, which include the popular casements, have sashes that swing outward. Because they're easy to operate, they're particularly good for hard-to-reach areas.

■ **Fixed** windows are sold alone or in combination with windows with movable sashes. Traditionally glazed with a single large pane of glass, fixed picture windows are now available with muntins.

■ **Rotary** windows have sashes that rotate on pivots on each side of the frame. Some are designed to be installed in sloping surfaces, such as the walls of a finished attic.

Special designs. Remodeling plans often call for special window shapes and sizes. Many are available ready-made.

■ **Bay** windows project from the wall, adding space to the interior, providing a place to enjoy the outside, and enhancing the view. A bay window has a fixed center window flanked by two opening windows attached at an angle. Variations include *bow* windows, which have more than three sections; *oriels,* which project from the upper story

A Selection of Window Types

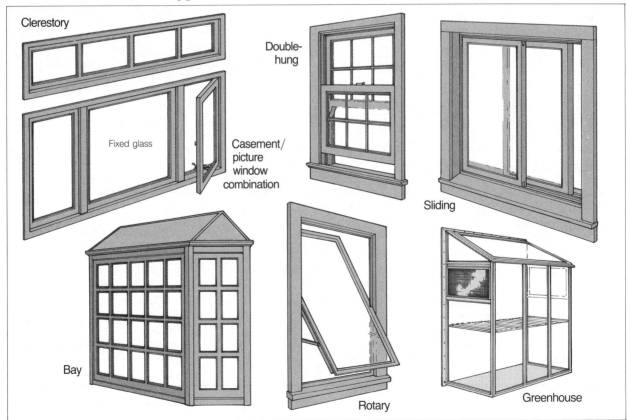

Clerestory

Fixed glass

Casement/ picture window combination

Bay

Double-hung

Rotary

Sliding

Greenhouse

Fig. 5

of a house; and *popouts,* custom-designed windows that cantilever from the wall of a house.

■ **Clerestory** windows, also known as ribbon windows, run along a wall near the ceiling. These windows often have fixed glass, though some may have sliding or hinged sashes.

■ **Cathedral** windows, large expanses of fixed glass, are used in rooms with very high ceilings. Admitting extra light and view, they generally follow the slope of the roof.

■ **Greenhouse** windows, popular in kitchen and bathroom remodels, are relatively small baylike units with glass walls and a glass roof. Designed to fit standard-size window openings, they provide a bright environment for growing plants, as well as capturing more light and a wider view than an ordinary window.

Materials. Windows may be wood, aluminum, vinyl, or steel, or a combination. Because wood is a good insulator, condensation isn't a problem, but regular maintenance is essential; also, wood can shrink and swell. Vinyl- or aluminum-clad wood windows require less maintenance than all-wood types.

Aluminum windows, though more durable than wood, can have a problem with condensation unless they're insulated. Vinyl windows, relatively new to the market, have excellent weathering resistance and are maintenance-free. Steel windows, seldom used in homes because of their expense, must be equipped with a thermal break to reduce problems with condensation.

Energy considerations. Typically, windows are either single or double glazed. Double glazing (two panes separated by a moisture-free air space) has a 95 percent higher resistance to heat flow than single glazing. In very cold climates, you may even want to consider triple glazing.

Glass with a reflective surface or a metalized polyester film (which can be applied to already installed windows) helps with sun control. The reflective sheen bounces back as much as 75 percent of the sun's heat.

Adding a skylight

A striking accent in any room, a skylight adds light, views, and, in some cases, ventilation without affecting privacy or taking up any wall space. When insulated and properly oriented to take advantage of the sun's heat, a skylight can also help to warm your house in winter.

Skylight design. Though you can have a skylight custom-made to fit a special situation, the most economical and usually the most reliable skylight is a prefabricated unit. Manufacturers offer skylights in an assortment of shapes and sizes. Several examples are shown in **Fig 6.**

Skylights with flat surfaces can be glazed with glass or plastic. Domed skylights are always glazed with some type of plastic, a material that molds easily into complex shapes. Use double glazing for energy conservation.

Some models can be opened to allow for ventilation, an advantage if you live in a warm climate; most open to about 45° and are equipped with insect screens.

Planning constraints. The location of framing members or proximity to a load-bearing wall may prevent you from placing the skylight where you want it. If you have easy access to your attic, check for potential problems in placement.

If there's an attic or crawlspace between the ceiling and the roof, you'll need a light shaft to direct the light through the attic to the room below. The longer the light shaft, the larger the skylight must be to achieve the same level of lighting on a given area. The light shaft may be straight, angled, or splayed.

An Array of Skylights

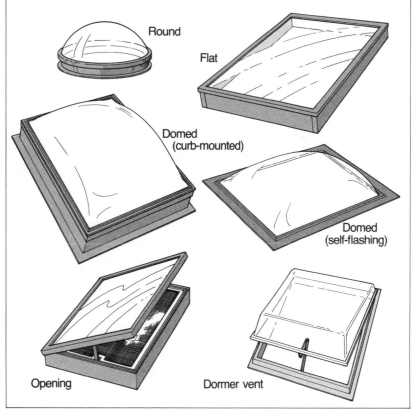

Round

Flat

Domed (curb-mounted)

Domed (self-flashing)

Opening

Dormer vent

Fig. 6

Flooring Choices

No matter what your remodeling situation, there's sure to be a flooring material that both complements your interior design and meets your needs. For help, study the design and material guidelines below. Also, it's a good idea to visit flooring dealers, home improvement centers, or flooring material suppliers; most dealers are happy to provide samples so you can see how they look in your home.

Planning guidelines

Confused by the array of flooring types available today? Here are some guidelines to keep in mind as you're making your selection.

■ **Aesthetics.** The flooring material's design, texture, even the way it feels underfoot can communicate the mood and style of a room. An area carpeted in a low, thick plush becomes a warm and inviting gathering place. A room laid with bold masonry blocks can appear to bring the outdoors into the house. Avoid designs, colors, or patterns that you may tire of quickly.

■ **Wear.** Determine the kind and amount of traffic the flooring is expected to bear. For high-traffic areas, such as hallways, entryways, kitchens, and bathrooms, select the most durable materials you can find. Areas that receive less wear can be covered with less rugged grades.

■ **Cost.** All the standard flooring materials come in various grades, with cost directly related to quality. A good rule of thumb is to install the best quality you can afford.

■ **Comfort.** Some flooring materials will be softer underfoot than others. If you object to a cold, hard surface, don't use ceramic tile or masonry.

Wood or resilient flooring provides a less firm surface. Softest of all is carpeting.

■ **Noise.** Soft flooring materials, such as vinyl, rubber, and carpeting, deaden sound. Wood, ceramic tile, and masonry surfaces tend to reflect sound rather than absorb it.

■ **Safety.** Avoid slippery finishes whenever possible. In kitchens and bathrooms, don't use flooring that becomes slick when damp. Loose rugs laid on hardwood floors should have nonskid backings or pads.

Flooring materials

Understanding the basic characteristics of the various flooring materials and how they can be used will help you make your decision.

Wood. A traditional flooring material, wood remains popular today because of its warm, natural look and its resiliency and long life—advantages that offset its high original cost. Such floors are usually made from hardwoods. The hardwood that's most commonly used today is oak; maple, birch, and beech are also available but are found much less often. One popular softwood choice for flooring is vertical-grain fir.

Almost all wood flooring can be classified into three basic types—*strip*, composed of narrow tongue-and-groove boards laid in random lengths; *plank*, tongue-and-groove boards produced in various widths and random lengths; and *wood tile*, wood flooring laid in blocks or squares, often in a parquet pattern.

Wood flooring may be purchased with a factory-applied finish or unfinished for sanding and finishing in place. When properly sealed, wood floors resist stains, scuffs, and scratches; if worn, they can be refinished. You'll need a very carefully prepared subfloor and a moisture-free environment.

Resilient. The development of resins and synthetics has created a family of floor coverings called re-

silient flooring. Generally made from solid vinyl, rubber, or polyurethane, they're flexible, moisture- and stain-resistant, easy to install, and simple to maintain. Another advantage is the seemingly endless variety of colors, textures, patterns, and styles available.

Note, however, that resilient flooring is relatively soft, making it vulnerable to dents and tears. Often, though, such damage can be repaired.

Ceramic tile. Made from hard-fired slabs of clay, ceramic tile is available in dozens of patterns, colors, shapes, and finishes. Its durability, easy upkeep, and attractiveness are definite advantages, but the surface is very hard and reflects noise.

Tiles are usually classified as *quarry tile*, commonly unglazed red-clay tiles that are rough and water-resistant; *pavers*, rugged unglazed tiles in earthtone shades; and *glazed tile*, available in glossy, matte, or textured finishes and in many colors.

Masonry. Used for centuries, masonry materials are even more practical flooring choices today, thanks to the development of sealers and finishes. Easy to maintain, masonry flooring is also waterproof and virtually indestructible. You'll need a structurally strong subfloor underneath.

Stone masonry flooring—marble, slate, limestone, granite, or flagstone—is usually installed only in entryways, kitchens, and bathrooms, or used as decorative flooring around fireplaces. Brick, a relatively inexpensive type of masonry, is becoming an increasingly popular choice for interiors. Its mass and heat-retaining property make it ideal for passive solar designs.

Carpeting. Like resilient flooring, carpeting is available in a huge array of colors, styles, and materials, with prices that vary widely. Though wool and other natural fibers are still popular, synthetics such as nylon, acrylic, and polyester dominate the market because of their low price, easy maintenance, and durability.

Flooring combination *takes advantage of each material's strengths: sheet vinyl for easy upkeep and comfort underfoot, ceramic tile for moisture protection in the plant bay. Tilelike vinyl pattern harmonizes with the real thing.*

At first glance, *this oak floor appears to be made from random-size planks. Actually, it's more economical strip flooring, routed at intervals of two to four strips. Architect: Peter C. Rodi / Designbank.*

Elegant geometry *is created by this juxtaposition of two ceramic tile patterns. White tiles mate perfectly with the staggered array of blue tiles marching resolutely to the tub. Architect: William B. Remick.*

Walls, Ceilings & Doors

Walls divide interior space; ceilings give rooms a sense of height or confinement; doors lead from one space to another. The way these boundaries are placed and treated gives your house its particular character and style.

Wall coverings & design

When you change your walls you alter a room dramatically. Add the warm luster of solid board paneling and the room becomes a serene hideaway for reading and relaxing. Remove an interior wall and two small rooms become one large one. Add a wall where none existed before and a new room is created.

Wall coverings. Depending on the finished look you want, you'll probably choose between two different materials—gypsum wallboard and paneling.

■ **Gypsum wallboard,** by far the most widely used, can be both a finishing material and a base for other coverings. Once installed and taped, it's often textured with a texturing compound in any of a variety of ways and then painted. Choose the water-resistant type for use in tub surrounds and other damp areas.

Wall coverings that use wallboard as a base include simulated brick, ceramic tile, glass, fabric, and wallpaper. Wainscoting combines wallboard with wood or other materials. Also available is wallboard predecorated with a vinyl covering.

■ **Paneling** is another popular wall covering. It's durable, easy to install, and requires no maintenance. The two most common types are sheet and solid board paneling. Generally, both can be applied over new stud walls, over existing walls that aren't bumpy or crooked, or over furring strips.

Sheet paneling may be made from plywood, hardboard, or plastic laminate. Plywood paneling comes unfinished, prefinished, or vinyl-faced. Many natural and decorator finishes are available. You can also find hardboard products that simulate brick, stone, wood, marble, or tile.

Because of its texture, natural fragrance, and subtle variations in color and grain, solid board paneling is particularly warm and inviting. Hardwoods commonly used for the boards include birch, maple, teak, and walnut. Popular softwoods are cedar, fir, pine, and redwood.

Generally, the edges of the boards are milled to overlap or interlock. No matter what the milling, boards may be graded "clear" for a smooth, formal appearance or "knotty" for a rough, informal look.

Structural considerations. Removing or adding a wall can have an even more dramatic impact on your home than changing the wall covering. But remember that when you move walls around, you're affecting your home's basic structure. If you're removing a bearing wall, for example, you'll have to add a beam over the opening and support it with posts on either side.

Note also that the walls of your house enclose and provide pathways for its mechanical systems—plumbing pipes, electrical wires, and heating ducts. If you remove even a small wall, you may need to reroute those systems.

But a wall doesn't have to be eliminated altogether. Consider removing just the top half to open up a partial view of an adjoining room and gain a feeling of spaciousness. Half-walls can direct and separate foot traffic, block drafts, and provide a backdrop for furniture almost as effectively as a wall that runs from floor to ceiling.

Ceiling treatments

Ceilings are often overlooked when remodeling ideas are being considered. But an unusual ceiling treatment can add a strong note of drama to an area or room. Think of your ceiling as another decorative element of your room.

Ceiling materials. Though your choices of coverings for ceilings may be more limited than those for walls, you can still make a major design statement by choosing a particular material.

■ **Gypsum wallboard** is today's standard, though the large, heavy panels are somewhat awkward to install. Wallboard not only is inexpensive but also accepts paint and surface textures well. Use a light-color paint in rooms used during the day; those used primarily at night become cozier with a darker ceiling. Wallpaper and fabric are also often used over wallboard.

■ **Ceiling tiles,** made from mineral and wood fibers, may be square or rectangular and are available in several decorative and acoustic styles. Easy to install, the tiles can be applied either directly to a ceiling that's in good condition or to furring strips nailed to ceiling joists.

■ **Suspended panel ceilings** consist of panels supported in a metal grid hanging from wires or hangers. Panels may be acoustic or decorative fiberboard, transparent, or translucent. Such a ceiling can effectively hide defects or any new wiring or pipes.

■ **Paneling,** both sheet and solid board, can be applied to ceilings as well as to walls (see at left).

Making structural changes. Removing the ceiling partially or entirely exposes the rafters above and opens a room to a new loftiness. However, taking out even a portion of a ceiling requires careful engineering to redistribute the roof's load. You'll also need to reroute any pipes, wires, or ducts running above the ceiling. It's best to consult an architect or structural engineer if you're contemplating such a design.

Door types & styles

Whether you choose a standard style or a one-of-a-kind model, the door you use can affect the mood of the room. Though there are many different designs from which to choose, some doors have special applications. Indoor and outdoor living areas, for example, are most often connected by *French* or *sliding* doors; *accordion,* or folding, doors allow you to temporarily close off one living area from another. For a look at some of the different styles of doors, see **Fig. 7.**

Modern manufactured doors come in two basic types: panel and flush. *Panel* doors consist of solid vertical stiles and horizontal rails, with filler panels in between. *Flush* doors, on the other hand, are built from thin face and back veneers—typically 1/8-inch plywood—attached to a solid or gridlike hollow core. Many different styles and finishes are available for either type of door.

Areas containing glass in a door are called lights. Safety hazard glass (tempered) is required for any light over 3 inches in diameter.

Exterior doors. Solid-core doors offer the most security and are often required by code. A wood door 3 feet wide or more should be at least 1¾ inches thick.

Weatherizing the top and bottom of the door, as well as its visible surfaces, is an important consideration. Be sure to apply weather stripping where necessary. A door clad with aluminum or vinyl minimizes maintenance of the exterior finish.

Front door intercoms and one-way peepholes allowing the person on the inside to see out provide extra security.

Interior doors. Doors used in the interior of your home are often the hollow-core type.

If space does not allow for a swinging door, consider bifold, pocket, or bypass sliding doors. A *bifold* door, which runs in a track, is hinged in the middle and folds out. A *pocket* door slides into a recess in the wall next to the opening. *Bypass sliding* doors, often used for closets, move past each other in tracks.

Fire doors may be required between any living space and the garage, or for closets containing a hot water heater or furnace. Check your local building code for specifics.

Typical Door Styles

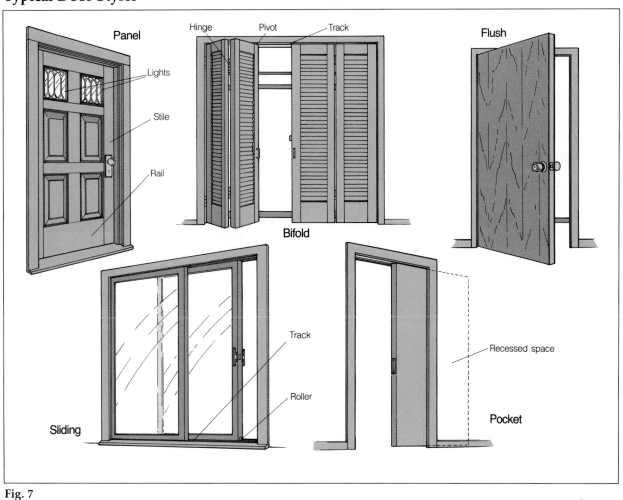

Fig. 7

Tailor-made wall system *accommodates both a music library and instruments that make music. At left, a vertical row of open shelves organizes sheet music for easy access. Standard bookshelves house stereo components, as well as records and books. As shown at right, bifold doors open to reveal a cavernous compartment for a cello. Design: John Kolkka.*

Storage

Finding room for all the things in our lives ranks high as a reason for remodeling. Clearing away clutter instantly provides more space. But where is it all to go? The challenge is twofold: making better use of existing space and combining it with creative solutions for additional storage.

First, you'll need to determine your needs and priorities. Take a look at each room in your house. If, for example, you love to cook, you'll need more than average space for utensils, special pans, and other equipment. If you plan a sewing room, you'll need storage space for supplies, as well as for your sewing machine and ironing board.

The second step is to choose the right kind of storage for your needs. The choices include built-ins, such as cabinets, drawers, and closets, large freestanding modular systems (available commercially), and small, movable storage units.

The last step is to decide where to put the additional storage. If you're creating new space in the course of remodeling, the choices may be obvious. But if you're staying within the confines of existing walls, you'll need to be a little more creative.

Look around carefully for any "wasted" space—over the washer and dryer, under the stairway, inside closets, in the basement, garage, or attic. Even consider installing shelves over windows and doors—they make eye-catching spaces to stow additional treasures.

Storage guidelines

No matter what type of storage you plan, follow these simple guidelines to maximize space and accessibility.

■ **Store frequently used items** between knee and eye level in the area where you use them most.

■ **Use closed storage** if you want to conceal clutter, open storage to display decorative articles or objects that need to be readily accessible.

■ **Design cabinets and shelves** to the user's height and reach (within reasonable limits).

■ **Customize** existing shelves and cabinets with such storage aids as door racks, turntables, drawer dividers, and pull-out shelves.

■ **For easy access,** arrange canned and packaged goods in a single row on a door rack or on shallow shelves.

Storage solutions

Storage solutions can be as creative as using the space between studs or designing shelving, cabinets, and closets that extend from wall to wall.

Plan your storage units carefully—their size, style, and arrangement will determine not only their usefulness but also how they blend in with their surroundings. Make sure they're not so big as to overwhelm the rest of the room, nor so small that they're relatively useless.

Inside-the-wall storage. Putting walls to work frees floor space. Have you ever thought of using the shallow space between the vertical 2 by 4 studs of a wall to add storage? Framing into a wall and extending to, or beyond, the wall on the other side can give you extra inches of precious storage space.

If you're planning to use just the width and depth between two studs (usually 3½ inches deep by 14½ inches wide), no extra support is necessary. But if your plans call for removing a stud to create a wider storage area, you'll need to add a horizontal header above to help bear the roof weight. (Check your local building code for information on the size header required.)

Shelving. The type of shelving you'll use will depend on the appearance you want, the load the shelves will bear, and the distance they'll span between supports. Shelves can be made from 1- or 2-by lumber, par-

ticleboard, hardwood, or glass. Support 1-by lumber every 32 inches for light loads, every 24 inches for medium loads (books, glasses, some audio equipment).

Most hardwoods and ¾-inch plywood will stay straight at 36 inches. For longer spans or such heavy loads as TVs and large stereo setups, use 2-by lumber.

Design the depth of your shelving according to what you plan to display. For books, you'll need shelves that are at least 8 inches deep; larger volumes may require 12 inches. TV and stereo units usually need 16 to 24 inches of depth.

Cabinets and drawers. Kitchen cabinets are typically built to standard dimensions, as shown in **Fig. 10** on page 25. Bathroom vanities are usually 32 inches high and 21 inches deep.

Wall systems, popular additions in nearly any room of the house, can be customized to meet your specific storage needs. Units often extend from floor to ceiling and combine cabinets and drawers with open shelving. Modular wall systems are available commercially, or you can design your own custom-built unit.

Visiting showrooms and home improvement centers will give you some idea of the materials, door and drawer styles, hardware options, and arrangements currently available.

Closets. Adding a built-in closet where none existed before can considerably increase your storage space. One option is to build a closet in a popout. Or, if you can afford to lose some floor space, you can simply add one inside existing walls. Such a closet can be a built-in unit made from plywood, like a wall-to-ceiling cabinet, or it can be framed and covered with wallboard or another wall covering of your choice.

Whichever type you choose, allow an inside depth of at least 26 inches. If you're planning a walk-in closet with rods on both sides, figure on 7 feet from side to side: 2 feet for each closet rod and 3 feet of clear space between rows.

Basic Design Principles

Integral to any remodeling project is interior design—the arrangement of all the interior elements, their shapes and sizes, and their colors. As you draw up your plans, keep the design guidelines outlined below in mind; they'll help ensure the aesthetic success of your remodel.

Line, shape & scale

Three keys to planning a balanced, visually pleasing design are line, shape, and scale. You'll need to consider each of these elements to achieve the effect you want.

Line—the dominant theme. A room can incorporate many different types of lines—vertical, horizontal, diagonal, curved, and angular—but often, one predominates and characterizes the design. Vertical lines lend a sense of height, horizontal lines add width, diagonals suggest movement, and curved and angular lines impart a feeling of grace and dynamism.

Repeating similar lines gives a room a sense of unity. Drawing elevation sketches of your walls, such as the one shown in **Fig. 8,** is the best way to consider the lines of your design. It's not necessary for everything to align perfectly, but the effect is far more pleasing if a number of elements do align—particularly the highest features in the room.

Depending on the shape and size of your room, you may want to emphasize or subdue certain lines to create a particular effect. For example, you can make a narrow room appear wider and more spacious by adding horizontal lines—rows of open shelves, tiles on a kitchen backsplash, or long towel bars in a bathroom.

Shape—a sense of harmony. Continuity and compatibility in shape also contribute to a unified design. This doesn't mean repeating the same shape throughout the room—carried too far, that becomes monotonous. Instead, even when the sizes of objects are different, their shapes can be similar or their arrangement balanced for an overall effect.

Study the shapes created by doorways, windows, stairs, cabinets, furniture, appliances, fixtures, and other elements in your room. Are these shapes different or is there a basic sense of harmony? Consider new ways to complement existing shapes or add compatible new ones.

Scale—everything in proportion. When the scale of a room's elements is in proportion to the overall size of the room, the design appears harmonious. A small kitchen, for instance, seems even smaller when fitted with large appliances and expanses of closed cabinets. Open shelves, large windows, and a simple design visually enlarge a room.

Wall cabinets that extend all the way up to a standard 8-foot ceiling can make a room appear top-heavy and small unless cabinet doors are divided into sections, with smaller units at the top. Reposition shelving so top shelves are relatively close together and shelves at the bottom are farther apart.

Consider the proportions of adjacent elements as well. Smaller objects arranged in a group help balance a larger item, making it less obtrusive.

Color, texture & pattern

The most intimidating element in design is also the most exciting—color. When you think of colors, consider both your personal preferences and the particular area you're remodeling. Though you may love a certain bold, bright color, living with it daily may be another matter.

Textures and patterns work like color in defining a room's space and

An Elevation Sketch

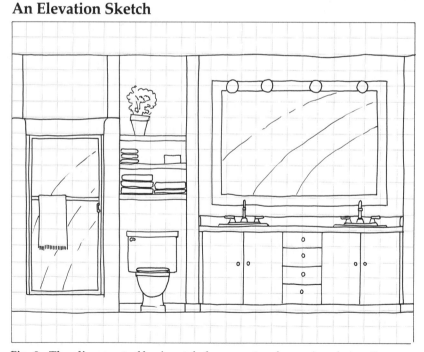

Fig. 8. The alignment of horizontal planes *creates a harmonious design. For example, the toilet tank top and vanity door tops are at the same height; the first shelf and the towel bar on the shower door are in alignment.*

style. The same color applied to contrasting textures can appear to differ in hue.

Thinking about color. In order to determine the most effective way to use color, you'll first need to understand the color wheel (see **Fig. 9**). From the primary colors of red, yellow, and blue come all the other colors, or hues. Mixing adjacent primary colors on the wheel creates the secondary colors—orange, green, and purple. Adjacent primary and secondary colors can then be mixed to create the tertiary colors.

Rarely is a color used exactly as it appears on a color wheel. Here are some terms to help you understand color gradations.

■ **Value** refers to a color's lightness or darkness—from white to black.

■ **Intensity** refers to a color's brightness or dullness; a pure color has the most intensity.

■ **Tints** are colors that have white added to them.

■ **Shades** are created by adding black to a hue.

■ **Tones** result from adding gray to a color.

Color schemes. How you choose to combine colors—your color scheme—helps to set the mood of the room.

■ **Monochromatic** color schemes (using different shades of one light color) are usually restful and serene.

■ **Contrasting** colors, on the other hand, add vibrancy and excitement to a design. A color scheme with contrasting colors may be too overpowering unless the tones of the colors are varied.

■ **Analogous** color schemes (using closely related colors) may provide more variety than monochromatic schemes; they typically include three to five hues of one primary color.

■ **Complementary** color schemes use hues directly opposite each other on the color wheel. The effect can often be dramatic. This use of color usually works best if one of the colors is used much more lavishly than the other.

Neutrals—white, black, gray, and beige—don't appear on the color wheel. They may be added to a particular color scheme without altering the basic color relationship, since they don't count as additional colors.

Designing with color. Skillful use of color weaves magic throughout a house, affecting how you perceive space and how you feel in that space.

A neutral color on walls, ceiling, and trim expands a small room visually; richer, warmer colors make a large space more intimate. Oranges, yellows, or colors with a red tone impart a feeling of warmth; blues, greens, or colors with a blue tone make an area seem cool.

Properly applied, color can accentuate or camouflage architectural features. If you want to highlight a special area, combine bold splashes of color and light. Subtle colors used

Hues, Tints, Shades & Tones

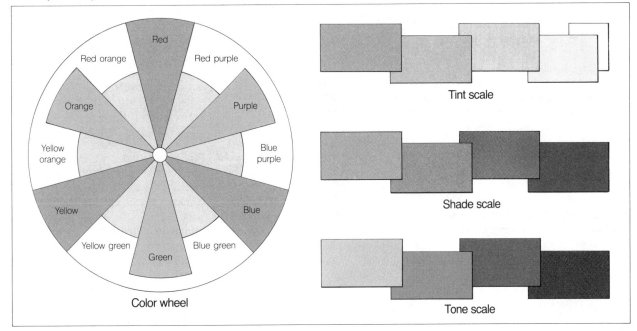

Fig. 9. The color wheel *(left) illustrates the relationship between primary, secondary, and tertiary colors. Color scales (right) show variations of hues: tints are made by adding white to hues, shades by adding black, and tones by adding gray.*

throughout a room can hide awkward details.

Many other variables, such as surfaces, textures, and surrounding colors, also affect color. For example, a color appears glossy on a hard, smooth surface; yet on a more absorbent surface, the same color looks duller.

As you narrow down your selections, make a sample board to see how your choices work together.

Texture and pattern. Rough textures absorb light and lend a feeling of informality. Smooth textures reflect light and suggest elegance or modernity.

Pattern choices must harmonize with the room's predominant style.

Though pattern is usually associated with wall coverings or upholstery, even such natural substances as wood and brick create patterns.

Though variety in textures and patterns adds interest, too much variety can be overwhelming. It's best to let a strong feature or dominating pattern be the focus of your design, choosing other surfaces to complement, not compete with, it.

SAFETY & SECURITY

Remodeling time presents a good opportunity to inspect and evaluate home safety and security systems. Walk around your house and garage, checking for security weaknesses; study your remodeling plans with the same thought in mind.

In some communities, the police will make a security inspection of your home and offer suggestions for improvements.

Safe entries
To secure your home against intruders and make it safe for guests, position bright outdoor lights near entries and low levels of light to outline paths and walkways. You may also want to attach lights to a time switch or a photoelectric cell that turns them on when someone passes through an invisible beam.

Alarm systems
Electronic alarm systems can be effective adjuncts to other safety measures. All systems incorporate three basic components: the alarm, a sensor that discovers the intrusion, and a control that engages the alarm.

Self-contained systems, such as those mounted on doors or plugged into a wall outlet, guard individual rooms. They're activated by motion detectors or by changes in air pressure incurred, for example, when a door or window is opened.

More elaborate systems, with separate entry sensors for each room, hidden alarms, and key- or code-activated controls, guard a complete house. They're usually connected to a security office or police station.

Heavy hardware
The flimsy construction of many door locks makes it easy to pick, jimmy, or break them. Securing your doors and windows with high-quality hardware and dead bolts or a self-locking dead latch discourages intruders.

To keep a sliding sash or door from being lifted out, insert three sheet metal screws, evenly spaced, into the groove of the upper track. Adjust the screws so they just fill the space between the groove and the top of the door or sash.

The easiest way to keep an inside panel from sliding is to drop a dowel or piece of metal tubing into the empty portion of the lower track. Cut the dowel or tubing ¼ inch shorter than the distance between the panel and the jamb. Manufactured track grips, metal stops that straddle the lower track, also secure inside panels.

A spring bolt lock has a pin that snaps through a hole drilled in the edge of the lower track and bottom of the sash. Use this lock on either inside or outside panels.

Window guards
Making window panes difficult to cut through or break strengthens the defense against intruders. Tempered glass, which crumbles rather than splinters when broken, is five times stronger than ordinary glass. Laminated glass (plastic laminate between two panels of glass) is even stronger.

Replacing glass with acrylic or polycarbonate makes the pane almost unbreakable, but plastic has some disadvantages. It scratches more easily, is more expensive, and may yellow after a few years.

You can buy wedge locks, key-operated cam latches, and pin locks to secure double-hung windows. The existing hardware on crank-operated casement windows is usually adequate to keep the windows closed, but you can buy cranks that lock.

Fire protection
Local codes may require that you install at least one early warning smoke detector in your home when you remodel. Be sure it's centrally located on the highest point of the ceiling near a hall serving the bedrooms. Consider installing heat detectors as well; they provide early warning of fires near hot water heaters or furnaces.

Fire extinguishers are particularly useful in or near the kitchen, the usual location of any flash fire.

Natural surfaces *in this master bathroom enhance the connection to the outdoors. Mirrored wall, strong vertical lines, and high ceiling enlarge the space. Sleek brass fittings and uncluttered design contribute to its cool, restful mood. Architect: Donald K. Olsen.*

Kitchen Design

Whether your ideal kitchen contains a wood stove and open shelves or is the epitome of sleek modernity, it's probably the most important room in the house, as well as the most expensive to equip. More elements—appliances, fixtures, plumbing, wiring, and cabinetry—fit into a given space in the kitchen than anywhere else in your home. Careful planning is essential.

Planning constraints

Before you can transform your existing kitchen into an ideal one, you'll need to consider a few facts about plumbing and wiring that may help you resolve layout decisions. Some alterations are simple and inexpensive; others are more complicated and costly. For example, if your kitchen is on a concrete slab and you want to extend plumbing or wiring to a kitchen island, you'll probably have to drill through the slab—an expensive proposition, especially if you have heating pipes running through the slab.

Electrical considerations. Requirements for electrical circuits serving a modern kitchen and dining area are prescribed by the National Electrical Code. Receptacles and switches for small appliances and the refrigerator must be served by at least two 20-amp circuits. Light fixtures are not connected to these circuits but share one or more 15-amp circuits.

If you're installing a dishwasher and/or garbage disposer, you may need a separate 20-amp circuit for each. Most electric ranges use a 50-amp, 120/240-volt major appliance circuit. Wall ovens and a separate cooktop may share a 50-amp circuit. Additionally, you'll need receptacles adjacent to every countertop and every 12 feet along a wall.

Depending on your present service capacity, you may just need to route a circuit or two; or you may have to add a new service entrance panel.

Plumbing and gas requirements. You'll need to make plumbing changes if you move your present sink and related appliances, plumb a sink into a new kitchen island, or add a new fixture, such as a second sink.

Extending supply pipes for new fixtures is a relatively easy job if you have access. If the proposed new fixture is close enough (by code) to the existing soil stack, you can probably use it to drain and vent the fixture. Otherwise, you'll need to add a branch drain and perhaps even a secondary stack.

If you plan to use an existing gas connection, the new range or cooktop must be within 6 feet of the shutoff valve.

Kitchen design & layout

Before you can work out the layout of your remodeled kitchen, you'll need to consider some important design guidelines.

Design considerations. Kitchen designers recommend basic guidelines for comfort and efficiency. **Fig. 10** on the facing page illustrates many of the major principles and suggests some minimum clearances. Of course, you don't need to adhere to all of these ideal conditions for your kitchen to work well for you.

■ **Four centers** are basic to most kitchens: cleanup, cooking, preparation or mixing, and cooling or food storage. Other more specialized areas—a baking or serving center, for example—can increase kitchen efficiency. In addition, you may want to include a planning/work center or an entertaining center with a second sink and small refrigerator.

■ **The work triangle,** formed by the sink, range, and refrigerator, should be located so the distance between any two of them (measured from center front to center front) is no less than 4 feet and no more than 6 to 9 feet, with the total of the sides of the triangle measuring no more than 26 feet. A greater distance means unnecessary walking; a shorter one means cramped work space.

Traffic should not intersect any of the legs of the triangle.

■ **Appliances** require different-size spaces, depending on make and model. For planning purposes, though, allow 36 inches for a refrigerator or double sink, 24 inches for a dishwasher or single sink, and 30 inches for a range or built-in cooktop.

The dishwasher should be on one side of the sink, with at least 20 inches of space in front for loading. Because a microwave oven takes up valuable work space, it probably shouldn't be placed on a counter. If you intend to use it mainly for thawing frozen foods or heating leftovers, it can be located near the refrigerator; if it's used mostly for main dishes, consider placing it near the cooking or mixing center.

■ **Plan heights of work surfaces** according to the heights of the cooks. Standard height is 36 inches—you'll have to make your own adjustment to standard base cabinets if you require a different height.

A surface 3 inches below elbow height is suitable for most tasks; however, tasks that require a downward force, such as chopping, mixing, or rolling dough, are more easily performed at a counter 6 or 7 inches below elbow level.

■ **Counter space** must be sufficient for each task. If you're right-handed, allot the largest amount of space to the right of the sink and a lesser amount on the left. Reverse the configuration if you're left-handed. If kitchen space is limited, you can let different functions share a counter; when combining work surfaces, choose the larger of the two minimum dimensions and add 18 inches.

The lengths of work surfaces will affect storage possibilities. Any space beneath the counters that is not taken up by an appliance will be available for cabinets or drawers.

■ **Small appliances,** equipment, tools, and supplies should be stored near the area where they're used. You'll save steps if dishes are stored in the cleanup center where they're washed, for example. The cleanup area should also include storage for cleaning supplies, dry foods such as onions and potatoes, foods initially prepared at the sink, and the utensils needed to cook those foods.

■ **Provide adequate clearance** in aisles and near eating areas. Between opposite work counters, allow at least 48 inches. Expand that clearance by an additional 6 to 16 inches if two or more people are likely to share the kitchen. If the dining table is near a passage, allow at least 32 inches for walking past a seated person. When your table is positioned away from passages, counters, or appliances, you'll need only 26 inches minimum clearance behind each seated person.

Laying out your kitchen. Though most kitchen layouts are similar to

Kitchen Planning at a Glance

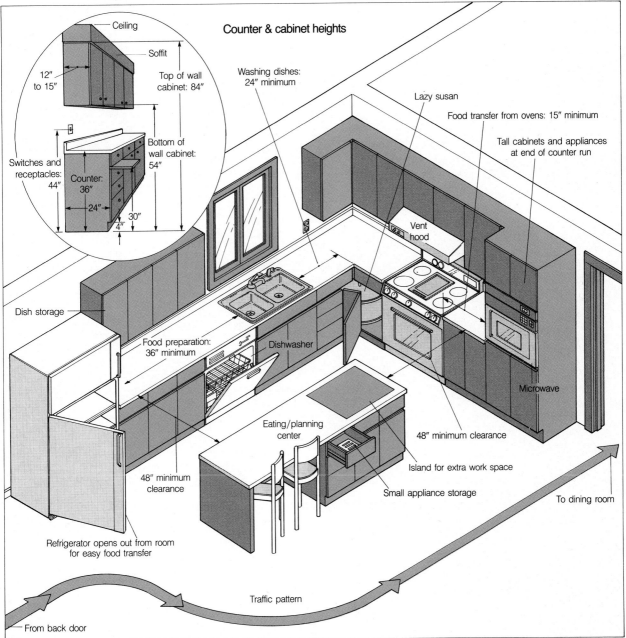

Fig. 10

Basic L-shaped kitchen plan *benefits from the addition of an island, which provides for separate work areas while maintaining a compact work triangle. The island also offers an alternate location for a cooktop or sink and helps direct traffic away from food preparation areas. Ample counter space provides plenty of room for a cook and several helpers. Design: European Kitchens & Baths.*

Sample Kitchen Layouts & Work Triangles

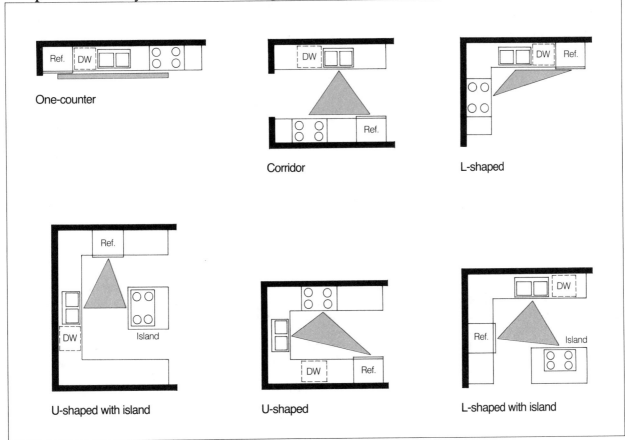

One-counter

Corridor

L-shaped

U-shaped with island

U-shaped

L-shaped with island

Fig. 11

the basic ones shown in **Fig. 11,** let the shape of your room and your own needs determine the final plan.

Using actual dimensions, if possible, make cutouts to scale of all major and minor appliances you'd like to use in your kitchen (indicate the location of door handles on the cutouts). Move the cutouts around on your floor plan until you find an arrangement you like.

In assigning space, decide where you'd like to perform what activities. If a window offers a pleasant view, would you rather enjoy it while eating or while washing dishes? Would you like to cook or prepare food on an island or peninsula? Imagine all the possibilities and then draw circles on the plan to represent the locations of different work areas.

Consider major or minor structural changes that would increase your options for locating activity centers. To help visualize how a proposed

change will affect the room, create a mock-up of the situation. Close a door, relocate a table, or set up an island, and go through the motions of working with the new arrangement.

When you're ready to block out work areas, use the standard counter depth of 24 inches. Match the longest surface with the most space-consuming chores. Add pull-out boards for additional work surfaces. Indicate the best positions for wall cabinets with a dotted line approximately halfway in from the lines representing work surfaces. Show any storage wall or walk-in pantry, too.

If you want an eating area in the kitchen, think about how you'll use it. Do you just want a simple counter for quick breakfasts or occasional meals? Or do you want a separate table for regular meals? If you're using a separate table, be sure to place it away from the traffic flow.

Special work or hobby areas can share space with the eating counter or kitchen table. Such an area can double as an office/menu-planning center. If there's a gourmet cook in your family, you may want to design entertainment, baking, pasta-making, or other specialized areas. If two people share cooking tasks, plan centers far enough away from the work triangle to keep the cooks from getting in each other's way.

Trace the work triangle and door openings, indicating the traffic flow. If the traffic must intersect the work triangle at any point, it's best to have it cross the path to the refrigerator.

To redirect traffic, try moving a door, angling a peninsula, or adding an island. Also check whether any appliance doors interfere with traffic.

When you've settled on the best layout for your kitchen, copy it down on a fresh copy of your floor plan.

Bathroom Design

A far cry from the strictly utilitarian room down the hall, today's sumptuous bathrooms often resemble spas, with whirlpool baths, saunas, and exercise equipment taking their place alongside the sink and toilet. Whether you're planning to expand your bathroom or you simply want to upgrade your fixtures, the information below will help you devise an efficient bathroom design.

Planning guidelines

Bathroom products are available in a huge array of colors, sizes, and shapes. Study the products to be sure of getting the ones that will work best for you. Also be aware of important plumbing, electrical, ventilation, and heating concerns. Here are some general guidelines to consider.

Choosing products and materials. When you shop for bathroom fixtures, tile, vanities, and light fixtures, consider function, durability, and aesthetic appeal as well as price. Ceramic tile, for example, is more expensive than some other wall coverings, but it requires minimum maintenance and can last a lifetime. Vanities with basins are more expensive than wall-hung basins, but vanities provide more storage space.

Materials that are good choices for the bathroom include glass, marble, glazed ceramic tile, plastic laminate, fiberglass-reinforced plastic, vitreous china, and porcelain-enameled steel and cast iron. Surfaces with lustrous finishes, such as glazed ceramic tile, are less likely to show water spots and splashes than glass and plastic laminate.

Using wood in a bathroom can pose a problem: untreated, wood will discolor, warp, stain, and decay if exposed to water. If you use wood, thoroughly protect it on all sides with a good sealer.

Construction considerations. Normally, you can move your sink a few inches with only minor plumbing changes. And your existing supply and drain lines can usually support a second sink. You can also extend existing supply and drain lines if the distance from the vent is less than the maximum distance allowed by code. If not, you'll have to install a secondary vent—a major undertaking.

If your bathroom has a wood floor with a crawlspace or basement underneath, it's relatively simple to move the plumbing and wiring. But if it's on a concrete slab, moving utilities is much harder, since you'll have to break up and remove the concrete.

Repositioning electrical receptacles and switches or adding new boxes for light fixtures may involve opening walls or the ceiling. At least one receptacle must be adjacent to the new sink area, and all bathroom receptacles must be protected with ground fault circuit interrupters (GFCIs), circuit breakers that cut off power immediately if the current begins leaking along the circuit.

Ventilation fans are relatively easy to add or relocate. These units are installed between ceiling joists or wall studs and may require ductwork to the outside. Since local codes may specify the placement of exhaust fans within the bathroom, consult your building department.

If you want to extend your existing heating system to the bathroom, check with a professional to be sure your system can handle the additional load. You can relocate a hot air register in the floor or in the vanity kickspace by changing the ductwork beneath the floor; ducts for wall registers can be rerouted in the stud wall. If you're adding a register, locate it where the ductwork can be extended easily from the existing system and where you won't sacrifice wall space.

Another option is to equip your bathroom with an electric space heater, which can be recessed in the wall or ceiling.

Minimum clearances

Local building codes specify minimum required clearances between,

Standard Heights, Minimum Clearances

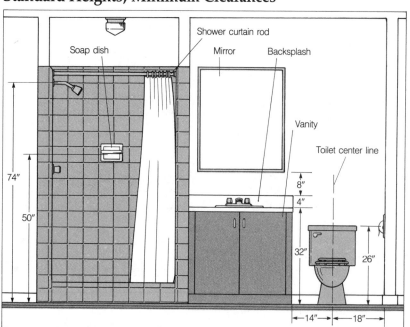

Fig. 12

beside, and in front of bathroom fixtures to allow adequate room for use, cleaning, and repair. **Fig. 12** (see facing page) shows standard heights, minimum clearances, and recommendations for the positioning of accessories.

Generally, you can locate side-by-side fixtures closer together than fixtures positioned opposite each other. If a sink is opposite a bathtub or toilet, 30 inches is the minimum distance allowed between them.

Laying out your bathroom

Generally, a workable layout provides for good access to the room, easy movement within the room, and the convenient use of fixtures and storage units. Be sure to note the dimensions of existing fixtures or their replacements and remember to put all your design ideas down on copies of your floor plan.

You may also want to make cutouts (to scale) of all bathroom elements. You can then move the cutouts around within the perimeter of the floor plan to see how each layout will work.

Typical layouts. The four most common layouts are categorized by the arrangement of fixtures. For an illustration of each one, see **Fig. 13.**

■ **A one-wall** bathroom layout suits a long, narrow room—as narrow as 4½ feet. It's economical because all the plumbing is in one wall.

■ **In an L-shaped** bathroom, fixtures are arranged in an L; a bathtub usually occupies the short leg. Commonly used for bathrooms that are 5 by 7 or 5 by 8 feet, this design provides ample floor space. All the plumbing is in one wall.

■ **A corridor** bathroom provides easy access; fixtures are located along two opposite walls. It's a practical arrangement for a small bathroom tucked between two bedrooms, with a door to each. The corridor should be at least 30 inches wide. Two walls require plumbing.

Four Bathroom Layouts

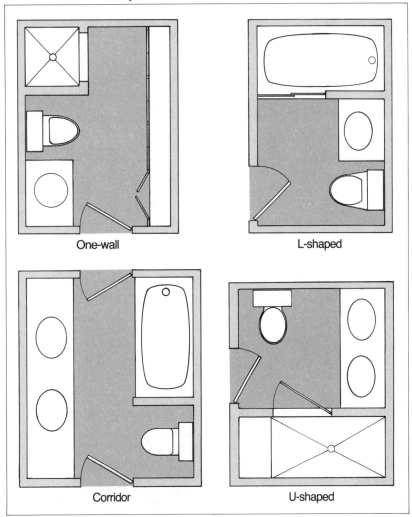

One-wall

L-shaped

Corridor

U-shaped

Fig. 13

■ **A U-shaped** bathroom requires a square room; fixtures are often placed along three walls. Though practical to use, this layout requires plumbing in all three walls.

Arranging fixtures. Position the largest unit—the bathtub or shower—first, allowing space for convenient access and easy cleaning. Next, place the sink (or sinks). The most frequently used fixture in the bathroom, it should be positioned out of the traffic zone. Be sure there's ample room in front for reaching the sink and plenty of elbow room on the sides.

If possible, locate the toilet away from the door. Often, the toilet is

positioned beside the tub or shower. If space permits, you can improve privacy by adding a partition or by putting the tub or toilet in a separate compartment.

Planning storage space. Consider what you need to store in the bathroom, how much space you need, and how to organize it. If you have a bathroom vanity or cabinet, you can equip it with racks, shelves, pull-outs, and lazy susans for supplies. Or why not display colorful towels and stacks of soap on open shelving?

If you have sufficient space in your bathroom, you may want to outfit a floor-to-ceiling cabinet as a linen closet or design a built-in hamper.

Attic, Basement & Garage Conversions

When it seems that the only solution to a lack of space is adding on, take a fresh look at the "rooms" in your house that aren't now being used as living spaces—the attic, basement, and garage.

With a little imagination and work, these underutilized areas can be turned into pleasant living spaces. And because these spaces are already sheltered, you'll probably spend far less money to convert them into comfortable, livable rooms than you would to build an addition.

Room at the top

Providing you have sufficient headroom in your attic, it's a good candidate for a conversion. However, there are problems you will have to overcome: temperature fluctuations—stifling heat in summer and icy air in winter; dampness and humidity; the awkwardness of sloping walls, sharp roof peaks, and unfinished floors; inadequate lighting; and lack of access from below.

Following are some suggestions for dealing with these problems. Keep in mind, too, that you may need to conceal or reroute ducts, vents, and wires running through the attic.

Insulation and ventilation. Insulation prevents warm air from escaping though the roof in winter and slows down the accumulation of heat from outside in summer. In all but the driest climates, use insulation with an attached vapor barrier. This prevents humid house air from condensing inside attic walls and roof materials.

New attic windows or an opening skylight will provide adequate ventilation. If necessary, you can use a house fan to push or draw hot air up and out of the attic.

To heat the attic, either extend the ductwork from your home's heating system or install a wall heater.

Structural concerns. Your first step is to determine whether or not the existing attic floor joists are sufficiently strong to support the new use planned for the space. If not, you'll have to reinforce the joists before installing the flooring.

To square off the steeply sloping walls, you can build short knee walls (check your local building code for minimum height requirements). You can also add partition walls to divide the space, if desired.

To create a flat ceiling, you may have to install collar beams. Then you can finish it with the material of your choice. Note that at least 7½ feet of headroom over a minimum of half the floor area is required by code.

Bringing in light. Opening up the attic with a gable wall window or skylight allows in natural light. Or you can build a shed or gable dormer. Though a gable dormer is more attractive, a shed dormer is easier to build and provides some extra living space.

To provide for switches, receptacles, and light fixtures, you'll need to extend wiring. You may even have to add an additional 15- or 20-amp circuit if your existing system isn't sufficient to handle the extra demand. Make sure to plan for a three-

An Attic Overview

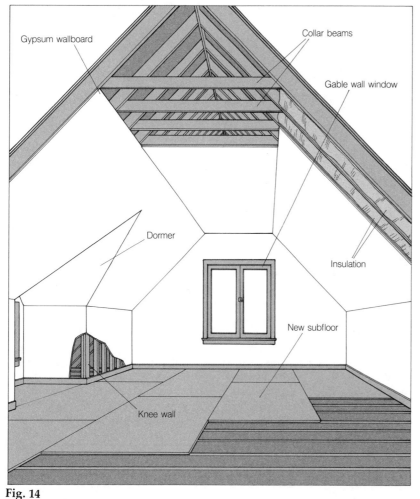

Gypsum wallboard

Collar beams

Gable wall window

Insulation

Dormer

New subfloor

Knee wall

Fig. 14

Efficient and organized, *this office space in a converted basement profits from bright white surfaces embellished with natural wood trim. L-shaped work center looks out on a garden path that flanks the basement wall. Interior design: Gail Woolaway & Associates.*

... *conversions*

way switch both above and below the attic opening.

Attic stairways. The minimum headroom for a stairway is 6½ feet. Be sure to take this into account when you're locating your opening. Also, the opening should be sufficiently large and any existing stairway strong enough for the new use intended for it.

Down below

Because basements are usually isolated from the outside and from the rest of the family living space, they make ideal retreats. If you're looking for peace and quiet, think about fitting out a study, home office, or bedroom in the area under your house.

Headroom and moisture are usually the main problems in dealing with basement conversions. Access is generally not a major concern, since most basements already have stairways linking them to the upstairs. Just be sure yours is up to code for the area's new use. You will have to plan an effective lighting scheme for the basement, since there probably isn't any major source of natural light.

Once you've solved all the problems, you can build up the walls, apply the flooring, and finish the ceiling (see **Fig. 15**).

Providing for headroom. If the ceiling is less than 7 feet high, you'll have to lower the floor or raise the house. The latter option is expensive, the former hard work because it usually has to be done by hand. Excavating more than a few inches below the present floor level could undermine the foundation; check with a professional to find out what's involved. Sometimes, it's possible to add retaining walls to shore up the footings.

Dealing with moisture. Most basement moisture problems are the result of improper drainage away from the house and foundation. Though a serious flow of moisture can't simply be plugged up from inside, many minor moisture problems can be solved.

Masonry sealers are designed to stop seepage and may be applied to walls or a concrete slab. Sweating pipes can be wrapped with insulating tape or special jackets and a vapor barrier. Insulating basement walls will eliminate most condensation problems. And minor leaks can be stopped with an application of waterproof cement.

Finishing the walls, floor, and ceiling. Two basic ways to build up masonry walls are with furring strips or standard 2 by 4 framing. Furring strips are easier to apply, but walls built from 2 by 4s provide extra room for thicker insulation and for electrical wiring. Insulation should include a vapor barrier. If yours doesn't, add a layer of polyethylene over the studs and insulation. You can then apply the wall covering of your choice.

If you can't cure your cold, leaky basement floor, seal it, apply a vapor barrier, and then build another floor above it, using 2-by sleepers and a plywood subfloor. A simpler flooring job, if your slab is dry and level, entails brushing on a chemical sealer. The finished flooring can then be installed.

Overhead framing, pipes, and ductwork can often be hidden by dropping the ceiling (if there's sufficient headroom), installing acoustic tiles, or adding a wallboard ceiling.

Basic Basement Improvements

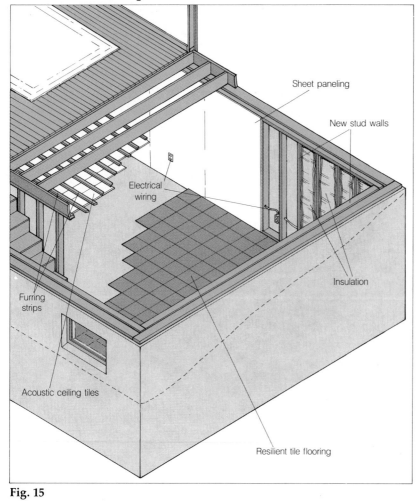

Sheet paneling

New stud walls

Electrical wiring

Furring strips

Insulation

Acoustic ceiling tiles

Resilient tile flooring

Fig. 15

Or you can simply leave the joists exposed.

Moving into the garage

Transforming the garage into valuable living space can be an economical way to expand your home. Most of the major construction work has already been done, and, best of all, the garage's architecture probably harmonizes with the rest of your home.

You can convert your garage into anything from a family room to a bedroom, studio, or workshop. Before you start to draw up plans, check your local building code—it may distinguish between space used for sleeping and space used for non-habitable purposes, such as a workshop. Many communities also require some kind of covered parking for cars, so you may need to add a carport or another garage.

The work involved in converting a garage includes adding insulation and utility runs, replacing the garage door with windows or a wall, and providing an adequate subfloor for finished flooring (see **Fig. 16**).

Insulation and utility runs. To make the space comfortable, you can add rigid foam panels in the ceiling or fur out the rafters to get the depth necessary for overhead insulation. You'll also want to add insulation—fiberglass batts, blankets, or rigid board insulation with a vapor barrier—between wall studs.

Running ductwork, wiring, and plumbing, if necessary, into an attached garage isn't much of a problem. Generally, you can simply extend your home's utility runs where they're needed.

If it's a detached garage, however, you'll have to run overhead or underground electrical wiring and extend plumbing to it. Outdoor pipes must be placed below the frost line (check your local code), and fixtures that require plumbing must be higher than the drainage system. To heat the room, you can install a space heater or a wood stove.

Garage Upgrades

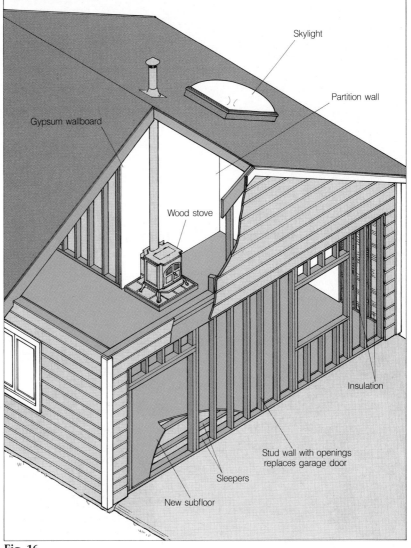

Fig. 16

Replacing the garage door. Once the garage door has been removed, you'll need to frame in a new wall, using standard stud construction to match the existing framework. To bring in natural light and provide ventilation, you may want to plan for a window or two in the wall.

The exterior will need to be finished so it disguises the conversion. One method is to simply re-side the entire wall. Or you can patch the new wall with siding that matches the existing material.

Though it's a big job, you may want to break up your old driveway and landscape the area in front to make the conversion blend in with the surroundings.

Adding a new floor. Most garages start off with barren concrete slab floors. First clean the floor of any oil residue. Then, if your floor isn't completely dry and level, seal the slab, apply a moisture barrier, and build the floor up with sleepers and a plywood subfloor; conceal any utility runs beneath the subfloor. Or pour a new, thin layer of concrete over the existing slab.

If your slab is completely dry and flat, you can attach the finished flooring directly to it.

Overhead glazing *and small-paned casement windows turn a sitting room into a sunspace. On sunny winter days, the sunspace not only heats itself but also helps to heat the rest of the house. In summer, the windows open for ventilation. Sunspace architect: Gerry Ives/Lamb & Ives.*

Adding a wall of glass *in place of the old swing-up door transformed a garage into this solar-heated office. Dark tile laid on the concrete slab stores heat during sunny days for release at night and on cloudy days; mini-blinds control both solar gain and natural lighting. Solar design: David R. Roberts of Dr. Solar.*

Your Final Plans

Once you've experimented with moving walls around, cut out scale models of furniture, appliances, and fixtures to test new room arrangements and traffic patterns, and considered all the design elements, you're ready to finalize your plans.

But before you start drawing floor plans and mapping elevations, you may want to estimate the amount your remodel will cost. If the figure exceeds your remodeling budget, it's time to rethink your goals and look for compromises. Deciding not to move a bearing wall or using a less expensive floor covering, for example, can reduce costs considerably.

Drawing a floor plan

To draw your floor plan to scale, you'll need dimensions of all the elements in the space you're remodeling.

Though most architects use graph paper with a scale of ¼ inch to 1 foot, you may find it easier to use paper with ½-inch squares; this gives you more room for writing down dimensions and labels. Using your original floor plan as a guide, if possible, mark off the dimensions of the space you're altering. Be sure to show any windows, doors, recesses, or projections in the space. For a sample floor plan, see **Fig. 17.**

Once you've drawn the space, indicate on the plan any gas, sewer, or water connections, showing how they'll reach any fixtures or appliances. Also mark the approximate locations of light fixtures, switches,

and receptacles and show which switch operates which light source; indicate whether it's a one-way or multiple switch.

Mapping elevations

A head-on view, an elevation shows how a room looks to a person standing in the middle of the floor, facing one wall.

On a rough sketch, draw the elements on each wall, measure carefully, and record the figures. Be sure to include windows, doors, electrical receptacles, switches, and any heating or cooling devices. Then redraw your elevation sketches on graph paper (for an example, see **Fig. 17**).

Don't forget to note such small details as a hanging light fixture over an eating area or the height of a backsplash.

Working Drawings: Floor Plan & Elevation

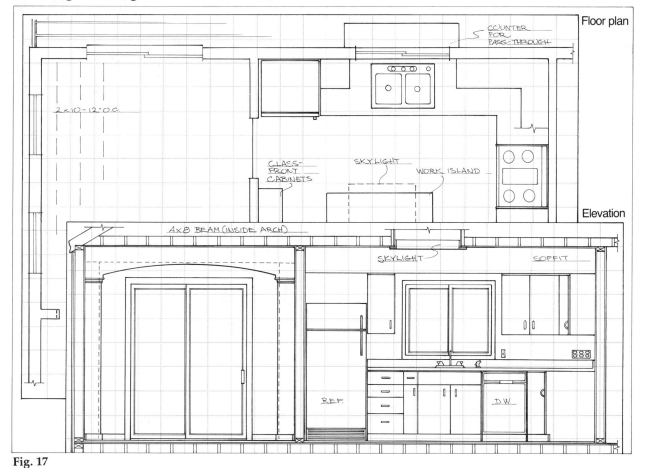

Fig. 17

Getting Started

Depending on your skills, your time, and your budget, you may want to do the remodeling work yourself or have a professional do some or all of it. Knowing how to choose a qualified professional you feel comfortable with is the key both to the successful completion of the job and to your own and your family's happiness while the work is being done. Even if you're not planning to seek professional help, the information below explains how to begin the process.

Remodels can be inconvenient at best and totally disruptive at worst. Throughout this section, you'll find some helpful hints from homeowners who have successfully survived a remodel.

Choosing & working with professionals

Your involvement with professionals—architects or designers, contractors, and subcontractors—can vary widely, from simply calling someone in occasionally to turning the entire job over to them.

Architects and designers. Architects are licensed professionals whose training includes education in design from aesthetic, functional, and engineering points of view. A designer also has professional training but is not licensed. Your architect or designer may design the project, provide working drawings and specifications, and then leave the construction and its supervision up to you. Or, the professional can do everything from designing through monitoring construction.

Your architect or designer should be technically and artistically skilled and also someone with whom you feel comfortable. Get references from friends, professional associations, or local building professionals. Interview each candidate, examining their portfolios as well as other homes they've designed. Once you've made your choice, the next meeting should be in your home, where the planning will begin.

> **The more planning you do, the fewer headaches later. Make as many early decisions as possible, including things like light switch locations and ways doors will swing. By the time construction is underway, you'll be sick of deciding.**

Contractors. A general contractor is a licensed professional builder whose responsibility is the actual building of a structure. Many contractors can also design (or help you design) a project. To do the actual building, contractors normally employ carpenters and arrange for other work, such as plumbing and wiring, to be done by subcontractors.

You can get the names of contractors from architects, from friends, from trade associations, or from material suppliers. Ask each contractor you're considering for several references; then talk to those clients about the contractors and arrange to see their work, both from the outside and, if possible, from the inside.

> **Our first contractor charged us heavily for every change we made in the plans after work began. Next time we'd study them beforehand—measuring and visualizing.**

Once you've narrowed down your list to two or three, interview each one to see if you feel comfortable with them. Check on their financial condition. Also call your local Better Business Bureau to find out if any complaints have been filed against them. Make sure each one is licensed and has liability and workers' compensation insurance.

Submit your plans and specifications to each contractor for bids. The specifications should be as detailed as possible, including materials, appliance numbers, fixtures, and so forth. All contractors should bid on the same specifications.

You don't have to take the lowest bid. It may be worth it to pay more for certain pluses, such as higher-quality work or a more amicable relationship with the contractor.

> **Our family room / kitchen remodel was fairly simple, yet we had no idea how many subcontractors it would involve: carpenters, roofers, sheet-metal installers, a plumber, an electrician, a cabinet-maker, a drywall installer, taper, texturer, tile setters, a mason, a glazier, a cabinet stainer, and flooring installers.**

Drawing up a contract. Once you've accepted a bid, you and the contractor will write up a contract. It's always a good idea to consult a lawyer before signing any contract for work on your property. As the working agreement between you and your contractor, the contract is very important—you can refer to it if any differences arise.

■ **Construction materials** should be listed in the contract, even minor things like drawer pulls and cabinet hinges. Anything not included and added later will increase your cost. An option is to include an allowance for finish details, such as cabinets and flooring, to give you more time to make your final decisions.

■ **A time schedule** for the project—a beginning date and a completion date—may be stipulated in your contract. The contractor obviously can't be responsible for delays caused by strikes or material shortages, and you have no effective legal way to enforce a schedule. Your best leverage is a good working relationship with the contractor—and the important stipulation that the final payment will be withheld until the work is completed.

■ **Payment,** of course, is covered in the contract as well. Usually, payment is made in installments as the work progresses or with an initial payment at the beginning and the balance at the end. Withhold some portion of the final payment until after the lien period (see below) has expired and until the final inspection has been completed.

Protection against liens. Under the laws of most states, people who perform labor or supply materials for a building can file a lien against it if they're not paid. If the contractor doesn't settle the claim, the building's owner may be liable. To be valid, liens must be filed within a specified time after construction is completed, and the time limit that a lien remains in effect is also specified by law.

> ❝ *We moved into the garage during our re-model. We were quite comfortable, with a bed, a refrigerator, an electric cooktop, a stereo, a chest of drawers, and a dowel hung from the ceiling for our clothes.* ❞

To protect yourself, you can pay suppliers of material and labor directly, you can require evidence of such payment from the contractor before making your payments, or

you can require the contractor to post a bond.

> ❝ *Put everything in writing—sizes and colors and installation and model numbers. Don't leave anything out. And, no matter how nice or needy the builders are, hold onto that last check until everything's done. Once you've paid them in full, they may never come back.* ❞

Working with a contractor. In the course of a remodeling project, it's normal for problems to arise. Don't be dismayed by disagreements you might have with your contractor. Clearly, you have a personal attachment to the project not shared by your contractor.

Keep a close eye on the work and the materials being used. Feel free to ask questions—it's your house and your money—but try not to get in the way of the work. And you should try to be around home at least some part of every day so the contractor can ask you questions. Don't give instructions to the contractor's employees or to subcontractors; always deal directly with the contractor.

If you plan to hire a contractor but want to do some of the work yourself, be sure your contractor agrees. You may be required to spell out your responsibilities in the contract, and you may have to sign a written statement releasing the contractor from any liability for your work.

Acting as your own contractor

Acting as your own general contractor means that you'll be responsible for everything from obtaining permits to hiring subcontractors to arranging for building inspections. But before you do anything else, be sure to obtain workers' compensation in-

surance to cover your liability for work-related injuries to any hired help.

When you hire subcontractors, use the same care you'd exercise in hiring a general contractor. Check references and insurance coverage; then get bids, work out detailed contracts, and carefully supervise the work.

Ordinances & codes

Every community has zoning ordinances and building codes to protect standards of health, safety, and land use. Remodeling done to your house must comply with these standards. Your building plans must be approved by officials before you can begin work, and the work in progress will be inspected periodically.

> ❝ *One month prior to beginning work, don't eat in any fast-food restaurant. There will be many nights when the sight of the mess is more than you can handle at home.* ❞

If professionals are doing the work, you may never come in contact with the building inspector or planning commission. They should take care of obtaining the necessary permits and inspections for you. If, on the other hand, you do all the work yourself, you'll need to deal directly with local officials.

Zoning ordinances. Designed to regulate land use, zoning ordinances separate commercial, industrial, and residential areas, establishing boundaries to prevent business from migrating into residential neighborhoods.

Building codes. Building codes are concerned principally with construction practices—structural design and strength and durability of building materials. The codes state what you can and cannot do when you build.

...*getting started*

If a proposed remodel doesn't conform to the building code, it may still be approved. The head of the building department has the authority to permit suitable alternatives, provided they do not weaken the structure, endanger the safety or security of the occupants, or violate the property rights of the neighbors.

Shopping for financing

Before making any loan arrangements, you must have finished plans and specifications for your remodel plus accurate estimates. Then you can research the various types of loans available in your area to learn their terms. You can borrow for home improvements from a variety of sources: commercial banks, savings and loans, mortgage banks, and credit unions.

Start with a lender you've used before. Your past or present business there may be all you need to get a home improvement loan.

You may also be able to finance your project by refinancing your present mortgage, obtaining a second mortgage, or remortgaging your home if it's paid for.

STEPS IN REMODELING

Are you ready to get to work? Before plunging into your project, you should have a clear idea of the sequence of steps necessary to complete the job. As the scale of your remodeling project increases, the need for careful planning becomes more critical. Before work begins, double-check the priorities listed below.

- Establish the sequence of jobs to be performed and estimate the time required to complete each one.
- If you're getting professional assistance for any part of the work, make sure you have firm contracts and schedules with contractors, subcontractors, or other hired workers.

- Obtain all required building permits.
- Arrange for delivery of materials; be sure you have all the necessary tools on hand.
- If electricity, gas, or water must be shut off by the utility company, arrange for it before work is scheduled to begin.
- Find out where you can dispose of refuse and secure any necessary dumping permits. Or rent your own dumpster.
- Be sure there's a storage area available for temporarily relocating furniture, fixtures, appliances, and any other possessions that will be in the way of the remodel.

- Measure fixtures and appliances for clearance through doorways and up and down staircases.

You can use the lists below to plan the basic sequence of tasks involved in dismantling the area being remodeled and in putting it all back together again. Depending on the scale of your job and the specific materials you select, you may need to alter the suggested order or perhaps even skip some steps.

Your goal is to maintain an operating household during as much of the time as possible. With careful scheduling and planning, the remodeling siege can be relatively comfortable for the entire family.

Removal sequence

1. Accessories, decorative elements
2. Furniture
3. Contents of cabinets, closets, shelves
4. Fixtures, appliances
5. Countertops, backsplashes
6. Cabinets, shelves
7. Floor materials
8. Light fixtures
9. Wall coverings
10. Wiring, plumbing, heating
11. Framing

Installation sequence

1. Structural changes: walls, doors, windows, skylights
2. Rough utility changes—wiring, plumbing, heating
3. Wall and ceiling coverings
4. Light fixtures
5. Cabinets, shelves
6. Countertops, backsplashes
7. Floor materials
8. Fixtures, appliances
9. Furniture
10. Decorative elements

Scattered tools, dust, and debris *can make a work area hazardous during remodeling. Moreover, you'll have to put up with noise, occasional lack of water and electricity, and perhaps even workers in your home. Knowing what to expect will make your remodeling project easier to survive.*

Handsome bath, *remodeled from a dressing room and a small bath, is faced with tongue-and-groove clear cedar. Vanity top and tub enclosure are marble. Mirrored wall conceals storage and visually enlarges the room. A series of skylights and down-lights provides illumination.*

A Gallery of Home Remodels

Every homeowner dreams of a better house, and every house has within it the seeds of a better home. When remodeling is successful, it unlocks a house's true potential, and dreams become reality.

The next 31 pages present, in full color, the flowering of 11 residences—houses that have bloomed into more fully realized homes. In each case, owners and designers looked at what was and saw what could be. This chapter will help you see through their eyes.

You'll find new bedrooms, bathrooms, even an attic. Above all, you'll find kitchens and family rooms. These are the most frequently remodeled rooms in the house and, especially with older homes, the ones where the greatest improvements can be made.

In most of the homes, little or no space was added. As these projects demonstrate, successful remodeling has more to do with refining space than with adding it. Even when some space was added, rethinking and reorganizing the existing interior was the key to the project.

For each house, we present three-dimensional floor plans and photos showing key views. Plans and photo captions are linked by colored arrows. On the plans, the arrows show the direction the camera faced when the photos were taken. Matching arrows on the captions tie the photos to the plans.

This chapter lets you profit from the successful experience of others. Read, look, and learn— and above all, enjoy.

Sun-filled atrium *reaches upward in space formerly occupied by a sunroom. For other views of this remodel, turn to pages 54–55.*

Chapter Two

Their children raised, these homeowners transformed the old bedroom wing into a dream of a master suite.

Architect: Don Brandenburger, A.I.A. Interior design: Legallet-Trinkner.

▼**Light and air** *fill the new bathroom. Skylights and clerestories bounce light everywhere. Porcelain fixtures complement the pale wood. Polyurethane seals the floor against moisture.*

Before: *Two bedrooms, two bathrooms, an extra room, closets, hallways—all were fine for a family, but now the kids were grown.*

After: *Generous master suite includes a luxurious bath, a new laundry room, and a replanned bedroom.*

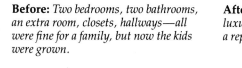

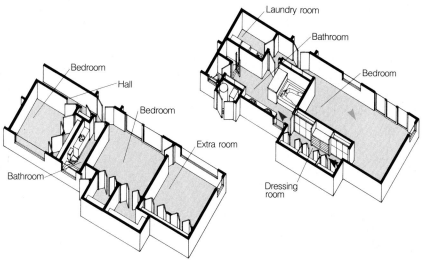

▼▼ **Seven-foot wall** *divides the bedroom (left) from the dressing room (right). Exposed collar beams in the bedroom add interest to the original ceiling, now sheathed in wood. New skylights bring the dressing room to life without sacrificing privacy.*

Back to the Drawing Board

An awkward floor plan kept this home from being all it could be. Now, with a revised plan and raised ceilings, it lives up to its potential.

Architect: Donald King Loomis. Interior design: Ruth Livingston.

▼**New family room and kitchen** *share light and air gained by raising the ceiling to the original roof line. New plan provides for both a breakfast nook and an eating bar. Tile floor and casual furniture can take what a family of active swimmers can dish out.*

Before: *Floor plan of this large home squandered space on an over-generous laundry, a superfluous "maid's room," and a poor traffic pattern in and around the bath/laundry core. Moreover, the home lacked a family room.*

After: *Kitchen moves next to the large, new family room. Maid's room becomes a pantry, and laundry occupies the old kitchen area. Redone entry features a new powder room and foyer. Bath, which now includes a dressing area and a door to the family room, retains an all-important door to the backyard pool area.*

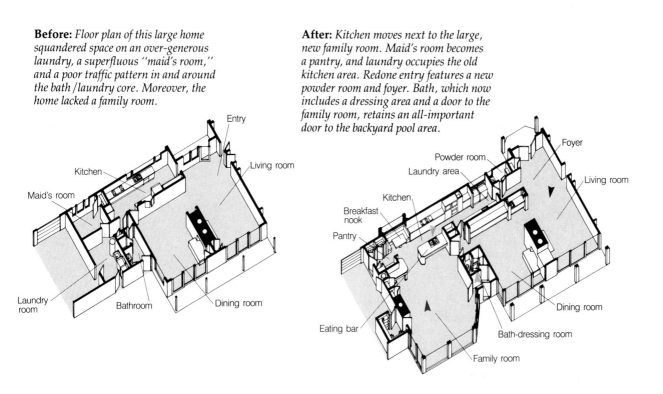

Before labels: Entry, Living room, Kitchen, Maid's room, Laundry room, Bathroom, Dining room

After labels: Foyer, Powder room, Laundry area, Living room, Kitchen, Breakfast nook, Pantry, Dining room, Eating bar, Bath-dressing room, Family room

◄ **Both the peninsula counter** *and the light soffit above divide the kitchen from the family room. Transition of forms and surfaces is deftly managed in both architecture and cabinetry. Flat ceiling in the family room shows where space was added.*

. . . back to the drawing board

▼Raised ceiling *in the living room and dining room exploits the original hipped roof and gives the home a whole new look and feel. Skylights at the apex dramatize the chimney core and fill the rooms with light.*

▲Bath-dressing room *shares a tile floor with the family room and kitchen. Bath opens to backyard, providing a buffer zone for swimmers re-entering the house.*

A Model of Efficiency and Grace

A conventional kitchen-breakfast area is transformed into a bright new kitchen-family room.

Interior design: Ruth Livingston.

▼ **Multipurpose island** *directs traffic, provides areas for cooking and eating, and offers ample storage space. With windows on just one wall, skylights and light surfaces are vital aids in balancing light.*

Before: *Nearly half this 16- by 30-foot kitchen-breakfast area was devoted to circulation—hardly an efficient use of space.*

After: *New plan channels traffic along one wall and between the kitchen and the new family-room area. A relocated doorway and new kitchen island are the keys.*

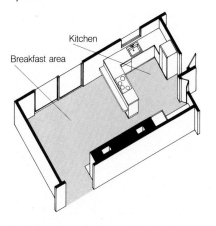

Kitchen

Breakfast area

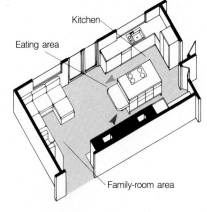

Kitchen

Eating area

Family-room area

▼**New mini-family room** *features generous shelves, built-in seating, and a slide-out TV. New fixed-glass window and relocated door replace the old sliding glass door.*

The Case of the Migrating Kitchen

This kitchen moved south for light, air, and view.
Now it's a hub for family living.

Architect: Moyer Associates.

Light-filled kitchen *takes over prime space once occupied by a laundry room, bath, and service porch. L-shaped plan with island routes traffic around work areas. New dining bay is just visible at left; deck was added outside the French doors.*

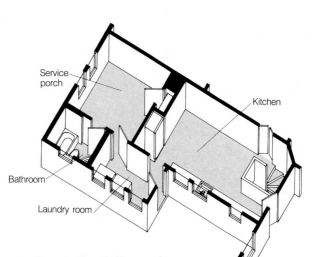

Service porch

Kitchen

Bathroom

Laundry room

Before: *Kitchen was like a hallway to the back of the house. Prime space at the rear was wasted on seldom-used utility rooms.*

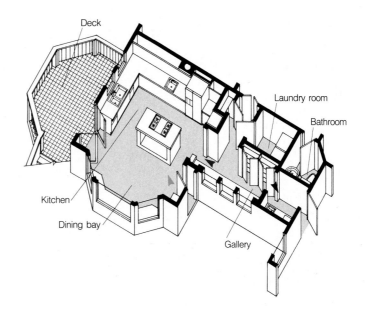

Deck

Laundry room

Bathroom

Kitchen

Dining bay

Gallery

After: *Bath and laundry room moved north when the kitchen migrated south. Stairs to the lower level were relocated to an adjoining hall. Kitchen had small windows in one wall; new location allows a skylight and generous glazing on two sides.*

. . . migrating kitchen

New kitchen *becomes a focus for family living. View from the breakfast table shows an efficient new work area, with generous appliance garages at rear. Dramatic hood caps the handsome new island. Hollow beams conceal exhaust ducts and wiring.*

▼ **New gallery** *connects the kitchen and formal dining room (unchanged in the remodel). Tiled counter houses a separate sink and provides a convenient service area for entertaining. Storage above and below includes cubbyholes for wine.*

Airborne

Indoor and outdoor spaces meet in an
inspired glass room.

Architect: Alan Dreyfuss.

▼**Soaring family room** *replaces a small
sunroom, den, and hall and creates a gracious link between the inside and the out-
of-doors. Stately column carries loads
once borne by the now-vanished walls.
Bright tile floor is impervious to sun.
New French doors invite a stroll
in the garden.*

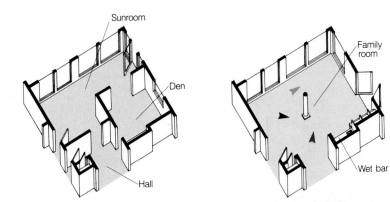

Sunroom

Den

Hall

Family room

Wet bar

Before: *Three small areas—hall, den, and sunroom—cluttered the back of the house.*

After: *New 18- by 22-foot family room merges indoor and outdoor space—and shares the character of both. Gone are three old walls.*

▲ **Entertainment center** *and wet bar nestle into the sheltered wall opposite the atrium.*

◄ **Glass-roofed atrium** *replaces the old sunroom and second-floor deck; former exterior window is just visible at top. On hot days, a powered sunshade runs down curved tracks just under the glass. Transom windows open for ventilation.*

A GALLERY OF HOME REMODELS   55

High Achiever

This attic remodel makes the most of what was once just empty space.
Architect: Glen William Jarvis.

▼**Compact but still luxurious,** *new bath features twin basins and a 5- by 7-foot whirlpool tub. Rotary windows provide light, air, and a completely private view of the bay beyond.*

▲**View from the bath** *shows a new gable window and rotary roof windows that bring in light and air. Entry is at far left, bed alcove under the exposed beams.*

Steep roof, empty attic *provided the raw material from which an elegant master bedroom suite was created.*

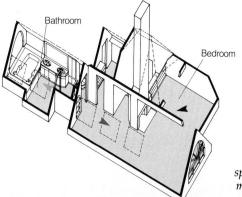

Bathroom

Bedroom

▼Bed alcove, *with its fireplace and spectacular view, is both cozy and dramatic. Large beams above replace attic stud walls.*

Yankee Ingenuity

Country charm meets modern planning in a thoroughly contemporary project clothed in the garb of yesteryear.

Architect: Ken Whitehead.

▼**Cheerful country ambience** *belies the modern plan of the new family room. New bay replaces the old porch; though it adds only 37 square feet, the effect is dramatic. Pine flooring adds an essential, authentic touch.*

Before: *Awkward kitchen and breakfast room were disrupted by traffic. Outside, a bare-bones concrete porch lurked in the shadows of the second story.*

After: *Traffic flows along the walls of this generous new kitchen-family room. Added space comes from the old porch, a new bay, and a small addition near the pantry. New fireplace borrows space from the library. Added bath tucks into the end of the old kitchen.*

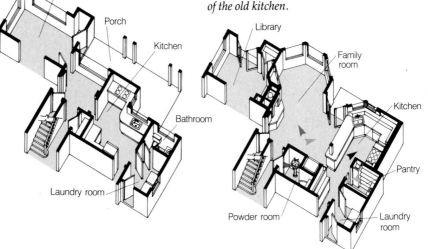

Library
Porch
Kitchen
Bathroom
Laundry room

Library
Family room
Kitchen
Pantry
Powder room
Laundry room

▼**Efficient new kitchen** *is out of the way, yet conveniently close at hand. For the cook, the U-shaped plan saves steps; two-way counter makes serving— and socializing—easy.*

. . . Yankee ingenuity

▼**Restaurant range** *dominates the kitchen; vital heat shielding is built into the brick sheathing and flanking cabinets. Windowsill shelf provides a roof for garages that hide appliances behind sliding doors.*

▼ **New pantry** *takes over the site of the former half-bath and borrows space from the laundry room. Small cleanup sink under the new fanlight is a helpful addition.*

▲ **Painted wainscoting** *and pine flooring carry the country theme into the new bath. Its location, formerly given over to a closet and part of the old kitchen, is more convenient than before.*

Fresh Face, New Space

The old deck comes inside, three rooms get a
brand-new look—and the house is reborn.

Architect: Donald King Loomis. Interior design: Ruth Livingston.

▼**Family-room expansion** *incorporates
the old deck (raised ceiling over the new
sitting area shows where it used to be).
Unified colors—in the new tile floor and
hearth, the paint, and even the
furniture—tie everything together and
make the spaces look larger.*

Before: *Kitchen, family room, and dining room were functional but rather small. Deck was the key to unlocking the home's potential.*

After: *Deck was roofed and wrapped in glass; sliding glass doors were removed, bringing the space indoors. Kitchen was enlarged slightly and windows were added, providing light, more room to work, and a new pantry.*

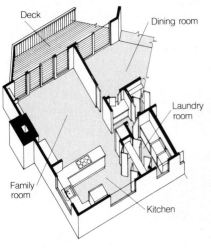

Deck

Dining room

Laundry room

Family room

Kitchen

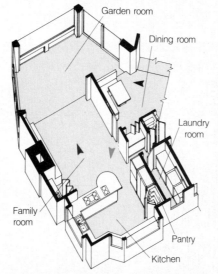

Garden room

Dining room

Laundry room

Family room

Pantry

Kitchen

▲ **Expansive, fixed-glass windows** *treat diners to a spectacular view.*

◄ **Unifying surfaces and colors** *extend into the remodeled kitchen. Countertop tile is the same as on the floor. Semicircular counter extension provides a landing spot for quick meals and snacks.*

Upstairs, Downstairs

A complex, two-story core remodel revitalizes this fine old home.

Architect: William B. Remick.

▼**Graceful new kitchen** *offers light, air, and solid practicality, thanks to white paint, clear finishes, and strategic lighting. Painted board ceilings maintain the character of the house. Over the railing at right is the breakfast mezzanine, with a new pantry beyond. Turn the page for floor plans.*

▲ **An ideal social space,** *new kitchen is a model of beauty and function. Mezzanine breakfast area keeps the family in touch with the cook, yet out of the way. New door into the dining room (at left) greatly improves the traffic flow. New bay window floods the room with light; gleaming dark granite countertops provide contrast.*

▼**Brand-new coffee bar** *backstops the dining room and offers lots of storage, too.*
Stain-resistant countertop is a practical choice.

Before: *Downstairs rooms were small and uncoordinated, and circulation was awkward. Upstairs baths were cramped.*

After: *Gracious downstairs spaces flow into one another. Revised and enlarged bathrooms upstairs provide all the modern amenities.*

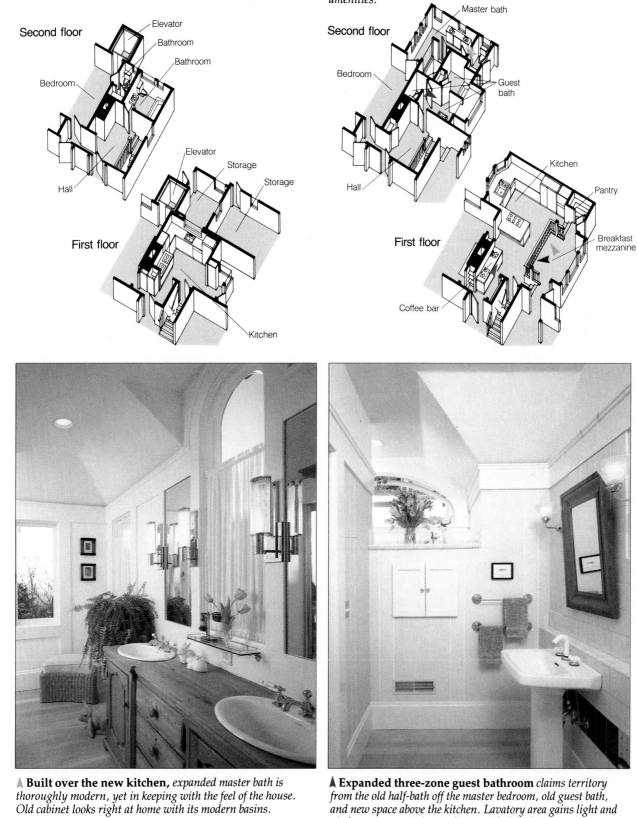

Second floor

Elevator

Bathroom

Bathroom

Bedroom

Elevator

Storage

Storage

Hall

First floor

Kitchen

Second floor

Master bath

Bedroom

Guest bath

Hall

Kitchen

Pantry

First floor

Breakfast mezzanine

Coffee bar

▲ **Built over the new kitchen,** *expanded master bath is thoroughly modern, yet in keeping with the feel of the house. Old cabinet looks right at home with its modern basins.*

▲ **Expanded three-zone guest bathroom** *claims territory from the old half-bath off the master bedroom, old guest bath, and new space above the kitchen. Lavatory area gains light and air from a new window it shares with the tub area.*

Traffic Manager

This kitchen remodel corrects traffic flow in
three rooms simultaneously.

Architect: Moyer Associates.

▼**Skylit kitchen** *makes optimum use of
modest space. Traffic flows past the new
island, well away from work areas. Every
inch of wall space provides storage.*

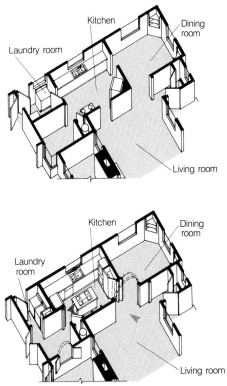

Before: *Badly placed doors forced traffic through the middle of the kitchen and living room, at the same time isolating one room from another.*

Kitchen

Dining room

Laundry room

Living room

Kitchen

Dining room

Laundry room

Living room

After: *New plan relocates openings to guide traffic along walls and let spaces flow into each other. Arched doorways tie everything together.*

▲ **Arched openings** *link the kitchen, dining room, and living room (see plans). Effect is both dramatic and efficient—three doorways in one.*

New Light, New Life

Transforming a pair of "afterthought"
spaces utterly changed the character of
this house.

Architect: Hiro Morimoto.

Before: *Long, narrow family room, attached only to the dining room, was dark and uninviting. Little-used sunroom (a grade-level screened porch added many years before) was even narrower.*

After: *New family room, breakfast area, and bath transform the old plan. Two walls were moved out slightly, adding just 70 square feet, but allowing a new fireplace and generous window seat. Kitchen door (which didn't move) and dining room doors (which did) give easy access to the expanded, revitalized space.*

▼ **Sunken seating area with fireplace** *replaces the old sunroom and becomes the focal point of the new family room. Graceful display shelving divides it from the breakfast area. Post and beam replace the old exterior bearing wall.*

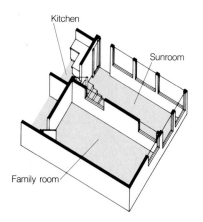

Kitchen
Sunroom
Family room

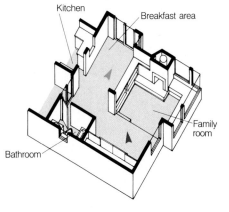

Kitchen
Breakfast area
Family room
Bathroom

➤ **Breakfast area** *features a raised roof that enlarges the space. Strategically placed gable window and skylight bring in light without sacrificing privacy. Pass-through to the kitchen sees service at mealtime.*

Posts and beams *allow this kitchen to be opened up to the rest of the house; raised ceiling, high clerestory windows, and gallons of white paint contribute to the spacious, airy feeling. Architect: Richard Sygar.*

How Your House Works

Beneath your floors, above your ceilings, and behind your walls a complex but orderly structural core and network of systems give your house stability and make it "work" for you.

The structural core—the foundation and framing—is the basic shell to which the exterior and interior finishing materials are applied. Concealed within this basic framework are all the systems that make the house function.

The electrical system lights your home and conducts power to your appliances. The plumbing system brings water and gas to all the water- and gas-using fixtures and appliances in your home. Finally, a system of ducts and flues distributes heat throughout the house and vents out the products of combustion.

When you remodel, you'll often need to alter your house's structure or its network of systems in one way or another. A wall may have to come down, added kitchen appliances and lighting may require a new circuit, or a new bathroom may require tapping into your plumbing and heating systems.

Before you start any remodeling project, it's important to familiarize yourself with your house's structure and its systems. In this chapter, we describe and illustrate three different types of framing—platform, balloon, and post and beam. We also give you an overview of typical electrical, plumbing, and heating systems.

Once you understand how your house works, you're ready to transform the house you have into the home you've always wanted.

Basic House Structure

Whatever style your house may be—from Cape Cod to California bungalow—its basic structure is probably one of three types of framing: platform (the most common), balloon, or post and beam. If you're contemplating a remodeling project that involves cutting into the framing, it's important to know which kind you have. Here's an overview of each type.

Platform framing

Platform framing, shown in **Fig. 1**, is the standard method used for house building today. The "platform" consists of the foundation and floor; walls are built up from this solid base. If the house is taller than one story, additional layers of floor platforms and walls are stacked atop the first-floor walls. Finally, ceiling and roof framing complete the structure.

Foundation. The foundation begins with wide concrete footings on which the foundation walls or posts rest. Atop the foundation walls lie wood mudsills, which provide a solid transition from the concrete below to the wood framing above and help distribute the house's weight evenly along the foundation. Most foundations include at least one interior concrete wall or a girder that helps bear the load above.

Floor structure. Floor joists, spaced 16 or 24 inches on center, rest on opposite mudsills or overlap an interior foundation wall or girder. Joist headers protect the joist ends and prevent them from twisting. Over the joists is a subfloor, made from either solid boards or plywood sheets.

One variation on the platform design is the concrete slab foundation; the continuous slab doubles as foundation and subfloor, and the walls are attached directly to the slab.

Walls. The framing begins with exterior stud walls, formed by vertical, evenly spaced 2 by 4 or 2 by 6 wall studs (usually 16 or 24 inches on center) that run between a horizontal sole plate and parallel top plate. At the top of window and door openings, headers distribute the load normally borne by studs. Cripple studs, rough (window) sills, and trimmer studs help strengthen openings.

Walls may be either bearing or nonbearing. A bearing wall helps support the house structure; a nonbearing, or partition, wall does not. In most cases, at least one main inte-

Platform Framing

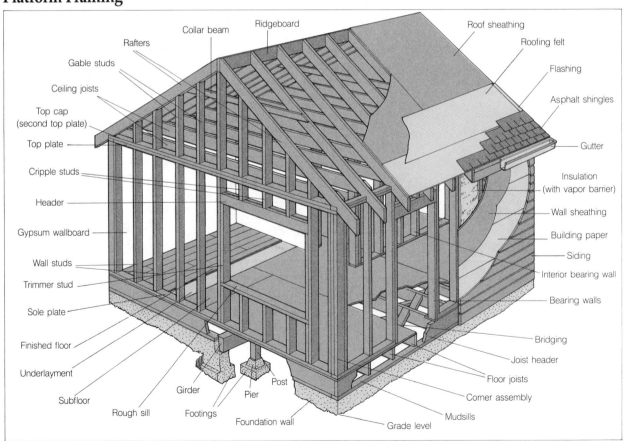

Fig. 1

rior wall is bearing, as are all exterior walls that run perpendicular to ceiling and floor joists.

Where walls intersect, extra studs or blocking help tie them together.

Walls are fastened through their sole plates to the subfloor and joists below. A second set of top plates, sometimes called top caps, overlaps the first and provides extra rigidity.

Ceiling. Framing the ceiling is a layer of joists running parallel to the floor joists below. If there's no second story, these are lighter ceiling joists; otherwise, they're another set of heavy-duty floor joists. The interior bearing wall supports the joists above as the girder did below.

Roof. The framing for a gable roof consists of matching pairs of evenly spaced rafters that meet at a central ridgeboard. Rafters are often bridged with horizontal collar beams or ties. At the open ends, gable studs are angled to meet the rafters.

An increasingly popular alternative to standard roof framing involves engineered trusses, which combine joist, rafters, and diagonal bracing into single triangular units.

Exterior finishing. Once the house is framed, the framing is enclosed in sheathing, which helps strengthen the structure and provides a nailing base for siding and roofing materials. Wall sheathing is usually plywood sheets; roof sheathing may be plywood, solid boards, or spaced boards, depending on your finished roofing material. A layer of building paper usually covers wall sheathing; roofing felt often goes atop the sheathing on the roof.

Interior finishing. Interior finishing encompasses many elements, from insulation to flooring. Insulation stops warm air from escaping in winter and slows down heat accumulation in summer.

Ceiling materials are fastened directly to ceiling joists or to a grid suspended from them. Gypsum wallboard is applied directly to wall studs; paneling is attached to studs, furring strips, or another backing. Plaster walls have a gypsum, fiberboard, or lath backing.

Finished flooring is applied either to an underlayment fastened over the subfloor or directly to the subfloor.

Balloon framing

Standard practice until about 1930, balloon framing is still used in some two-story houses, especially those with masonry exteriors. The chief difference between balloon and platform framing is that, in balloon framing, the exterior bearing wall studs extend continuously from the mudsill on top of the foundation wall to the doubled top plate two stories above, as shown in **Fig. 2.**

To determine if your house has balloon framing, look in the basement or crawlspace for the mudsill atop the foundation wall. If you see paired joists and studs resting on the sill, your house was built with balloon framing. (If joists alone are visible below the subfloor, you have platform framing.)

Post & beam framing

The framing for post and beam houses consists of sturdy posts (up to 8 feet apart) that hold up beams, which, in turn, support planks forming the floor and roof deck (see **Fig. 3**). The posts—a minimum of 4 by 4 lumber—either sit atop a standard foundation wall or extend down to individual piers and footings.

Two trademarks of post and beam houses are the open-beam ceiling and, because the spaces between the posts needn't bear any weight, the use of large expanses of glass.

Balloon Framing

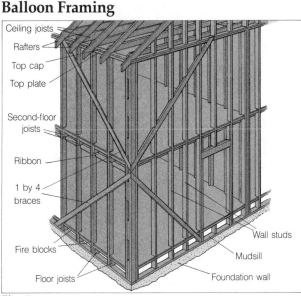

Ceiling joists
Rafters
Top cap
Top plate
Second-floor joists
Ribbon
1 by 4 braces
Fire blocks
Floor joists
Wall studs
Mudsill
Foundation wall

Fig. 2

Post & Beam Framing

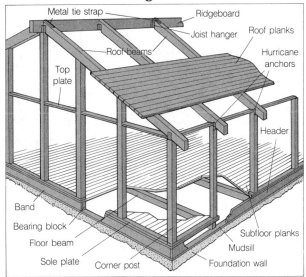

Metal tie strap
Ridgeboard
Joist hanger
Roof planks
Roof beams
Hurricane anchors
Top plate
Header
Band
Bearing block
Floor beam
Sole plate
Corner post
Subfloor planks
Mudsill
Foundation wall

Fig. 3

The Electrical System

That maze of cables and wires running behind the walls, under the floors, and above the ceilings of your home may appear jumbled—but it's really a well-organized system of circuits that brings electricity to the lights and appliances in the house.

Before you attempt to alter or expand this system, it's essential to familiarize yourself with its operation. On these pages, we give you a quick course in electrical terms and systems. For an illustration, see **Fig. 6.**

How your home is wired

Today, most homes have what's called three-wire service. The utility company connects three wires—two "hot," one neutral—through a meter to your service entrance panel. These wires provide both 120- and 240-volt capabilities. One hot wire and the neutral wire combine to supply 120 volts, the amount used for most household applications, such as lights and small appliances. Both hot wires and the neutral wire can form a 120/240-volt circuit for such needs as a range and dryer. The two hot wires alone combine to make a 240-volt circuit.

Some older homes have only two-wire service, with one hot wire at 120 volts and one neutral wire. Two-wire service does not have 240-volt capacity.

Service entrance panel and subpanel. If your power is supplied overhead, the utility company connects its wires to yours at a weatherhead anchored either on the roof or on the side of the house below the roofline. If you have underground service, the wires are buried in a rigid metal conduit. (Both types are illustrated on page 166.)

The wires pass through a utility company meter to the service entrance panel, which may be located outside your house adjacent to the meter or on an inside wall directly behind the meter. This panel is the control center for your electrical system. Inside you'll usually find the main disconnect (main fuses or main circuit breaker), the fuses or circuit breakers protecting individual circuits, and the grounding connection for the entire system.

After entering the panel and passing through the main disconnect, each hot wire connects to one of two hot bus bars, as shown in **Fig. 4.** These bars accept the amount of current permitted by the main disconnect and allow you to divide that current into smaller branch circuits at the distribution center. The neutral wire is attached to a neutral bus bar, which is in direct contact with the earth through the grounding electrode conductor.

Your home may also have one or more subpanels from which branch circuits originate. A subpanel is an extension of the service entrance panel; the two are connected by hot and neutral subfeeds.

Simple circuitry. The word *circuit* represents the course that electric current travels; carried by the hot wire, it passes from the service entrance panel or subpanel to one or more devices using electricity and then returns to the panel by way of the neutral wire.

The devices are normally connected by parallel wiring, as shown in **Fig. 5.** The hot and neutral wires run continuously from one housing box to another; separate wires branch off to individual switches, receptacles, and fixtures.

The hot wire of each 120-volt branch circuit originates at a branch circuit fuse or circuit breaker connected to one of the hot bus bars. A 120/240- or straight 240-volt circuit, which requires both hot wires, is connected through the fuse or breaker to both hot bus bars. All neutral wires originate at the neutral bus bar inside the panel.

Safeguards in the system

The service entrance panel and any subpanels in your home are equipped with either fuses or circuit breakers. These are the safety devices that keep the branch circuits and anything connected to them from overheating and catching fire.

Just as the electrical system is protected from fire by fuses or circuit

Service Entrance Panel

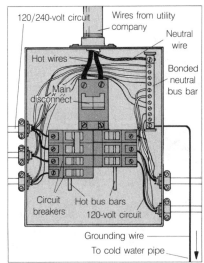

Fig. 4. Power enters *your home through the service entrance panel, where it's divided into branch circuits.*

Parallel Circuitry

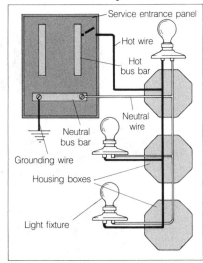

Fig. 5. In parallel wiring, *hot and neutral wires run continuously from one electrical device to another.*

breakers, the people who use it are protected from shock by the grounding system.

Fuses and circuit breakers. A fuse has a thin metal strip through which current passes into a circuit. The metal has a low resistance to heat, and when the current passing through exceeds the rating of the fuse, the metal melts, breaking the circuit. To restore power, you must replace the fuse with one of the same type and amperage rating.

Circuit breakers are heavy-duty switches that serve the same purpose as fuses. When a circuit carries more current than is safe, the breaker switches to RESET. On most breakers, the switch has to be pushed to OFF and then to ON after the circuit trips.

A special kind of circuit breaker—the ground fault circuit interrupter (GFCI)—is installed in bathroom, outdoor, and garage locations. If there's a current leakage, or "ground fault," the GFCI opens the circuit instantly, shutting off the electricity.

Grounding. The National Electrical Code requires that every circuit have a grounding system. Grounding ensures that all metal parts of the wiring system will be maintained at zero volts. In the event of a short circuit, a grounding wire carries current back to the service entrance panel and ensures that the fuse or circuit breaker will open, shutting off the flow of current.

The grounding wire for each circuit is attached to the neutral bus bar and then is run with the hot and neutral wires; individual "jumper" wires branch off to ground individual metal devices and boxes as required.

An Overview of the System

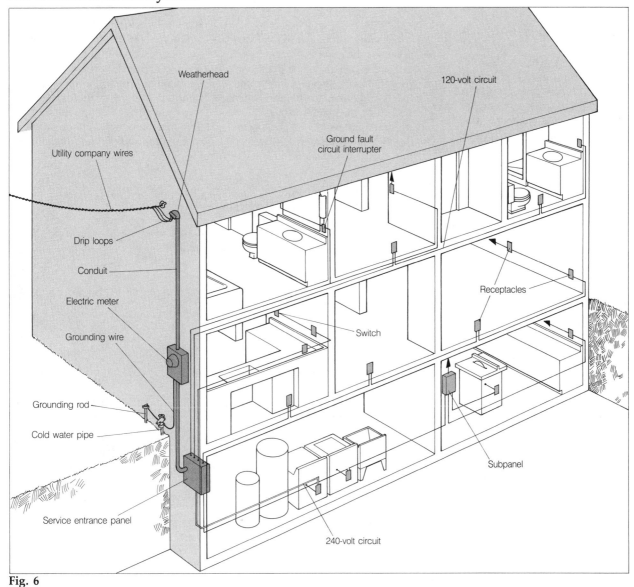

Weatherhead

120-volt circuit

Ground fault circuit interrupter

Utility company wires

Drip loops

Conduit

Electric meter

Grounding wire

Grounding rod

Cold water pipe

Service entrance panel

Receptacles

Switch

Subpanel

240-volt circuit

Fig. 6

The Plumbing System

The plumbing system brings water and gas to your house, distributes them to the places where they'll be used, and carries away waste water. It's comprised of four subsystems—the water supply system, the drain-waste system, the vent system, and the gas system. (Often, the drain-waste and vent systems are referred to collectively as the DWV system.)

Here's how the plumbing system works. For an illustration, refer to **Fig. 8.**

The supply system

The supply system carries water from a utility main or other source into your house and around to all your water-using fixtures and appliances, such as sinks, toilets, the dishwasher, and the washing machine. In most homes, a water meter monitors usage from the water utility; a main shutoff valve, usually located near where the main water supply pipe enters the house, turns the water for the house on and off.

Once inside the house, the supply pipe divides into two branches, one supplying the water heater and the other remaining cold. If the system is equipped with a water softener, it may be located either on the main supply line before it divides or on the branch supplying the water heater.

For most of their distance, hot and cold water pipes run parallel and horizontally until they reach the vicinity of water-using fixtures and appliances. There, vertical branches, called risers, connect the fixture or appliance to the water system. Risers are usually concealed inside walls. Horizontal pipes are fastened to floor joists or buried under a concrete slab.

Ideally, supply pipes should be installed with a slight pitch in their runs so that all pipes can be drained through a valve or faucet at the lowest point.

Some water-using fixtures and appliances have their own shutoff valves; this allows you to shut off the water to repair or replace them without cutting off the water supply for the entire house.

The drain-waste system

The drain-waste system takes advantage of gravity to channel waste water and solid wastes to the sewer line. Drainpipes lead away from all fixtures at a carefully calculated slope. If the slope is too steep, water will run off too fast, leaving particles behind; if it's not steep enough, water and waste will drain too slowly and may back up into the fixtures. The normal pitch is ¼ inch for every horizontal foot of pipe.

The workhorse in the drain-waste system is the main soil stack, a vertical section of 3- or 4-inch-diameter pipe that carries waste away from toilets and other fixtures and connects with the main house drain in the basement or crawlspace, or under the slab. From here, the wastes flow to a sewer or septic tank.

Venting Systems for Fixtures

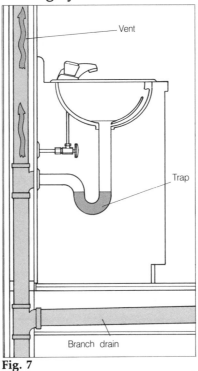

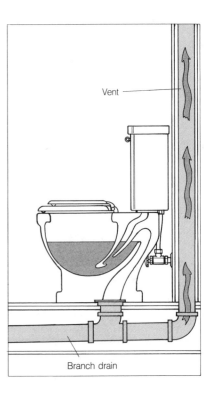

Fig. 7

Since any system will clog occasionally, cleanouts are placed in the drainpipes. Ideally, there should be one cleanout in each horizontal section of drainpipe, plus a U-shaped house trap, sometimes located outdoors, to give access to sewer or septic tank connections. A cleanout is usually a capped 45° Y fitting or 90° T fitting, designed for cleaning with a snake.

The vent system

To prevent dangerous sewer gases from entering the home, each fixture must have a trap in its drainpipe and must be vented (see **Fig. 7**). A trap is a bend of pipe that remains filled with water at all times to keep gases from coming up the drain.

The vents in the drain-waste system are designed to get rid of sewer gas and to prevent pressure buildups in the pipes. The vents come off the drainpipes downstream from the traps and go out through the roof. This maintains atmospheric pressure in the pipes and prevents the siphoning of water from the traps.

Each plumbing fixture in the house must be vented. Usually, a house has a main vent stack (which is the upper part of the main soil stack) that runs up to the roof, with additional 1½- to 2-inch vent pipes connecting to it. In many homes—especially single-story ones—widely separated fixtures make it impractical to use a single main vent stack. In this situation, each fixture or fixture group has its own secondary vent stack.

The gas system

The gas system is composed of two subsystems—the supply system, which carries gas under pressure from the utility company main through a meter to all the gas-using appliances in your house, and the vent system, which exhausts the products of combustion from the house.

Both subsystems are similar to the water supply and DWV systems, but because gas is combustible, certain important safety features are built into the gas system. Supply lines at such appliances as water heaters and furnaces should have valves that shut off automatically when pilot lights go out, so unburned gas can't enter the house. Where pipes run underground, they must be specially coated.

In addition, every gas-using appliance should have a vent or flue running directly to the outside.

An Overview of the System

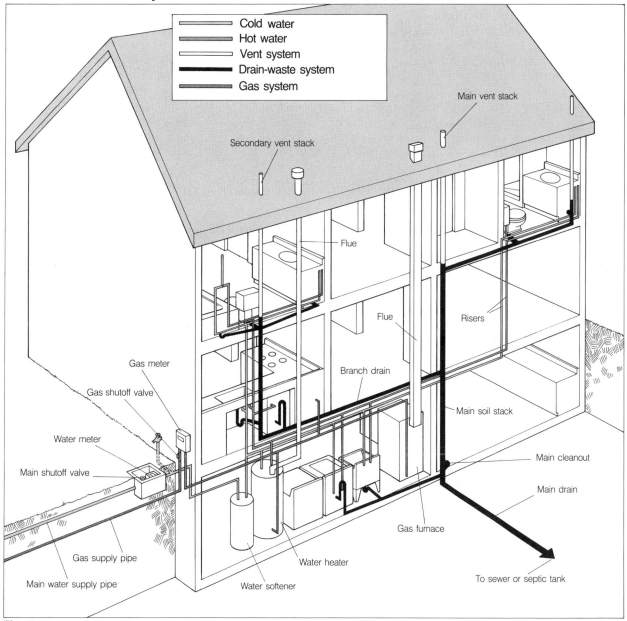

Fig. 8

Heating Systems

Heating systems vary considerably, but all have the same purpose—keeping your house warm when temperatures outdoors drop.

Most homes today are centrally heated either by a forced warm air system or a hot water system. Steam heat, found in older homes, is rarely installed now. In areas where electricity is cheaper than gas or oil and in some remodeling projects, electric-fired boilers or furnaces or electric room heaters may be used.

Sometimes, homeowners choose to supplement their conventional heating system with some sort of solar heating system.

The various heating systems and their components are explained below.

Conventional heating systems

Conventional heating systems all function in the same basic way. Each system is equipped with a control, a heat producer, a heat exchanger, and a heat distributor.

The control, called a thermostat, signals a need for heat. The signal turns on the heat producer, usually an oil or gas burner or an electric heating element; the heat warms the transfer medium—air, water, or steam—in the heat exchanger: a furnace if it heats air, a boiler if it heats water or produces steam.

The transfer medium moves by gravity or is forced through ducts (warm air) or pipes (water or steam) to the heat distributors located in the living area. These heat distributors are registers in a forced warm air system and convectors or radiators in a hot water or steam system. In a hot water radiant heating system, the water moves through tubing concealed in the room's ceiling, walls, or floor.

Return ducts or pipes carry the medium back to the heat exchanger. When the temperature of the living area reaches the level set on the thermostat, the thermostat automatically shuts down the system.

Forced warm air systems. With these systems, a blower pulls air into the cold air return and return duct, through a filter, and into the furnace, where the air is heated. The blower then distributes the warmed air back to the rooms through warm air ducts and outlets or through registers. (See **Fig. 9** for an illustration of how the system works.)

Some older homes have gravity warm air systems, which rely on the buoyancy of hot air to distribute heat. Compared to the gravity system, forced warm air systems are much more efficient and can be extended fairly easily. In addition, forced air systems can use the ductwork of gravity systems, so if you have a gravity furnace, you can replace it with a forced air unit without replacing the whole distribution system.

Hot water systems. These systems are particularly good choices if you don't want air blown through your house—to reduce the circulation of dust, for example, when someone in the house has dust-related allergies. Hot water heating systems range from gravity types, found in older homes, to the most common modern system—the hydronic system.

In all hot water systems, water heated in a boiler travels through a network of pipes to the heat distributors, usually radiators or convectors, where the heat is given off. An expansion tank containing air and water is usually mounted above the boiler. The air acts as a cushion to maintain even water pressure in the system.

In older homes, the movement of water through the pipes is controlled by gravity—warmer, lighter water rises and takes the place of heavier, cooler water. In the more efficient hydronic systems, a pump forces heated water through the pipes.

Steam systems. These systems are similar to hot water systems. Water is heated in the boiler, and the steam rises through pipes to the radiators above. When cooled, the steam condenses into water and flows back to the boiler. Sometimes, old steam lines can be used when the system is upgraded to a more modern hydronic system.

Radiant systems. Radiant heating uses a house's structure—its walls, floor, or ceiling—to radiate steady, even heat into rooms. One example is radiant slab heating, where pipes carry hot water to heat the concrete slab floor in which they're embedded. Because it works well with relatively low water temperatures, such a system can be used with solar heating. However, it's not easily integrated with other heating systems.

Room heaters. Room heaters can take many forms. They may be baseboard heaters, small wall or ceiling heaters, or electric radiant heating panels. Duct heaters are also available.

Baseboard heaters are commonly used in newly remodeled spaces or in hard-to-heat areas. Some baseboard heaters have resistance coils that glow red hot; others have a resistance wire that heats a ceramic tube; still others have the heating element immersed in a sealed tube surrounded by fins that radiate heat into the room.

Wall and ceiling heaters, suitable for bathrooms and other small areas, are mounted in a wall or ceiling and are wired directly into the electrical system or connected to the gas supply line.

Radiant heating panels may be electrically heated glass panels mounted in walls or ceilings or special gypsum wallboard panels embedded with electric resistance wires and installed in place of regular wallboard. Both kinds are wired into the electrical system and are controlled by a thermostat.

Duct heaters can be turned on at the same time as the blower in a forced warm air system or can be operated by a separate thermostat located in an area requiring supplemental heat.

Solar heating systems

Though solar heating alone rarely provides enough heat to meet all of a home's energy needs, it's often used as a supplement to a conventional heating system. It retrofits easily to the hot water systems described on the facing page. Solar heating systems help to conserve energy and can result in considerable savings in energy costs.

There's a broad spectrum of solar heating options, from simple to highly complex. But no matter what they look like, all are either active or passive. Both types perform four distinct functions: they collect the sun's energy, store that energy as heat, distribute it through the rooms to be heated, and retain the heat on cloudy days or during the night.

In an active system, electrically powered pumps and fans move warm air or water through the house. This distribution is thermostatically controlled, so heat is delivered only when and where it's needed, just as with a conventional heater.

A strictly passive design relies on natural heat movement to distribute energy from the thermal storage mass to the areas the system was designed to serve. But many passive systems have been made more effective through the use of small fans and ductwork. Because they include a mechanical boost, these designs are known as hybrid systems.

A Forced Warm Air System

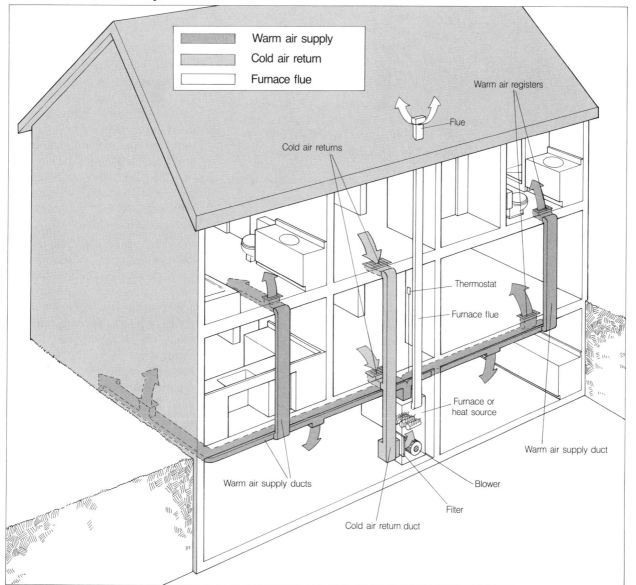

Fig. 9

Walls & Ceilings

The basic "shell" of any room—the walls and ceiling—is probably the first place you'll turn your attention to when you think about remodeling. That's because it offers a myriad of remodeling possibilities. You can do something very dramatic, such as removing a wall or raising a ceiling to achieve a more open feeling, or something much more modest, like brightening up your bathroom with ceramic tile walls or refurbishing your windows and doors with new interior trim.

Whatever your goals, you'll learn how to accomplish them in this chapter. In addition to basic information on walls, wall coverings, and ceilings, you'll get special help with extras like adding new closets or cabinets to already existing spaces.

Many of the simpler projects—for example, applying new wall coverings or even removing a partition wall—are ones you can tackle yourself with a minimum of outside help. But if your project involves altering the structure of your house, as in adding a shed dormer, removing a bearing wall, or raising a ceiling, you'll need to proceed with care; it's best to consult an architect or a structural engineer who can analyze the effect your proposed changes will have on the present structure and tell you whether or not they're feasible.

Even if you engage the services of a professional, it's always a good idea to be familiar with the basic structure of your house. For a short course in three common styles of house framing, turn to pages 74–75. If you need detailed information about framing a house from the ground up and the outside in, see the *Sunset* book *Basic Carpentry Illustrated*.

Removing a Partition Wall

Often, remodeling plans call for removing all or part of an interior wall to enlarge or open up a space. Before you decide to tear down a wall, it's important to understand the structure of your house. Begin by studying pages 74–75, where you'll find fully illustrated explanations of three types of framing.

It's crucial to determine whether the wall you want to remove is bearing or nonbearing. A *bearing* wall helps support the weight of the house; a *nonbearing* wall does not. An interior nonbearing wall, often called a partition wall, can be removed without special precautions. The procedure outlined below applies to partition walls only. If you're removing a bearing wall, see pages 84–85.

How can you distinguish between bearing and nonbearing walls? All exterior walls running perpendicular to ceiling and floor joists are bearing. Normally, at least one main interior wall is also a bearing wall. If possible, climb up into the attic or crawlspace and check the ceiling joists. If they're joined over any wall, that

wall is bearing. Even if joists span the entire width of the house, their midsections may be supported by a bearing wall. If you have any doubts about the wall, consult an architect, contractor, or building inspector.

Though removing a partition wall is not complicated, it can be quite messy. Cover the floors and furnishings with drop cloths and wear a painter's mask, safety glasses, and gloves. Check the wall for wiring, pipes, or ducts, all of which will have to be rerouted.

Removing the wall covering. If there's a door in the wall, remove it from its hinges. Pry off any door trim and ceiling or base molding.

The most common wall covering is gypsum wallboard nailed to wall studs. To remove it, knock holes in the wallboard with a hammer and then pull the wallboard away from the studs, using a pry bar. After one surface is removed, you can hit the other side from behind to knock it free.

If the wall covering is plaster and lath, chisel away the plaster until the lath backing—wood or metal—is exposed. You'll have to cut through the lath to break it up; then pry the lath and plaster away from the studs.

For paneling, cut starter holes with a saw and pry off the paneling.

Dismantling the framing. Remove the studs by sawing through each one (see **Fig. 1**); then push and pull them sideways to free the nails. To get at end studs (attached to studs or nailing blocks in adjacent walls), strip the wall covering back to the bordering studs and pry loose the end stud from the side.

To remove the sole plate, saw a small section out of the middle down to the finished floor level; chisel through the remaining thickness and insert a pry bar in the gap, as shown in **Fig. 2**.

To remove a top plate that lies parallel to the joists, cut the ceiling material back to the adjacent joists and pry off the plate (see **Fig. 3**). If the top plate is perpendicular to the joists, cut an even strip in the ceiling material, making certain that you don't cut into the joists; remove the plate in the same way.

Patching. Once the wall is dismantled, you may need to patch areas of adjacent walls, ceiling, and floors that have been damaged during the dismantling process. Though patching is straightforward, the real challenge lies in matching wallpaper, paint, or flooring. For wallboard techniques, see pages 92–94. Flooring information appears in the chapter "Floors & Stairs."

Removing Wall Framing

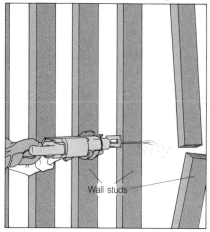

Fig. 1. **Saw through** *the wall studs; bend them sideways to free the nails from the top and sole plates.*

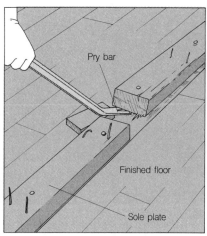

Fig. 2. **Pry up sections of the sole plate,** *using a pry bar, after cutting a gap with a saw and chisel.*

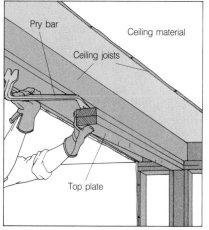

Fig. 3. **Pry out sections of the top plate** *after stripping off the ceiling material and sawing gaps in the plate.*

Removing a Bearing Wall

Because an interior bearing wall helps support the house structure above, removing all or part of this type of wall is trickier than removing a nonbearing partition wall. To complete the job, you'll need to follow this basic sequence: (1) build temporary support walls on both sides of the wall to shore up the house while you're working; (2) remove the wall covering, studs, sole plate, and top plate; and (3) provide permanent support around the new opening in the form of a sturdy beam and two posts.

The new beam can be solid 4-by or larger lumber, two 2-bys with ½-inch plywood sandwiched between them, or a steel I-beam. What size beam do you need? Check your local building code for the requirements in your area. Posts are typically wood 4 by 4s.

To determine whether the wall you wish to cut into is bearing or nonbearing, familiarize yourself with structural basics, as outlined on pages 74–75. All exterior walls running perpendicular to ceiling and floor joists are bearing. For more information, refer to page 83.

If you're not sure whether or not a wall is bearing, it's best to consult an architect or structural engineer. These professionals can also specify the beam and post sizes for longer spans and tell you if the job demands special precautions.

Before you begin, you'll also need to determine what utilities are concealed inside the wall. Electrical wires, plumbing pipes, and heating ducts must all be rerouted.

Building a Temporary Support Wall

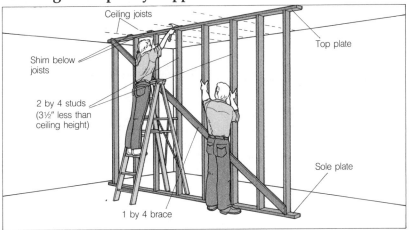

Ceiling joists

Top plate

Shim below joists

2 by 4 studs (3½" less than ceiling height)

Sole plate

1 by 4 brace

Fig. 4. Construct temporary support walls *to hold up the ceiling joists on both sides of a bearing wall before cutting into the wall.*

Removing the Wall: Two Details

Strip back wall covering

Saw through middle

End stud assembly

Sole plate

Fig. 5. Where the bearing wall *intersects another wall, saw through the middle of the stud assembly and pry out the pieces.*

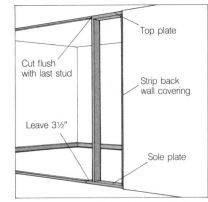

Cut flush with last stud

Top plate

Strip back wall covering

Leave 3½"

Sole plate

Fig. 6. If you're keeping *part of the wall, cut the top plate flush with the last stud, but let 3½ inches of the sole plate protrude.*

Building temporary support walls

To shore up the ceiling joists while you're working, you'll need to build two temporary support walls as shown in **Fig. 4**—one on each side of the wall section to be removed. To allow room for removing the wall itself, plan to erect these supports about 4 feet away.

For each support wall's sole plate and top plate, you'll need a 2 by 4. You'll also need enough 2 by 4s for studs, one at each end and one every 16 inches on center. Cut the plates for the support walls to length and mark the locations for the studs on both plates with a pencil and combination square.

Next, measure the height from floor to ceiling and cut studs to this length, minus 3½ inches. Nail each sole plate and top plate to the ends of the studs with 16-penny nails, two to each stud. Check the wall for square and then nail on a 1 by 4 diagonal brace, as shown.

Locate the ceiling joists (for help in finding joists, see page 95) and mark them. With a helper, swing the support wall up into place, parallel to the existing wall. While your helper uses a level to make sure the support wall is plumb on both the side and the end, drive shims between the top plate and the ceiling joists above until the wall is tight. If the ceiling joists sag in any spot, drive shims there until they're level.

Removing the wall

Take off any doors in the wall area you're removing, as well as any door trim, ceiling molding, or base molding. Since the work is messy, you may want to cover the furnishings with drop cloths.

Next, remove all wall materials. Where the wall adjoins an adjacent one, strip wall materials back to the bordering studs, as shown in **Fig. 5.** If you're taking out only part of the wall, strip wall materials back to the center of the stud beyond the last one you'll keep (see **Fig. 6**). For tips on removing the wall covering, see page 83. Need help finding studs? Turn to "Locating Studs & Joists" on page 95.

Dismantle the studs and sole plate, as described on page 83, and pry away the top plate from the ceiling material. Saw through and pry out the end stud assembly in the adjacent wall. If you're planning to keep part of the wall, cut the top plate flush against the last stud, but leave 3½ inches of the sole plate protruding, as shown in **Fig. 6.**

Adding the beam & posts

Before you add permanent support for the new opening—a beam and two posts—study **Fig. 7;** also examine the area beneath the locations of the new posts. Is there adequate bearing surface there for the weight of the structure? If joists sit atop a support girder or a wall below, you'll need to provide blocking between joists, as shown. If you don't have access, you'll need to remove a small section of the subfloor or of the basement ceiling below in order to install the blocking.

Assembling new beam and post supports. Cut the beam to the exact length; then notch either or both ends where they will be fastened below the adjacent wall's top plate. Lay the beam atop the sole plates below its intended position; measure the height from the beam to the ceiling joists at each end. Cut two posts to these lengths.

Now have several helpers elevate the beam into position. Slide both posts into position, check that they're snug and plumb, and toenail through the beam into the posts and plates at each end, using 10-penny nails. Add two studs at each wall intersection (see **Fig. 7**) to help secure the beam and provide a nailing surface for the wall covering. On a partial wall, nail through the end stud into the beam and post, using 16-penny nails.

Finishing up. The new beam can be finished and left exposed, trimmed with wood, or covered with wallboard and metal cornerbead.

Posts can be surfaced with wood trim or wallboard in the same way. You'll also need to patch existing wall, floor, and ceiling coverings. For wallboard techniques, see pages 92–94. To install floor covering, refer to the chapter "Floors & Stairs."

Installing the Beam & Posts

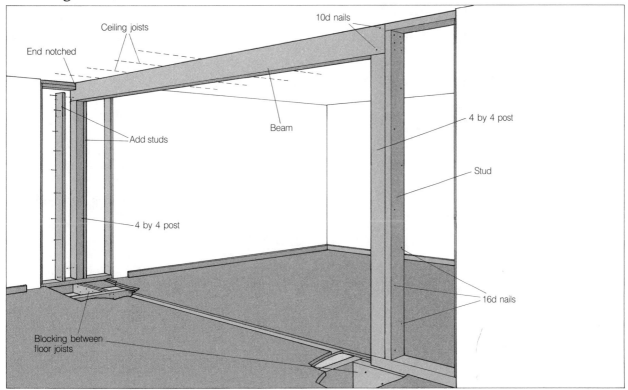

Ceiling joists

End notched

10d nails

Add studs

Beam

4 by 4 post

Stud

4 by 4 post

16d nails

Blocking between floor joists

Fig. 7

Building a Partition Wall

If your remodeling plans call for subdividing a large space or separating two living areas, you may need to build a nonbearing interior wall, or partition. Framing a wall (see **Fig. 8**) is a straightforward job, but you must measure carefully and continually check the alignment as you work.

Plotting the location. The new wall must be anchored securely to the floor, to ceiling joists, and, if possible, to wall framing at one end.

A wall running perpendicular to the joists will demand the least effort to attach. If wall and joists will run parallel, try to center the wall under a single joist; otherwise, you'll need to install nailing blocks every 2 feet between two parallel joists. Likewise, if the end of the new wall falls between existing studs, you'll need to install additional nailing blocks. To locate wall studs, use the method outlined on page 95; use the same method to locate ceiling joists.

Positioning the top plate and sole plate. On the ceiling, mark both ends of the center line of the new wall. Measure 1¾ inches (half the width of a 2 by 4 top plate) on both sides of each mark; snap parallel lines between corresponding marks with a chalkline to show the position of the top plate.

Hang a plumb bob from each end of the lines and mark these points on the floor. Snap two more chalklines to connect the floor points.

Cut both sole plate and top plate to the desired length. Lay the sole plate between the lines on the floor and nail it in place with 10-penny nails

Wall Framing Components

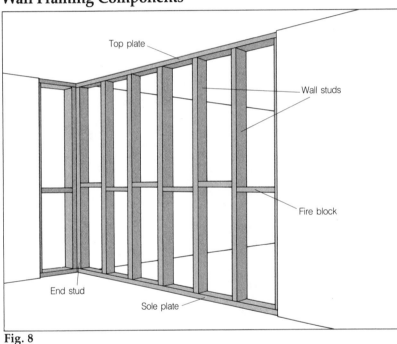

Top plate

Wall studs

Fire block

End stud

Sole plate

Fig. 8

How to Mark Stud Positions

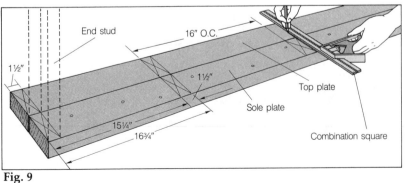

End stud

16" O.C.

1½"

1½"

Top plate

Sole plate

Combination square

15¼"

16¾"

Fig. 9

Top Plate Options

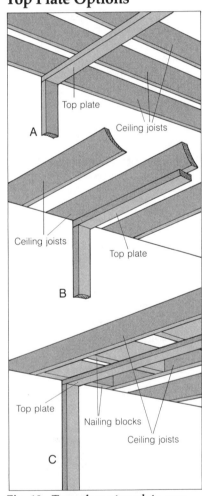

Top plate

Ceiling joists

A

Ceiling joists

Top plate

B

Top plate

Nailing blocks

Ceiling joists

C

Fig. 10. To anchor a top plate, *you may nail it to perpendicular joists (A), to the bottom of one parallel joist (B), or to nailing blocks installed between joists (C).*

spaced every 2 feet. (If you have a masonry floor, use a masonry bit to drill holes through the sole plate. Then insert expansion bolts.)

If you're planning a doorway (see page 129), don't nail that section of the plate; it will be cut out later.

Marking stud positions. Lay the top plate against the sole plate, as shown in **Fig. 9.** Beginning at an end that will be attached to an existing wall, measure in 1½ inches—the thickness of a 2 by 4 stud—and draw a line across both plates with a combination square.

Starting from the same end, measure and draw lines at 15¼ and 16¾ inches. From these lines, advance 16 inches at a time, drawing new lines, until the far end of both plates is reached. Each set of lines will outline the placement of a stud, with all studs evenly spaced 16 inches on center. Don't worry if the spacing at the far end is less than 16 inches. (If local codes permit, use 24-inch spacing—you'll save lumber—and adjust the initial placement of lines to 23¼ and 24¾ inches.)

Fastening the top plate. With two helpers, lift the top plate into position between the lines; nail it to perpendicular joists, to one parallel joist, or to nailing blocks (see **Fig. 10**).

Attaching the studs. Measure and cut the studs to exact length. Attach one end stud (or both) to existing studs or to nailing blocks between studs. Lift the remaining studs into place one at a time, checking plumb with a carpenter's level. Toenail the studs to both the top plate and the sole plate with 8-penny nails.

Your building code may require horizontal fire blocks between studs (see **Fig. 8**). The number of rows depends on the code; if permitted, position blocks to provide an extra nailing surface for wall coverings.

Finishing. After the studs are installed, add any electrical receptacles and switches (see pages 149–162), as well as any new plumbing (see pages 177–180). Once the wall has been inspected, finish it as desired.

PATCHING WALLS

Whenever you cut out a section of a wall during remodeling, you'll need to patch the affected area. Below are some tips for patching two of the most common types of walls—gypsum wallboard, and plaster and lath.

Gypsum wallboard. For a small hole, square up and trim any ragged edges neatly with a sharp utility knife. To provide backing for the new patch, cut a piece of lath slightly longer than the hole's width. Screw it to the back of the surrounding wallboard, as shown in **Fig. 11.**

Cut a patch of wallboard the same size as the opening; butter the edges with joint compound and attach the patch to the lath with drywall screws.

Using a 10-inch taping knife, spread joint compound across the joints; then smooth the compound and feather the edges out, removing any ridges. After it dries, sand it smooth and repeat. (If you're trying to match an existing texture, use a sponge, roller, paintbrush, or other tool while the last layer of compound is still wet.)

For a large hole, cut the surrounding wallboard out to the nearest studs and attach a new piece of wallboard (see pages 92–94).

Plaster and lath. To patch a small hole where the lath base has been cut out, remove loose plaster from around the hole, using a cold chisel and soft-headed steel hammer. To make a base for the new plaster, loop a wire through a piece of rust-resistant metal mesh. Roll up the edges, insert the mesh in the hole, and flatten it. Tightly wind the wire around a stick to hold the mesh; then dampen the hole's edges.

Using a putty knife, fill just over half the hole's depth with patching plaster, forcing it through the mesh (see **Fig. 11**). When the plaster is firm, remove the stick and clip off the wire. Score the plaster with a nail and let it dry. Then wet it again and apply a second layer of plaster to within ⅛ to ¼ inch of the surface. Score it and let it dry; then use a taping knife to apply finishing plaster, feathering the edges, and screed smooth. Texture it, if necessary, to match the surrounding wall. For a smooth surface, use a metal float dipped in water.

For a larger hole, install new lath and then finish as described above.

Two Types of Backing

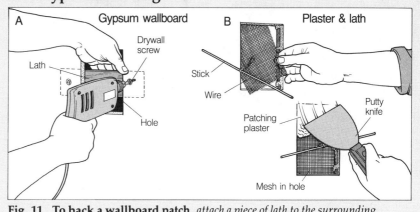

Fig. 11. To back a wallboard patch, *attach a piece of lath to the surrounding wallboard. For a plaster-and-lath wall, insert a piece of metal mesh in the hole (A); hold it in place with a stick and wire while you add new plaster (B).*

Framing Out an Attic

The classic attic shape—sloping walls and a sharp roof peak—presents a unique challenge for remodelers. If you're considering converting your attic into a finished room, you'll want to take a look at attic design. For ideas, see the planning chapter beginning on page 4.

To start the job, you'll need a solid subfloor, if you don't already have one; for details, see pages 116–117. The work entails closing off the eave space with short knee walls, squaring off the peak with collar beams, and perhaps dividing up the floor area with a partition wall. Here, we'll explain all three procedures.

Framing knee walls

A knee wall is simply a 2 by 4 sole plate and wall studs that run from the plate up to the rafters above. The only tricky parts to building one are laying out the sole plate and cutting the studs at the correct angle.

Your local building code may specify a minimum height for knee walls—usually 4 or 5 feet. Even if there's no requirement, it's not worth building walls much shorter. If your knee wall meets a partition wall partway across the room, try to place the intersection directly below a rafter.

To begin, measure the height up from the subfloor to the bottom edge of one rafter. The most accurate way to do this is to mark off the desired wall height on the string of a plumb bob; then move the marked string up and down the rafter's edge until the plumb bob's point just grazes the floor (see the inset in **Fig. 12**). Mark the spot on the floor. Repeat this procedure at the far end of the wall; again, mark the floor.

Snap a chalkline between the two marks on the floor; this line marks the inside edge of the sole plate. Measure and cut the sole plate to length. Nail through the plate into the subfloor and joists below with 16-penny nails. Add 10-penny nails between each joist (see **Fig. 12**).

Mark and cut the first stud square, a little bit longer than required. While a helper holds it in place against the rafter and sole plate, check it for plumb. Then trace the rafter angle on the stud and cut the stud along this line.

Position the stud between the sole plate and rafter, check it for plumb again, and nail the top to the rafter, using 8-penny nails. Check for plumb one more time; then toenail the bottom to the sole plate. Attach the remaining studs to the rafters and sole plate in the same way.

If the knee wall meets an end partition, you'll need to build a corner post assembly, as shown in **Fig. 12**. Simply attach a straight piece of 2 by 4 to each side of the end stud, using 10-penny nails in a staggered pattern.

Finally, cut and insert 2 by 4 nailing blocks between studs to provide an additional nailing surface for the wall covering.

Installing a flat, level ceiling

If you're closing off the ceiling in your attic room, you'll need to install collar beams to serve as new ceiling joists. Your attic may already have collar beams, but they may not be the right height—at least 7½ feet above the finished floor; they also may not be the right dimensions. For guidelines on spans and spacings, check your local building code. If you're replacing existing collar beams, remove the old ones and add new beams one at a time.

Take extra care when installing collar beams so they will all be at the same level. First, mark your plumb bob's string for the correct ceiling height. Then drop the plumb bob to the floor from the bottom of each rafter and mark the height on the rafter's face. At this height, measure the distance from outside edge to outside edge of each pair of rafters and subtract ½ inch; cut each beam to this length at an angle to match the slope of the roof.

Knee Wall Anatomy

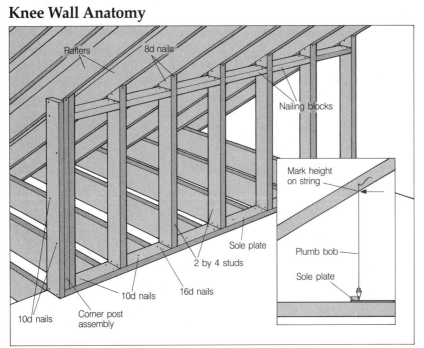

Fig. 12. A knee wall *is simply a sole plate and short studs cut to match the rafters' slope; nailing blocks help support the wall covering. To locate the sole plate, drop a plumb bob (see inset) from the correct height.*

With a helper, hoist each collar beam into position, lined up with your marks and about ¼ inch from each rafter edge; nail it to the rafters on each side with at least three 10-penny nails in a staggered pattern (see **Fig. 13**).

If you plan to add a partition wall, double the collar beams above the spot. Nail the second beam to the other side of the rafter; then insert blocking between the beams to provide a nailing surface for the partition's top plate.

Adding an attic partition wall

You build an attic partition in much the same way as a standard partition wall (see pages 86–87), but you'll need to custom-fit the top plate and studs to follow the angle of the knee walls and rafters, as shown in **Fig. 14**.

Start by installing the sole plate on the subfloor, directly below the collar beam assembly and running from knee wall to knee wall. Again, a plumb bob will help you find the location exactly.

The top plate is installed in three separate pieces. First, measure along the bottom of the doubled collar beams and cut a section of top plate to this length. Center the plate below the collar beams and nail it in place, using 16-penny nails spaced every 16 inches.

The next pieces you'll add are the sloping sections of the top plate between the collar beams and knee walls, as shown in **Fig. 14**. Build these areas up with 2-by nailing blocks attached flush with the rafter edges. Then cut two top plate sections to run from the knee walls to the top plate you just installed, carefully matching the angles to the existing pieces. Nail the sloping sections to the rafters.

To complete the wall, add studs at 16-inch intervals and extra studs below the joints between top plate sections. If you plan a doorway, frame it as detailed on page 129. Finally, face-nail the wall's end studs to the corner posts with 10-penny nails staggered every 12 inches.

Framing a Flat, Level Ceiling

Fig. 13. Collar beams *square off an attic's roof peak. After marking the height from the attic floor, measure the distance between the outside edges of matching rafters, cut the collar beams ½ inch short, and nail them to the rafters.*

Building an Attic Partition Wall

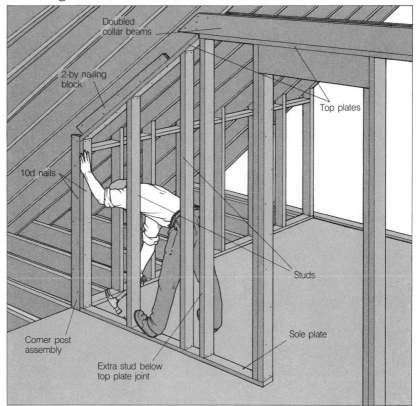

Fig. 14. A custom-shaped partition wall *cuts off the attic's length between knee walls. To build one, lay down the sole plate; then fit top plate pieces to doubled collar beams and rafters. Finally, cut and install studs to match the top plate's slope.*

Adding On a Shed Dormer

If you're after extra attic floor space, a required fire exit, or simply a new view, a dormer may be the answer. There are two types: a *gable* dormer and a *shed* dormer. Though the gable dormer's pitched roof is attractive, a shed dormer provides more usable space and is the simplest to build. The procedure is outlined below.

Can do-it-yourselfers plan and build a dormer? Yes, but planning is critical and working on the roof requires extra precaution. Before you dive in, show your plans to a structural engineer or architect to make sure your present house structure can handle the new load.

Sketching out a plan

A shed dormer requires a roof opening, a front wall, side walls, and new rafters. You'll need to decide where to place the opening, what the slope of the new rafters should be, and how much floor space and headroom you want.

To maximize floor space, the front wall is sometimes positioned directly above the bearing wall below; however, the dormer looks much better if it's moved back a bit, as shown in **Fig. 15**. Rafter slope should be integrated visually with the existing roofline and must be at least the minimum required by code for the roofing material you're using.

The front wall's height not only affects rafter slope but also available headroom: attic rooms typically must have 7½ feet of headroom over at least half their area, and there may be a minimum requirement of 4 or 5 feet at *any* given point.

To interrelate all these factors, first draw a side view of your existing

Dormer Framing

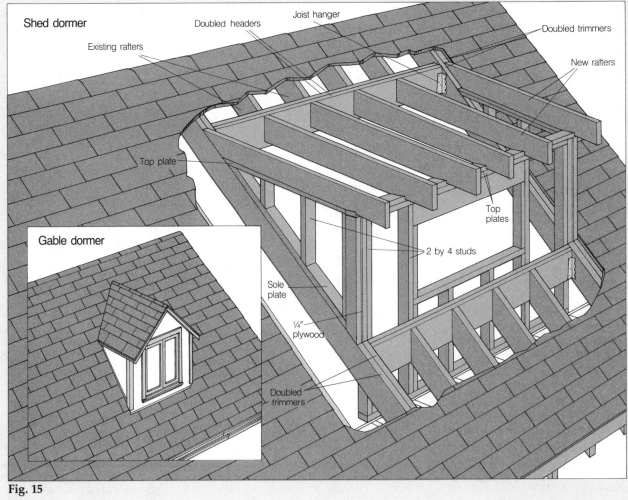

Fig. 15

roof. Figure the roof's half-span (the horizontal distance from top plate to ridge) and the vertical rise at the ridge; then lay these features out to scale. Next, lay tracing paper over your original plan and sketch dormer profiles, like the one shown in **Fig. 16,** to your heart's content. With this method, you can easily check the effects of any choices—such as front wall height or placement—on the remaining factors, such as rafter slope.

The basic building sequence

When you're ready to build, consider these general guidelines: choose a day with zero probability of rain, and where possible, do your work while standing on solid footing, such as the attic subfloor, rather than on the roof. Here's the basic procedure for building a shed dormer.

First, lay out the roof opening; plan to use the existing roof rafters for trimmers, if at all possible. Double the trimmers, as shown in **Fig. 15.** Using your layout as a guide, cut away the roofing materials and sheathing within the opening. (This process is similar to the first steps for installing a skylight; for details, see pages 140–141.)

Next, erect temporary support walls (see page 84) to support the roof rafters above and below the opening. Then cut the rafters within the opening and install doubled headers, fastening them to the trimmers with double joist hangers.

Frame the dormer's front wall, building it to the width of the opening (for techniques, see pages 86–87 and 134). Swing the wall up into place, plumb and brace it, and then nail it to the attic floor joists. Add corner posts at each end and nail a second top plate over the entire wall.

To lay out the dormer rafters, you'll need to figure three cuts: (1) the plumb cut (where the rafter meets the header), (2) the bird's mouth (the notch for the front wall's top plate), and (3) the tail cut (forming the dormer roof's overhang). You can figure these cuts by trial and error or by laying them out with a rafter square. For help with roof framing, see the *Sunset* book *Basic Carpentry Illustrated.*

Once one rafter fits, use it as a pattern to cut the rest. For the end rafters, the ends of which sit atop the trimmers, first cut the bird's mouths; then hold each rafter against its respective trimmer, trace the correct angle, and cut the ends.

Add the sole and top plates for the side walls; then cut angled studs to fit between the plates.

Finally, apply the exterior finishing materials (see **Fig. 17**). For help, see the *Sunset* book *Roofing & Siding.* Inside, you'll need new wall and ceiling coverings. Turn to pages 92–105 for instructions.

Planning: A Sample Sketch

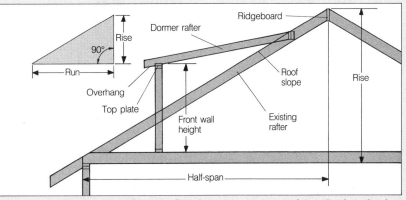

Fig. 16. To plot out your dormer, *first draw your present roof to scale; then sketch rafter and front wall profiles until you find the best combination.*

Closing Up the Exterior

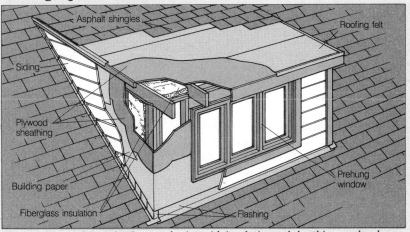

Fig. 17. A weathertight dormer *begins with insulation and sheathing, and ends with siding and roofing materials that match existing surfaces.*

Gypsum Wallboard

Whether you're covering up the framing of a new wall or looking for a way to freshen up an existing one, gypsum wallboard is a good choice. It's inexpensive and provides a smooth surface for paint, wallpaper, tile, plastic laminate, or paneling.

Wallboard can be applied to ceilings, too. If you're using it on both the walls and the ceiling, be sure to apply it to the ceiling first. The wall panels will help support the edges of the ceiling panels.

Standard wallboard is composed of a fire-resistant gypsum core sandwiched between two layers of paper. Some wallboard is water-resistant for use in bathrooms and other damp areas. Panels are usually 4 by 8 feet and ½ inch thick, but other thicknesses may be required by code.

Cutting and installing gypsum wallboard is a straightforward job, but concealing the joints between panels and in the corners demands patience and care. And the weight of full panels makes them awkward to negotiate. Wallboard is easily damaged; take care not to bend or break the corners or tear the paper covers.

To make a straight cut in wallboard, first mark the cutting line on the front paper layer with a pencil and straightedge, or snap a chalkline. Cut through the front paper and score the board with a utility knife (see **Fig. 18**).

Turn the panel over and break the core along the line by bending it back. Finally, cut the back paper along the bend and smooth the cut edge with a perforated rasp.

When fitting wallboard around obstructions, carefully measure from the edge of an adjacent panel or reference point to the obstruction. Transfer the measurements to a new panel and make the necessary cuts with a keyhole saw.

For small cutouts, such as those for electrical devices, first rub a bit of colored chalk (or even lipstick) on the edges of the opening or object. Position the panel and press in on the area; then saw along the outline left by the chalk. If the fit is too tight, trim the edges with a perforated rasp.

Gypsum wallboard for walls

Wallboard panels may be positioned either vertically or horizontally—that is, with the long edges either parallel or perpendicular to wall studs. Most professionals prefer the latter method because it helps bridge irregularities between studs and results in a stronger wall. You may not want to use this method, though, if your wall is higher than 8 feet—the extra height requires more cutting and creates too many joints.

Laying out the wallboard. Before installing panels, mark the stud locations on the floor and ceiling. Starting from one corner, place the first panel tight against the ceiling. If you choose the horizontal method, stagger the end joints in the bottom row so they don't line up with the joints in the top row.

Fasteners. Wallboard may be fastened to walls with nails, drywall screws, or construction adhesive supplemented by nails. Fastener

Cutting Gypsum Wallboard

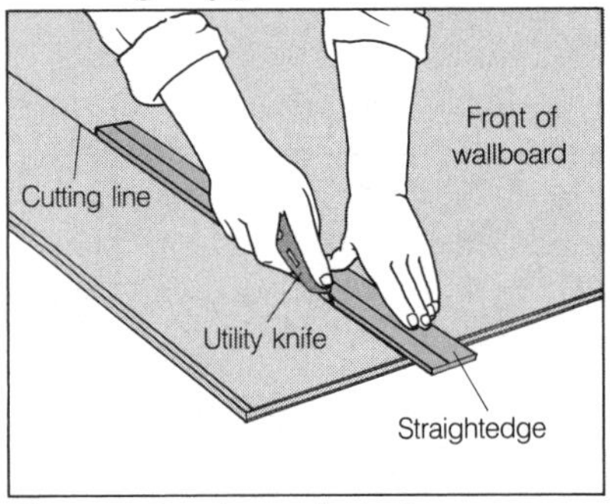

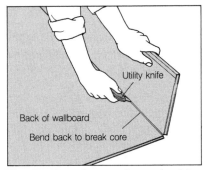

Fig. 18. **Cut through** *the front paper and score the core, using a utility knife.*

Fig. 19. **Turn the panel over,** *bend it back, and cut through the paper.*

Installing Panels on Walls

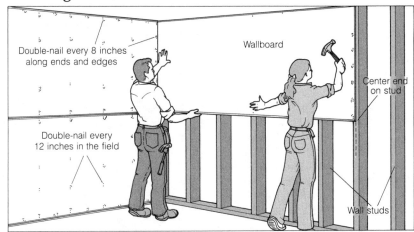

Fig. 20. **Lift the wallboard panel** *into position and center the edges over the studs. Then nail the panel to the studs, dimpling the surface slightly with the hammer.*

Taping Wallboard Joints

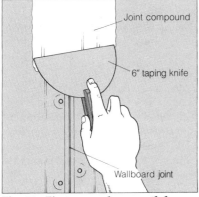

Fig. 21. First, spread a smooth layer *of joint compound over the joint with a 6-inch taping knife.*

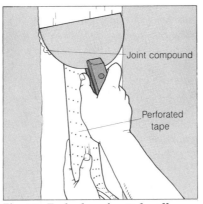

Fig. 22. Embed perforated wall-board tape *in the compound and apply another, thinner layer of compound.*

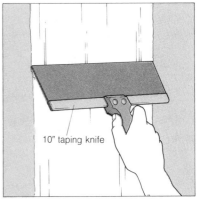

Fig. 23. After the compound *is dry and sanded, apply a wider layer with a 10-inch taping knife, feathering the edges.*

spacings are subject to local codes, but typical nail spacing is every 8 inches along panel ends and edges and along intermediate supports (called "in the field"). Be sure that nails are no closer to the edges than ⅜ inch.

Panels can also be double-nailed, ensuring that if one nail fails, its partner will hold the panel. When double-nailing, space a second nail 2 inches from each initial nail; you can space these pairs 12 inches apart in the field (see **Fig. 20**).

For best results when nailing, use ring-shank nails with ¼-inch-diameter heads. Choose 1¼-inch nails for ⅜- or ½-inch panels, and 1⅝-inch nails for ⅝-inch panels.

Drive the nails in with a claw or wallboard hammer. Your goal is to dimple the surface of the wallboard without puncturing the paper. If you do puncture the paper or miss a stud, drive in another nail; the hole can be patched and sanded later.

It's usually simplest to first tack a row of panels in place with a few nails through each; later, you can snap chalklines to mark the studs and then finish the nailing pattern.

If your wallboard will serve as a backing for a ceramic tile wall, sheet or board paneling, or cabinets, you may not need to hide joints and corners. But if you're planning to paint or wallpaper, you'll have to finish the wallboard.

Taping joints and corners. To finish wallboard neatly, you'll need perforated wallboard tape (buy tape that's precreased) and joint compound. Premixed joint compound is much simpler to use than the powdered variety.

Taping is done in three stages, as shown in **Figs. 21–23**. Let the compound dry between each stage. (See the manufacturer's instructions for drying time.)

To tape a joint between panels, first apply a smooth layer of taping compound over the joint, using a 6-inch taping knife and pushing the compound into the joint. Before the compound dries, embed wallboard tape into it and apply another thin coat of compound over the tape, smoothing the compound gently

with the knife. Use only enough compound to fill the joint and cover the tape evenly; excess compound just means more sanding later.

To tape an inside corner, apply a smooth layer of compound to the wallboard on each side of the corner. Measure and tear the tape to length, fold it in half vertically along the crease, and press it into the corner with a corner tool (see **Fig. 24**). Apply a thin layer of compound over the tape and smooth it out.

Cover exterior corners with a protective metal cornerbead cut to length and nailed through its perforations. You don't need to tape here: simply run your knife down the sharp metal edge to fill the spaces and cover the cornerbead with joint compound, as shown in **Fig. 25**.

Taping the Corners

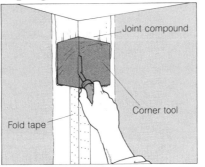

Fig. 24. To tape an inside corner, *fold the tape in half and press it into the compound with a corner tool.*

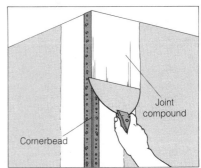

Fig. 25. Protect an outside corner *with metal cornerbead; finish with joint compound.*

... *gypsum wallboard*

Tape all remaining joints in the same manner. Then, using smooth, even strokes with the 6-inch knife, cover the nail dimples in the field with compound.

Allow the taping compound to dry for at least 24 hours; then sand lightly until the surface is smooth (be sure not to sand through the tape). Wear a painter's mask and hat against the dust and close off the room where you're working.

Then, using a 10-inch knife, apply a second coat of compound, feathering out the edges past each side of the taped joint.

Let the second coat dry. Then sand it and apply a final coat, using the 10-inch taping knife or an even wider finishing trowel to smooth out and feather the edges. After the compound dries, sand it once more with fine sandpaper to remove even minor imperfections.

Textured versus smooth finish. Though many people prefer the smooth look, texture can hide a less-than-perfect taping job. Also, as the house shifts and framing shrinks over time, any cracks between panels will be less apparent.

Texturing compounds are available ready-mixed or in powdered form. Some joint compounds double as texturing compounds; other effects may require special texturing materials. Ask your dealer for recommendations.

Professionals often apply texturing with a spray gun, but homeowners produce good results by daubing, swirling, or splattering the compound on with a sponge, paint roller, or stiff brush—whatever tool produces the desired appearance.

Let the compound set up until slightly stiff; then even it out as required with a wide trowel. Allow the finished surface to dry for at least 24 hours before painting.

Gypsum wallboard for ceilings

Though gypsum wallboard panels are heavy and awkward to install on ceilings, they're the most popular choice because they're inexpensive, they take paint and surface textures well, and one panel covers a large area. A few special techniques will help the work go smoothly—and will lead to a smooth result as well.

Basic ceiling application. Methods for installing a wallboard ceiling are basically the same as those for walls (see the preceding section). Choose ½- or ⅝-inch-thick panels and fasten them perpendicular to

joists with annular ring nails, drywall screws, or a combination of nails and construction adhesive. Nail spacings are governed by local codes, but typical spacing is every 7 inches along panel ends and at intermediate joists.

If you decide to double-nail—a smart choice for ceilings—space the first set of nails every 7 inches along the ends and every 12 inches in the field. Place the second nail 2 inches from the first one. Space nails at least ⅜ inch in from the edges.

Supporting the panels. Because you'll need to support the heavy panels while you're fastening them, installing a wallboard ceiling is a two-person job. First, position a pair of stepladders or set up a couple of sturdy sawhorses, laying a few planks across them to serve as a short scaffold to stand on. Then, with both you and your helper holding the ends of the panel in place with your heads, begin nailing at the center of each panel; place the next few nails where they'll take the weight off your heads (see **Fig. 26**).

As an alternative, you can construct one or two T-braces (see **Fig. 27**). The length of each brace should equal the height from the floor to the ceiling joists; when the panel is positioned, the extra length will help wedge the brace in place.

Tips for Installing Wallboard on the Ceiling

Fig. 26. It takes two people *to install a wallboard ceiling. Holding the ends of each panel in place with your heads, nail first in the center and then where it will take the weight off your heads. When double-nailing, place the second nail 2 inches away from the initial one.*

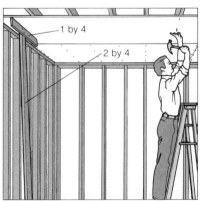

Fig. 27. T-braces, *used singly or in pairs, can also hold panels in position. Fashion a simple, sturdy brace from a 2 by 4 upright and a 1 by 4 crosspiece.*

Most walls and ceilings are not solid —they're made of gypsum wallboard, plaster and lath, or wood paneling laid over a framework of studs and joists (see **Fig. 28**). If you're planning to cut into an existing wall or if you're simply looking for a strong anchoring point, you'll need to locate those framing members behind the smooth facade of the wall or ceiling.

Studs and joists are spaced, according to building codes, at regular intervals—usually 16 or 24 inches on center. Once you've found one stud, locating the rest should be easy. Often, you can simply start from one of the four major corners inside a conventionally built house, measure in 14½ inches, and, using one of the methods outlined below, find the first stud there. If so, the next ones

should be at 16-inch intervals. Here's how to find studs.

Knocking firmly on the wall with the heel of your clenched fist will sometimes allow you to locate the studs. Rap sharply in the area where you think a stud should be. A solid sound means a stud is behind the wall; a hollow sound tells you to keep knocking.

Another method is to examine your wallboard or paneling closely— you can often see where nails have been driven into studs and joists. If the nails don't show, try using a stud finder (see **Fig. 29B**), an inexpensive device with a magnetized needle that dances as it nears a nail head.

If all else fails, drill exploratory holes in a likely but inconspicuous

spot, using a drill fitted with a small bit. Either drill a hairbreadth above the baseboard molding (be sure you're not hitting the sole plate) and fill the holes later, or take up the molding and drill where the hole will be covered later when the molding is replaced.

The same methods apply to finding ceiling joists. If the ceiling is suspended, simply push up a section and look for solid wood. If you're working on the top (or only) story of the house, you may have access to an attic or crawlspace where the joists are exposed. Either measure to one joist and transfer the measurement downstairs or drill a small hole in the attic next to one joist so the spot will be marked from below, as shown in **Fig. 29D**.

Framing Detail

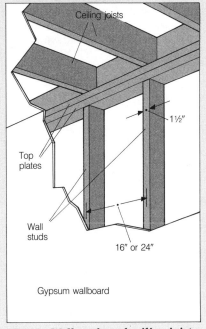

Fig. 28. Wall studs and ceiling joists *in most homes are spaced at regular intervals, usually 16 or 24 inches on center.*

Four Ways to Find Studs & Joists

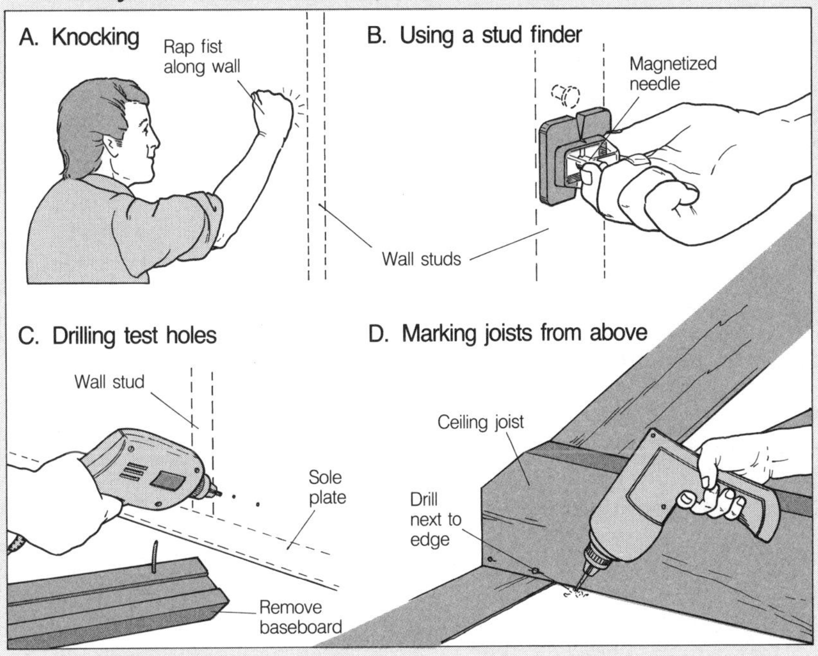

A. Knocking — Rap fist along wall

B. Using a stud finder — Magnetized needle — Wall studs

C. Drilling test holes — Wall stud — Sole plate — Remove baseboard

D. Marking joists from above — Ceiling joist — Drill next to edge

Fig. 29. To find the first stud or joist, *try one of these methods: knock until you hear a solid sound (A); look for nails or use a magnetized stud finder that detects nails (B); drill a test hole near or behind the baseboard molding (C); or mark joist edges by drilling a hole from the attic above (D).*

Paneling

Paneling can add warmth and character to any room, no matter what its style. Paneling is practical, too—it's an ideal way to conceal problem walls that would be very difficult or costly to repair. And paneling is durable, easy to maintain, and relatively simple to install.

The two types are sheet and solid board paneling. Sheet paneling can be plywood (created from thin layers of wood veneer), hardboard (made from compressed wood fibers), or plastic laminate. It comes in large panels—commonly 4 by 8 feet.

Solid board paneling, with its natural grain and texture, is particularly attractive. Boards vary in width from 3 to 12 inches and in thickness from ⅜ to ⅞ inch. Milled from both hardwoods and softwoods, they often come with edges that overlap or interlock.

Board paneling can be easier to use where extensive handling, maneuvering, and cutting are needed, such as around doors and windows. Sheet paneling is easiest to apply over large, unbroken surfaces. Whatever type of paneling you choose, arrange to store it (and any trim) in the room where it will be used for at least 2 days (ideally, a week to 10 days). This allows it to adapt to the room's temperature and humidity, which may prevent warping and buckling later on.

Installing sheet paneling

Sheet paneling can be laid over new stud walls, applied directly to existing walls that are in good condition, or attached to furring strips over old, bumpy walls. If you're paneling over bare studs, ask your dealer whether you'll need to back the sheets with gypsum wallboard or another material for rigidity and fire protection.

Estimating materials. To estimate the amount of paneling you'll need, measure the length of the wall you're covering (assuming it's a standard 8-foot height) and divide by the width of your panel—probably 4 feet. Round the figure off to the next higher number. The result is the number of panels you'll need. Unless a very large part of the wall is windows and doors, don't bother trying to deduct materials for them.

Preparing the wall. Unless you're applying paneling over a new stud wall, you'll have to check the wall to see if it's flat and plumb. To do this, use a carpenter's level. If the wall is flat and plumb, simply clean it thoroughly and, using an adhesive, attach the sheet paneling directly to the wall.

If the wall is very bumpy or significantly out of plumb, you'll need to apply furring strips, as described below.

If the wall is made of masonry, it will need to be waterproofed before you can apply the paneling in order to prevent condensation from damaging the paneling. Patch the surface with cement grout and then apply a waterproofing sealer. A vapor barrier paper or polyvinyl film between the masonry and the furring strips will further protect the paneling from moisture.

If you're paneling a basement with concrete walls, you may want to install a framework of 2 by 4 studs first so there'll be enough depth for receptacles and switches. In this case, don't use furring strips; instead, place blocking between the studs to provide a nailing base.

Furring and shimming. Furring strips, usually 1 by 3s or 1 by 4s, are attached to studs with nails long enough to penetrate the studs at least an inch. (For help locating studs, see page 95.) For masonry walls, use concrete nails or expansion bolts.

Nail the furring strips to the studs horizontally, either 16 or 24 inches on center (see **Fig. 30**). Check the manufacturer's instructions for recommended nail spacings. Be sure to leave a ¼-inch space at both the top and bottom of the wall when applying the strips. This will help prevent buckling if the house should settle.

Furring strips should be plumb and flat; you can make small adjustments with shingle shims. If the existing wall is severely out of plumb, you may need to block out the furring strips at one end.

When you add furring strips, you'll need to adjust door and window frames, receptacles, and switches to accommodate the increased wall thickness.

To adjust door and window frames, add material of sufficient thickness to the existing framework to accommodate the depth of the furring and paneling. A typical example is shown in **Fig. 31**. To move electrical boxes, which are usually mounted on the studs, you may have to cut away some of the existing wall covering.

CAUTION: Be sure to turn off the electric current before you move any electrical devices.

Planning your layout. For appearance's sake, cut the first and last panels on a wall the same width, unless you're using panels with random-width grooves. Prop the panels up along the wall to see how they'll fit. Whenever possible, center between-panel joints over door and window

Applying Furring Strips

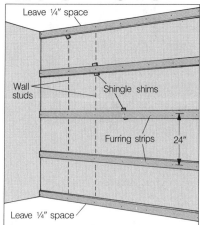

Leave ¼" space

Wall studs

Shingle shims

Furring strips   24"

Leave ¼" space

Fig. 30. Nail horizontal furring strips *to studs. If the furring isn't perfectly plumb and flat, use shingle shims for small adjustments.*

openings. At inside corners, plan to butt panels together. Outside corners, unless perfectly mitered, will require two pieces of trim or a corner guard.

Cutting paneling. Support the paneling on sawhorses; arrange several furring strips or 2 by 4s across the horses for extra support.

To cut the panels, use either a handsaw (choose one for fine cutting—10 to 15 teeth per blade inch) or a portable circular saw. Cut the panels *face up* if you're using a handsaw, *face down* if you're using a power saw. To avoid splintering the veneer when sawing by hand, use a sharp knife to score the cutting line first.

Scribing a panel. The first piece of paneling that you fit into a corner probably won't exactly match the contours of the adjoining wall. To duplicate the irregularities of the adjoining surface on the paneling's edge, prop the panel into place about an inch from the uneven surface; use shims, if necessary, to adjust level and plumb. Draw the point of a compass or wing dividers along the irregular surface so the pencil leg duplicates the unevenness onto the paneling. (For an illustration, see **Fig. 66** on page 111.)

Carefully trim the paneling along the scribed line with a coping saw, saber saw, or block plane.

Laying out an opening. Fitting a panel around any opening requires careful measuring, marking, and cutting.

Keep track of all the measurements by sketching them on a piece of paper. Starting from the corner of the wall or the edge of the nearest panel, measure to the edge of the opening or electrical device; then, from the same point, measure to the opening's opposite edge.

Next, measure the distance from the floor to the opening's bottom edge and from the floor to the opening's top edge. (Keep in mind that you'll install the paneling ¼ inch above the floor.)

Marking the side of the panel that will face you as you cut (face up for a handsaw, face down for a power saw), transfer these measurements to the panel. When marking the back of the panel, remember that measurements will be a mirror image of the opening.

Attaching sheet paneling. Though you can attach paneling with nails only, a combination of adhesive and nails is preferable.

To begin, cut a panel ½ inch short of the distance from floor to ceiling (this will allow for any eventual settling of the house). On furring or exposed wall framing, apply adhesive to the framing in squiggly lines (see **Fig. 32**). On a finished wall, apply adhesive directly to the wall, spacing the squiggly stripes a uniform 12 or 16 inches apart.

Drive four finishing nails through the top edge of the panel—4-penny nails for ¼-inch panels, 6-penny for panels up to ⅝ inch thick, and 8-penny for thicker materials. Position the panel on the wall, leaving a ¼-inch space at the bottom; drive the nails partway into the wall to act as hinge pins.

Pull the panel's bottom edge about 6 inches out from the wall and push a block behind to hold it there; wait for the adhesive to become tacky (check the manufacturer's directions for the specific time).

Then remove the block and press the panel firmly into place. To force the adhesive into tight contact, knock on the panel with a mallet or hammer against a padded block.

Drive the nails at the top all the way in; then nail the panels at the bottom (you'll eventually cover the nail heads and ¼-inch gap with molding). Thin paneling materials

Adjusting a Window Frame

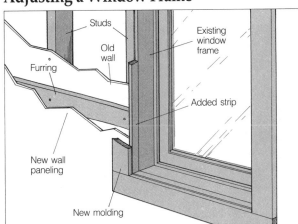

Fig. 31. To adjust a window frame's depth *to match your paneling, nail a strip of wood of equal thickness over the existing frame; then add new molding. Use the same technique to adjust a door frame.*

Putting Up Sheet Paneling

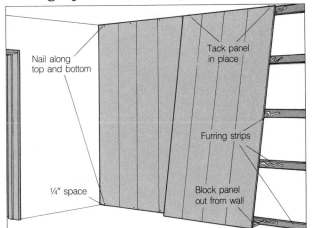

Fig. 32. To install a panel, *apply adhesive to the furring strips (or wall); then prop the panel into position and nail it partway into the wall along the top edge. When the adhesive becomes tacky, press the panel into place and finish nailing.*

require either glue or nails within ½ inch of the panel edges to prevent curling.

Installing solid board paneling

Like sheet paneling, solid boards can be attached to new stud walls, to existing walls in good shape, or to a gridwork of furring strips over old, bumpy walls. Though solid boards are usually installed vertically or horizontally, you can use a diagonal pattern or even one of your own design.

Estimating materials. To estimate the amount of paneling you'll need, first calculate the square footage to be covered by multiplying height by length. From this figure, subtract the area of any doors and windows.

Then decide on the pattern of application, as well as board width and edge-milling. Remember that a board's actual width is less than its nominal size; you may also need to subtract the width of the edge-milling.

Cutting and applying solid board paneling. You cut solid boards to fit into corners and around openings the same way as for sheet paneling (see page 97). To prevent splintering, cut finished boards *face up* if you're using a handsaw, *face down* if you're using a portable circular saw or saber saw.

You can either nail solid boards to your wall surface or attach them with adhesive. However, nailing is the preferred method. For standard 1-by boards, use 6-penny finishing nails and recess the heads ½32 inch below the surface with a nailset. Cover the nail heads, using a putty stick that matches the finish of the boards.

Where you nail depends on the board's milling. Typical nail placements are shown in **Fig. 33.** If you want to use an adhesive, apply it following the adhesive manufacturer's directions. Also, nail the top and bottom of each board after it's glued.

Vertical pattern. Unless you're attaching boards directly to an existing wall, before paneling vertically with solid boards you must attach horizontal furring strips to the studs every 24 inches on center or install nailing blocks between studs. (To locate studs, see page 95.)

Measure the width of the boards you're using and then the width of the wall. From these figures, calculate the width of the final board. To avoid a sliver-size board, split the difference so the first and last boards are the same. Plan to cut boards ½ inch shorter than the height from floor to ceiling.

When you place the first board into the corner, check the outer edge with a carpenter's level. If the board isn't plumb or doesn't fit the corner exactly, scribe and trim the edge facing the corner as described for sheet paneling (see page 97).

Attach the first board, leaving a ¼-inch space above the floor to allow for any settling of the house; then butt the second board against its edge and check for plumb before you nail it. Repeat this procedure with all subsequent boards.

To allow the last board to fit easily into place, cut its edge at a slight angle (about 5°) toward the board's back edge.

At inside corners, simply butt adjacent board edges together, scribing them if necessary. At outside corners, you can either miter the joints for a neat fit (cut the miters at an angle slightly greater than 45° so they'll fit snugly) or butt boards and conceal the joints with trim.

Horizontal pattern. Generally, you won't need to apply furring strips unless the wall is badly damaged or out of plumb. You can nail the boards to the studs directly, as shown in **Fig. 34,** or through existing wall coverings.

To avoid ending with a very narrow board at the ceiling, calculate and adjust its size as described for vertical board paneling, at left.

Starting at the bottom of the wall, temporarily nail the first board at one end, ¼ inch above the floor. Then level the board and complete the nailing. If you need to scribe and trim the board at its ends, follow the instructions on page 97. Minor inconsistencies can be covered later with molding.

Working toward the ceiling, attach the remaining boards. Cut the last board to width, leaving a ¼-inch space below the ceiling. If you have trouble fitting it, bevel its back edge slightly and pivot it into place.

Solid Board Applications

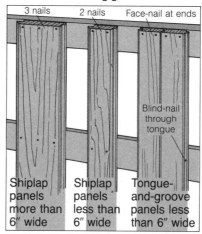

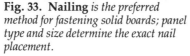

Fig. 33. Nailing *is the preferred method for fastening solid boards; panel type and size determine the exact nail placement.*

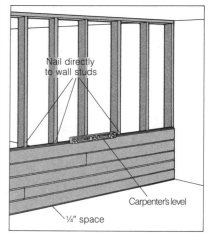

Fig. 34. Horizontal boards *can normally be nailed directly to wall studs; check often as you work to make sure the boards are level.*

Ceramic Tile Walls

Few wall coverings have the decorative impact and durability of ceramic tile. Glazed wall tiles come in every imaginable color and in many finishes and patterns. In addition to individual tiles, you can buy pregrouted tile panels, usually intended for use in shower and bathtub enclosures.

Tile is a natural choice for walls in kitchens and bathrooms and for bathroom tub and shower surrounds. Water, dirt, and grease can be wiped off quickly and easily to leave a sparkling clean surface.

You can install ceramic tile over new or existing gypsum wallboard, or even over wood paneling or tile as long as it's in good condition. After the surface is prepared, you need to carefully mark your working lines, install the tile, and then grout and seal it.

Ceramic tile may be set in either mortar or adhesive. Though tile set in mortar is the most durable choice for bathroom tub and shower enclosures, setting tile in mortar is usually a job for a professional. On these pages, we show you a good do-it-yourself approach to installing tile using adhesive.

Note: If your plans call for ceramic tile on the floor, too, install the floor tiles before setting tile on the wall. For instructions, see pages 122–123.

Removing old tile

Removing wall tile set in mortar is a very tough job. If possible, replace only those tiles that are damaged (for instructions, see the *Sunset* book *Remodeling with Tile*). If your old tiles are clean and smooth and the wall surface is flat, consider installing new tile over them. If you must remove old tile that's been set in mortar, it's best to have a professional do the job.

If your wall tile is set on gypsum wallboard with adhesive, you can more easily remove it yourself. Wearing goggles and a painter's mask, use a cold chisel and soft-headed steel hammer to chip through the tile and backing. Once you've removed small sections, insert a pry bar and pry off large sections of tile and backing until the wall studs are exposed. Be careful not to damage the studs.

Inspect the exposed wall framing for any water damage and replace framing members if necessary. Then install new wallboard (for techniques, see pages 92–94) as backing for the new tile.

Installing ceramic tile

It's important to plan and prepare carefully before you install tile. First, measure the walls you want to tile and sketch them to scale on graph paper. Choose and plan the placement of special trim pieces, such as bullnose, cove, and quarter-round tiles. (Some typical trim pieces are illustrated in **Fig. 35**.)

If you're tiling a bathroom, you must also plan for ceramic accessories—soap dishes, paper holders, and toothbrush holders. Your dealer can help you select trim pieces and accessories.

Once you've planned the design of your walls and selected tile, you're ready to prepare the surface and install your tile. (If you're using pregrouted tile panels, follow the manufacturer's instructions.)

Before you start, remove baseboards and window and door trim, wall-mounted accessories and lights, and, if necessary, fixtures such as sinks and toilets.

Preparing the backing surface. This is probably the most important step in installing wall tile successfully. The surface must be solid, flat, clean, and dry.

If you're using wallboard as backing in a bathroom tub or shower enclosure, be sure it's the water-resistant type.

First, clean off all dirt and grease. Repair any old tile and use an abrasive disc mounted on an electric drill to clean and roughen the surface for better adhesion. Remove old finish from wood and sand it smooth.

Then check the backing surface with a straightedge; if it's irregular, you may be able to level it with a mastic underlayment or another compound recommended by the tile adhesive manufacturer.

You may need to prime or seal new or existing wallboard backing. A primer or sealer (also called a bond-erizer) penetrates the backing, increasing water resistance and strengthening the bond between the backing and the new tile. Again, check the adhesive manufacturer's recommendations.

Marking working lines. Marking accurate horizontal and vertical working lines will help you keep tiles properly aligned and ensure that your finished wall will look level and even. The horizontal working line should be near the bottom of the wall, because tiling up a wall is easier than tiling down.

If you're not tiling around a tub, find the lowest point by setting a level on the floor at various locations against the walls to be tiled. At the lowest point, place a tile against the wall and mark its top edge on the wall. If you're installing a cove base, set a cove tile on the floor and place a wall

Standard Trim Pieces

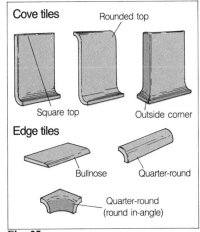

Fig. 35

. . . ceramic tile walls

tile above it (allow space for the grout joint); then mark the top of the wall tile. Using a level and straightedge, draw a horizontal line through the mark across the wall. Extend this line onto other walls to be tiled.

After marking your horizontal working lines, nail battens (1 by 2 wood strips) all along the walls, placing their top edges on the lines. These will be your horizontal guides.

If you're tiling around a tub, establish working lines there first. This way, you can plan for a row of full (uncut) tiles just above the tub. This works out best if the tub is level to within ⅛ inch. Locate the high point of the tub lip with your level and measure up one tile height plus ⅛ inch. Mark a level line on the wall

through this point; then extend it carefully across all adjoining walls (see **Fig. 36**). This will give you a bottom row of full tiles around the tub. (You can fill in any small gaps below them with caulking later.)

If your tub is not level to within ⅛ inch, you'll need to locate the horizontal working line from the low point of the tub lip; then follow the same method outlined above. You'll have to cut the bottom row of tiles to fit.

Then, on walls adjoining the tub, establish a line close to the floor. To do this, start at the working line you extended from the tub wall and measure down a full number of tiles, including grout joints. Leave a space at least one full tile high above the floor. Mark the horizontal working line for the wall through this point

with a straightedge and level, and nail on battens as described above.

To establish the vertical working line, locate the midpoint of the wall and mark it on the horizontal working line. Starting at this point, set up a row of loose tiles on the batten to see how they'll fit at the ends of the wall, as shown in **Fig. 37**.

If you'll end up with less than half a tile on both ends, move your mark half a tile to the right or left to avoid ending the rows with narrow pieces. Then extend the vertical working line through your mark and up the wall with a straightedge and level.

If you don't plan to tile to the ceiling line, mark the point where the highest tile will be set. Using a level, draw a horizontal line through this point across the wall.

Finally, be sure to mark locations of any ceramic accessories.

Setting the tile. The way you'll begin setting tiles depends on which bond you use—jack-on-jack (with joints lined up) or running bond (with staggered joints). Both are illustrated in **Fig. 38**.

For jack-on-jack, you set the first tile on the batten so one side is aligned exactly with the vertical working line. Additional tiles are set as shown, forming a pyramid pattern. For running bond, center the first tile on the vertical working line; then follow the pyramid pattern for the remaining tiles.

Prepare the tile adhesive according to the manufacturer's directions. You can select one of three types of thinset adhesive—organic- or cementbase (the two most commonly used types), or epoxy-base. Read the label or consult your dealer to find out which kind to use. Be sure to keep your working area well ventilated.

To determine how large an area to cover at one time, consult the adhesive container label for the "open time"—the length of time you have to work with the adhesive after spreading it. Apply the adhesive to the wall, combing it with a notched trowel to form ridges.

When you set the tiles, place each one with a slight twist—don't slide

Marking Working Lines for Tiling around a Tub

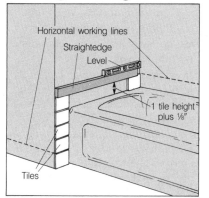

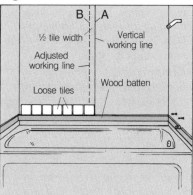

Fig. 36. Extend the horizontal working line *from one wall to the adjoining tub walls. Then measure down a full number of tiles and mark another line at least one tile height from the floor.*

Fig. 37. To establish the vertical working line, *first locate the midpoint of the wall (A); adjust the line (B), if necessary, according to the width of the end tiles.*

Patterns for Setting Tile

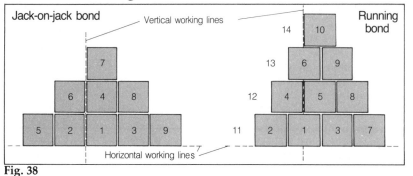

Fig. 38

it. Be sure to keep spacing for grout joints uniform. If your tiles don't have small ceramic spacing lugs molded onto their edges, drive nails into the wallboard to act as temporary spacing guides (see **Fig. 39**).

With either bond, continue setting tiles upward and toward the ends of the wall following the pattern you established. After laying several tiles, set them into the adhesive by sliding a carpet-wrapped piece of plywood across the tiles as you tap it gently with a hammer.

Cut tiles to fit at the end of each horizontal row and at the top near the ceiling. Use a glass cutter (see **Fig. 40**) or a rented tile cutter to cut straight pieces; use tile nippers to cut out irregular shapes. For the top row of a wainscoting or other installation that doesn't reach the ceiling, set bullnose or cap tiles.

When you come to a wall where there are electrical devices, turn off the power to them. Remove the cover plates and pull the devices from their boxes, but don't disconnect them. Cut and fit tiles around the boxes; then remount the devices flush with the new surface. If you're tiling around a sink, shower, or toilet, cut tiles to fit around any stubouts or faucet stems.

On inside corners, butt tiles together. On outside corners, set one column of bullnose tiles to cover the unfinished edges of the tiles on each adjoining wall. Around windows, finish off the sides and sill with bullnose tiles.

Install ceramic accessories in their spaces. Tape them in place while the adhesive sets.

Now check your work. If anything is out of alignment, wiggle it into position before the adhesive sets. Clean adhesive from the face of tiles and accessories, and from joint spaces.

When the adhesive has set, carefully remove the battens. Twist nail spacers as you pull them out from the wall.

Spread adhesive at the bottom of the wall where the battens were and set the remaining tiles, cutting them as needed (see **Fig. 41**).

Grouting the tile. Allow the adhesive to set properly—usually you must allow 16 hours for epoxy-base, 24 hours for organic-base, and 48 hours for cement-base adhesive.

Remove any excess adhesive from the tile joints. Then mix the grout recommended for your tile and spread it on the surface of the tile with a rubber-faced float or a squeegee, forcing it into the joints until they're completely filled (see **Fig. 42**). Scrape off excess grout, working diagonally across the surface.

Wipe the tiles with a wet sponge to remove any remaining grout. Rinse and wring out the sponge frequently, wiping until the grout joints are smooth and level with the tile surface. When the tiles are as clean as you can get them, let the grout dry until a haze appears over the surface. Then polish the haze off the tiles

with a soft cloth. Finish the joints with the end of a toothbrush handle.

Sealing the tile and grout. Installations with unglazed tile or with cement-base grouts need to be protected by a grout and tile sealer. Most sealers have a silicone base.

Follow the manufacturer's instructions for applying these sealers. Both tiles and grout should be dry. On new tile, wait at least 2 weeks before applying a sealer—this will give the grout a chance to cure completely. Apply only a moderate amount of the sealer, wiping off any excess to prevent the tile from discoloring.

Finally, replace any trim, accessories, or fixtures that you removed earlier. Use caulking to seal all openings or gaps between pipes or fixtures and tile.

Installing Wall Tile

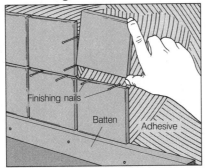

Fig. 39. To space wall tiles *that aren't molded with spacing lugs, drive nails into the wallboard between the tiles.*

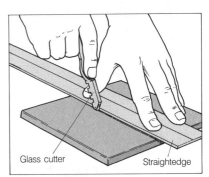

Fig. 40. To cut tile, *score it with a glass cutter; center the score mark over a nail or dowel and break the tile.*

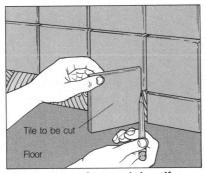

Fig. 41. To set the remaining tiles, *remove the batten from the working line, mark the tiles, and cut each one. Set in adhesive as for the other tiles.*

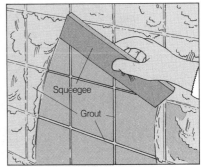

Fig. 42. Spread grout on the tile, *forcing the grout into the joints with a float or squeegee until they're full. Remove the excess grout.*

ADDING A BUILT-IN CLOSET

Few homes, whether new or old, have enough closet space. But if you have the floor space and some basic skills, you can construct a built-in closet that looks like it's been there since the beginning.

First, you'll need to make a frame and fasten it to the surrounding walls. Then you trim the door opening and add the doors of your choice. Finally, it's time for the fun part: customizing your new space with closet rods, shelves, drawers, and accessories. Some of the many storage options available are shown in **Fig. 45**. For additional information on storage, see the planning chapter beginning on page 4.

Built-in Closets: Two Types

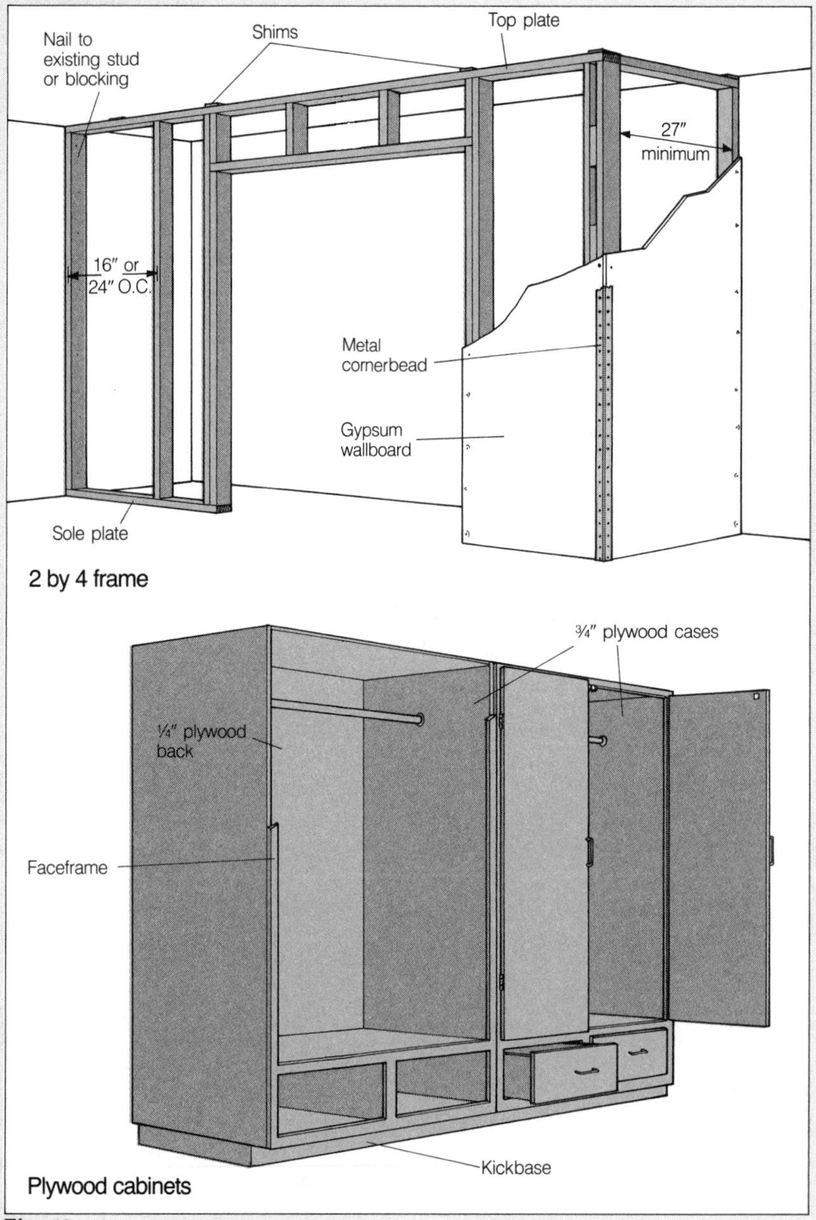

2 by 4 frame

Plywood cabinets

Fig. 43

Building the basic frame

You can frame a closet in two ways: either with standard 2 by 4 wall framing and the wall covering of your choice, or by installing floor-to-ceiling plywood cabinets (see **Fig. 43**). The first method is the simplest and blends right in with the room. Cabinets, on the other hand, create a "custom woodwork" look and allow a number of design options, such as split-level compartments and built-in drawers.

Whichever type you choose, be sure to allow an inside depth of at least 27 inches.

To build a 2 by 4 frame, space the studs 16 or 24 inches on center, using the techniques described on pages 86–87. To frame the doorway, turn to page 129. Be sure to have your doors—and the correct dimensions for the rough opening—on hand before you begin.

You'll need to size the "walls" about ¼ inch less than ceiling height. Once they're built, swing them into place and shim between the top plate and the ceiling joists. Nail the sole plate to the subfloor (*don't* nail inside the doorway) and then anchor the end studs to existing wall studs or to blocking inserted between the studs. Cut out the sole plate between the trimmers.

Next, add wall coverings to match the room. If you're installing gypsum wallboard (see pages 92–94), tape the seams between the new and old wallboard and protect any outside corners with metal cornerbead.

If you opt for plywood cabinets, you'll need to build them as multiple units (4 feet wide or less), carefully level and plumb them, and screw them to wall studs. Though not required, a kickspace at the bottom (see **Fig. 43**) adds a custom touch. For help with designing and building your cabinets, see the *Sunset* books *Bookshelves & Cabinets* and *Basic Woodworking Illustrated*.

Once the frame is intact, install a closet light fixture, taking care to position the light where it won't be blocked by any shelves added later. Check your local building code for any additional restrictions. For wiring details, see "Electrical Basics" beginning on page 142.

Hanging the doors

If you're building a small closet that has ample clearance in front, a standard interior door (see page 130) may be all you need. But for greater access, you may want to use one or two sets of either bifold or sliding doors, as illustrated in **Fig. 44.** Both types are simple to install, as long as your rough opening is square.

A standard 2 by 4 closet frame requires some prep work before you can hang the doors. Add standard head and side jambs (see page 130) and trim the opening as you would any standard doorway (see pages 108–109).

Bifold doors move in metal tracks mounted to the bottom of the head jamb; pivots turn in top and bottom brackets, as shown in **Fig. 44,** and a center guide at the top runs in the track. The doors come with all the necessary hardware.

Sliding doors run on rollers inside metal tracks; floor guides keep the doors in line below. Tracks are available to fit either ¾-inch plywood or standard 1⅜-inch interior doors. A trim strip, shown in **Fig. 44,** hides the track. The hardware you need is available in kit form, containing everything from tracks to mounting screws.

Closet Door Close-ups

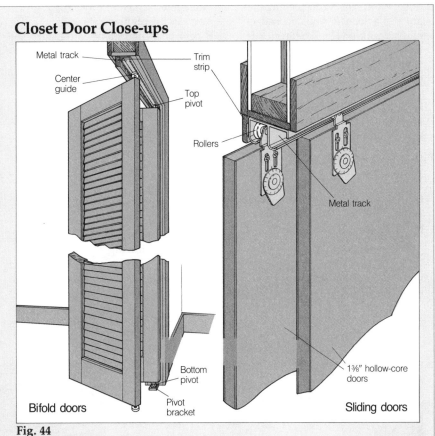

Bifold doors

Sliding doors

Fig. 44

A Variety of Closet Rods & Shelving

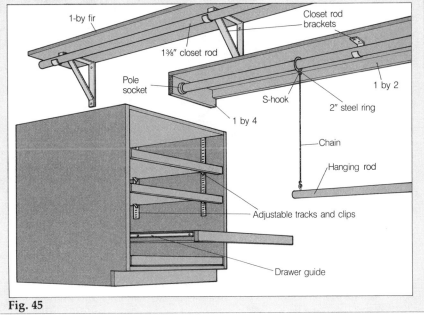

Fig. 45

Tile Ceilings

Square and rectangular ceiling tiles are available in several decorative and acoustic styles. If ceiling joists are exposed or your existing ceiling is bumpy, you'll have to add furring strips to the joists or ceiling before you can apply the tiles. Where a ceiling is flat and in good condition, tiles can be attached directly to the ceiling.

To estimate the number of tiles you'll need, follow the method described for suspended ceilings on the facing page. Plan to trim border tiles to equal widths along opposite edges of the room.

Before you install the tiles, open the boxes they came in and leave them in the room to be tiled for at least 24 hours; this allows the tiles to adapt to the room's temperature and humidity.

Tiling over furring strips. To form a solid nailing base for the tiles, you'll need to fasten 1 by 3 furring strips to the ceiling joists with 8-penny box nails, as illustrated in **Fig. 46.** (For help finding joists, see page 95.)

Position the first strip along the edge of one wall, perpendicular to the joists. Place the second strip so that the edges of the border tiles (allowing for their trimmed widths) will be centered on the strip. Then space each succeeding furring strip 12 inches on center.

If you're applying the furring to an existing ceiling, locate the joists and mark them. Nail on the strips.

Check the furring strips for level as you go. Level them, as necessary, by driving shingle shims between the strips and the joists (see **Fig. 47**).

To trim the tiles for the borders, cut them, face up, with a coping saw or sharp utility knife.

Place a border tile in the corner and nail one edge to the furring, as shown in **Fig. 48.** (You can add ceiling molding later to cover the nail heads.)

Then staple the flanges to the furring strips. Continue applying tiles in the same manner, working outward as illustrated in **Fig. 49** and being sure to center each tile on the furring strips.

Tiling over a ceiling. If you're applying tiles over an existing ceiling that's flat and in good condition, first mark your layout across the ceiling by snapping a chalkline for each row. Following the same sequence as described above, install the tiles by daubing a special adhesive on the back of each tile in the corners and in the center.

Attaching Tile to a Ceiling: Four Steps

Fig. 46. Where ceiling joists are exposed, *nail the first furring strip flush against the wall at a right angle to the joists.*

Fig. 47. Level the furring strips *by driving shingle shims between the strips and the joists. The furring strips must also be level with each other.*

Fig. 48. Nail the corner tile *to the furring at the wall edge where molding will cover the nail heads; staple the flange to the furring. Add the second tile as shown.*

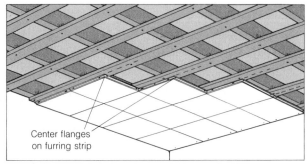

Fig. 49. Working outward from the border tiles *across the room, staple the remaining tiles, centering each tile on the furring strips.*

Suspended Ceilings

Easy-to-install suspended ceilings are a good choice when you want to finish off a room, where you need to conceal ductwork or pipes, or where you want to lower a too-high ceiling. Suspended ceilings consist of a metal grid supported from above by wire or spring-type hangers. The grid holds any of several types of removable ceiling panels.

The most common panel size is 2 by 4 feet, though panels are available in a variety of sizes. Panels may be acoustic or decorative fiberboard. Transparent and translucent plastic panels and egg-crate grilles are also made to fit the gridwork and admit light from above. Panels that accommodate special recessed fluorescent lighting units are also available from some manufacturers. All components are replaceable, and the panels can be raised for access to the area above.

Figuring your needs. To determine the number of panels you'll need, first measure your wall lengths at the proposed ceiling height. Draw the ceiling area to scale on graph paper. Block in the panel size you'll be using. Finally, count the blocked areas and parts of areas to get the number of panels you'll need.

For a professional-looking job, plan to have equal borders of partial panels on opposite sides of the room. To determine the width of border panels, lay out as many full panels as possible across the room and divide the remaining space by two. This figure will be the dimension of border panels against that wall and the one opposite. Repeat for the other room dimension.

Installing the ceiling. First, figure the finished ceiling height. It should be at least 3 inches below plumbing, 5 inches below lights; minimum height should be 7½ feet. Snap a chalkline around the room at your chosen level and install right-angle molding; place its base on the chalkline, as shown in **Fig. 50**.

Next, cut the slotted main runners to length with tinsnips or a hacksaw. Setting them on the right-angle molding at each end, support them every 4 feet with #12 wire attached to small eyescrews fastened into joists above (see **Fig. 51**). Lock 4-foot cross tees to the main runners by bending the tabs in the runner slots.

Set the panels in place and install any recessed lighting panels. Cut border panels as necessary with a sharp utility knife.

Installing a Suspended Ceiling

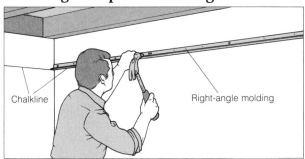

Fig. 50. After snapping a chalkline *around the room at your desired ceiling height, install right-angle molding, positioning its base on the chalkline.*

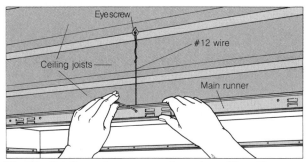

Fig. 51. Set the main runner ends *on the molding. Use #12 wire and eyescrews screwed into ceiling joists to attach the runners to the joists.*

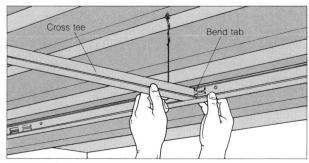

Fig. 52. To lock the 4-foot cross tees to the main runners, *insert the tabs through the runner slots and then bend the tabs.*

Fig. 53. Install the panels *by sliding them up diagonally through the grid openings and lowering them into place. Be careful handling the panels—smudges can be hard to remove.*

OPENING UP THE CEILING

Looking for a way to make a room seem bigger and brighter without blowing the lid off your remodeling budget? Consider opening up the ceiling. The options are many, from simply removing the gypsum wallboard ceiling up to complex, carefully engineered projects that redistribute roof loads.

How you choose to open up space depends on a variety of factors—your family's living patterns, your budget, your home's present layout and structure, and more. Whatever your choice, the keys to a good job are a thorough understanding of your roof structure and careful planning.

How a roof works

If you think of an isosceles triangle that's propped up at both ends of its base, you'll picture a cross-section of a typical gable-roofed house (see **Fig. 54**). The end supports are the bearing walls that carry the vertical load of the roof to the foundation. Horizontal ceiling joists tie the sloping rafters together, creating a rigid triangular shape. The weight from the slope pushes down and out on the walls. The joists lock everything together and keep the walls vertical.

Roof Geometry

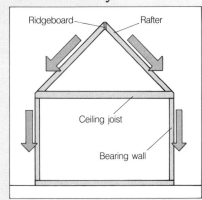

Ridgeboard

Rafter

Ceiling joist

Bearing wall

Fig. 54. A roof's weight *pushes down and out on the bearing walls; it's the ceiling joists that tie things together.*

Breaking the geometry

The drawings in **Fig. 55** show a number of ways to open up your ceiling. If you remove joists, the roof structure will be weakened unless you do something to maintain the integrity of the triangle or redistribute the roof's load. Options include removing only some of the joists and doubling up the others, tying the rafters together higher up with collar beams, or taking some of the roof load off the walls and carrying it with beams added at the ridge or along the rafters.

Unless ceiling joists are quite large, they probably don't span the entire width of a house. Instead, they're usually composed of two lengths (2 by 4s or 2 by 6s) that meet in the middle and rest atop a central bearing wall. In the example shown in **Fig. 55**, bottom right, the central bearing wall was extended to the ridgeline, only a portion of the attic is exposed, and the central wall carries some of the roof load.

When ceiling joists are removed, another way to make up for some of the loss in strength is to nail plywood to end walls or interior bearing walls; this helps redistribute weight loads and adds shear strength (against sideways stresses).

In newer tract homes, builders often use ready-made roof trusses that span the house from side to side with no central bearing wall. Interrupting these trusses would almost certainly require a more complex engineering solution.

Unless you plan to remove only the wallboard, making changes that affect the geometry and structural integrity of your home's roof requires the advice of an architect or structural engineer.

What are the drawbacks?

There are a few trade-offs when you raise the ceiling. For one, the in-creased volume of living space is bound to require more energy to heat and cool. In addition, ceilings often conceal a morass of pipes, wires, vent lines, and heating ducts, as well as insulation.

Most of the heating ducts and the plumbing and electrical lines can be rerouted. Pipes or wires that must run along exposed rafters can be hidden by boxing them in, as shown in **Fig. 56**.

But insulation remains a concern: where does it go? If the existing rafters are deep enough, you may be able to staple batts of 6-inch fiberglass insulation to them to get an R-19 ceiling; you'll then have to cover the underside with new ceiling materials to hide the insulation.

For shallower rafters, you can insert rigid foam insulation (2-inch-thick foam is rated at about R-14). Or, to gain additional depth, you can nail narrow furring strips to the bottom edge of each rafter and then add insulation as shown in **Fig. 57A**.

For older houses that often have only 2 by 4 rafters, structural engineers typically recommend a more drastic step, both for insulation and for strength. They suggest removing the roofing material and covering the existing roof deck with new plywood sheathing (see **Fig. 57B**). Next would come a layer of rigid foam insulation, then a new roof deck, and finally shingles.

When you open up the ceiling, heat recirculation can present a problem. One solution is paddle fans or recirculating ducts that draw trapped heat from the top of the room and drive it down to floor level. And because rafters are accessible, it's easy to add skylights to these overhead spaces. Besides providing natural light, an openable skylight can help vent trapped air in warm weather. For more information on skylights, see pages 140–141.

Removing the Ceiling: Different Ways to Go

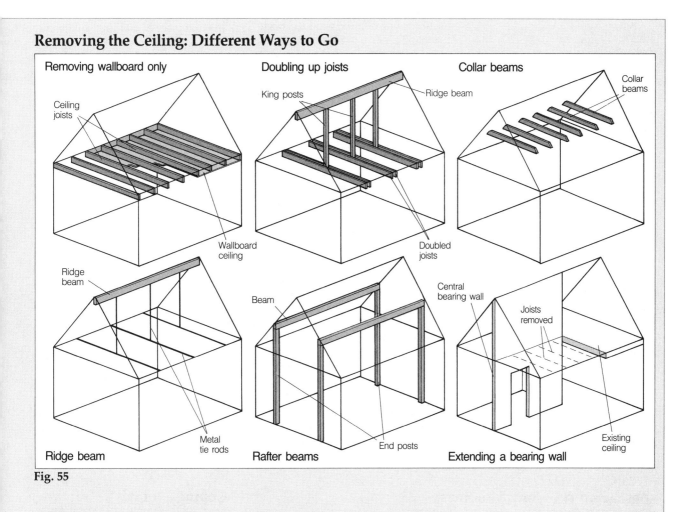

Fig. 55

Hiding Wires

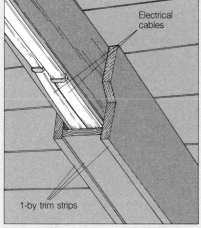

Fig. 56. Trim strips box in *this rafter, forming a tunnel for electrical cables.*

Insulating an Open Ceiling

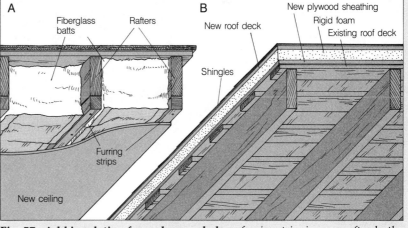

Fig. 57. Add insulation from above or below: *furring strips increase rafter depth if you're insulating from below (A); a new roof deck covers a layer of foam up top (B).*

Moldings & Trim

If you've installed new wallboard or paneling, you'll probably need to add standard lumber trim or decorative contoured moldings along the top and bottom edges to conceal any gaps between the walls and the floor or ceiling. Here, we explain how to install those moldings and also the casing used to trim doors and windows.

When ordering moldings and casing, remember that thickness is specified first, width second, and length last; both thickness and width are measured at the widest point.

Cutting moldings. A miter box and backsaw are most commonly used for neatly cutting trim. With a miter box, you can cut the precise 45° and 90° angles necessary for most joints. If you're doing a lot of cutting or are working with unusual angles, you may want to rent or borrow a power miter saw.

If you're using contoured molding, joints at inside corners along baseboards and ceilings must be cut to the proper curvature with a coping saw (see "Baseboards," below).

Fastening moldings. You can choose one of three ways to attach molding: nail it in place with finishing nails and recess the heads with a nailset; fasten it with color-matched nails; or blind-nail it.

To blind-nail, use a small knife or gouge to raise a sliver of wood large enough to hide the head of a finishing nail; don't break off the sliver. Pull the sliver to the side, nail into the cavity, and then glue the sliver into place. You can tape the sliver down with masking tape until the glue dries. Rubbing the spot lightly with fine sandpaper will remove all signs of fastening.

Baseboards. Once the finished floor is installed, you can attach baseboards and, if desired, a base cap and shoe (see **Fig. 58**). When you install these moldings, leave a slight gap between the flooring and the bottom of the molding, using thin cardboard as a spacer. Nail the moldings to the studs and sole plate, *not* to the floor.

Where two lengths of molding join along a wall, miter the ends to create a *scarf joint*. Nail through the joint to secure the pieces.

Contoured moldings require a *coped joint* at inside corners for a smooth fit. To form a coped joint, cut the first piece of molding square and butt it into the corner. Then cut the end of the second piece back at a 45° angle, as shown in **Fig. 59**. Next, using a coping saw, follow the exposed curvature of the molding's front edge while reinstating the 90° angle.

At outside corners, simply cut matching miters in each piece.

Door casing. Door trim may be either contoured molding or standard lumber. If you choose lumber, butt or miter joints together at the top; for molding, miter the joints.

Before installing the casing, lightly pencil a *reveal*, or setback line, ¼ inch from the inside edge of each door jamb, top and sides. Aligning the head casing with the pencil line, mark it where it intersects the side reveal lines. Miter the ends from these points or, if you prefer, add the width of the side casings and cut the ends square. Use 4- or 6-penny finishing nails to attach the casing to the jamb and 8-penny nails along the rough framing. Space nails **every** 16 inches.

Baseboard & Ceiling Moldings

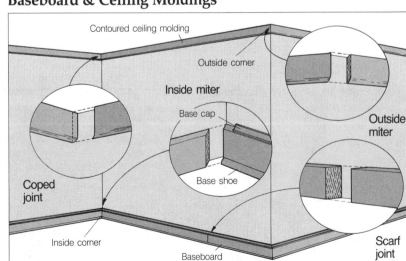

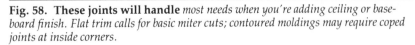

Fig. 58. **These joints will handle** *most needs when you're adding ceiling or baseboard finish. Flat trim calls for basic miter cuts; contoured moldings may require coped joints at inside corners.*

Coping a Joint

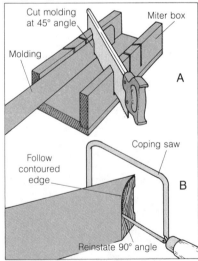

Fig. 59. **For a neat coped joint,** *miter the end at a 45° angle (A); then follow the exposed edge with a coping saw (B).*

Now measure for the side casing. If the door jambs are level and plumb, all should join snugly. If not, you'll have to adjust the angles of the side cuts to fit the top casing exactly. Then nail the side casings into position. If the finished floor is not yet in place, remember to leave room for it at the bottom of the casing.

Window casing and trim. Most window units require interior trim around the opening. Standard treatment consists of head and side casings, a stool atop the sill, and a bottom casing, or apron, below the stool.

Begin by penciling a ⅛- or ¼-inch reveal just inside the side and head jambs; then measure the width of your casing. Adding ¾ inch to the casing's width, measure this distance out from each side jamb's reveal and make a mark on the wall. Now measure the distance between these marks: this is the length you'll cut the stool. Use either a flat piece of lumber or a preformed rabbeted or flat stool that matches the slope of the finished sill.

Position the stool so that its ends line up with the marks on the wall; then mark the inside edge of each side jamb on the stool's back edge, as shown in **Fig. 60.**

Marking Window Trim

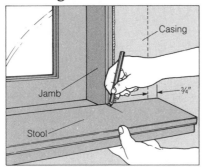

Fig. 60. Mark the inside edge *of each side jamb on the stool's back edge.*

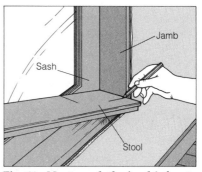

Fig. 61. Next, mark the jamb's front edge *on each end of the stool.*

Place one end of the stool against a jamb (the back edge flush with the window's sash) and mark the jamb's front edge on the stool (see **Fig. 61**). Mark the other end in the same way.

Using a combination square, extend each set of marks until they intersect; then notch the stool along the lines. Nail the stool to the sill with 6-penny finishing nails.

Next, square off one end of a piece of casing. Set that end on the stool, aligning the inside edge with the reveal. Mark the edge where the head jamb's reveal crosses it. If you're using flat lumber, cut the end square or miter it at a 45° angle. For molding, miter the end.

Nail the casing to the jamb with 4- or 6-penny finishing nails, and to the rough framing with 8-penny nails. Repeat for the other side casing.

For the head casing, cut one end of another piece of molding to fit the side casing. Make a trial fit and then cut as necessary so the casing follows the reveal. At the other end, make another trial fit; if all is well, cut the casing to length and nail it in place.

For the apron, cut a piece of molding that's the same length as the distance between the outsides of the side casing. Center the apron under the stool and nail it to the rough framing with 6-penny finishing nails.

Door Casing

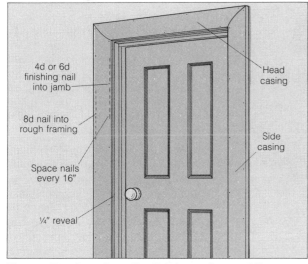

Fig. 62. To trim a door, *first lightly pencil a reveal line on each door jamb; align the casing edges with the reveal and nail the casing both to the jambs and to the rough framing.*

Window Casing & Trim

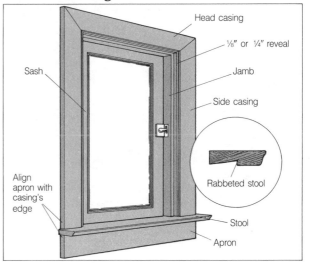

Fig. 63. Finished window trim *consists of the casing, stool, and apron. The outside edges of the casing and apron should be aligned; the stool extends slightly past this point.*

CABINETS: ADDING STORAGE WITH STYLE

Whether you're reviving an existing kitchen or bathroom or you're outfitting a brand-new space, cabinets can add both style and efficiency.

When it comes to kitchen cabinets, you'll find both wall and base units in a multitude of styles, sizes, and finishes. Oven cabinets, refrigerator or dishwasher panels, and free-standing kitchen islands are also available. Bathroom vanities hide plumbing, as well as offer cabinet and drawer space and even laundry bins to storage-shy bathrooms.

You can install cabinets with basic tools, though the work must be done carefully to achieve a professional look. Here's how.

Hanging wall cabinets

Kitchen wall cabinets range from 12 to 15 inches deep and from 12 to 42 inches high. The shorter cabinets are typically mounted above refrigerators and ranges. If you're installing both wall and base cabinets, it's easiest to install the wall cabinets first. Typically, wall cabinets are mounted so their tops are 84 inches off the floor.

First, locate and mark the wall studs in the area of your new cabinets. (For help in finding studs, see page 95.) Snap a chalkline to mark the studs' centers.

Next, to lay out reference lines for the top and bottom of the cabinets, measure up 84 inches from the floor (or the appropriate height for your wall cabinets). Because floors are seldom completely level, measure in several spots and use the highest mark as your reference point. Trace a line from this mark across the wall, using a carpenter's level as a straightedge (see **Fig. 65**).

Then measure down the exact height of the new cabinets from the top line and draw this line on the wall. Align the top of a 1 by 3 or 2 by 4 ledger strip with that line and tack it to the wall studs.

With a helper or two, lift the first cabinet into place atop the ledger. Drill pilot holes through the cabinet's nailing strip into wall studs; loosely fasten the cabinet to the studs with 3-inch woodscrews or drywall screws and finishing washers.

At this point, check the cabinet carefully for level and plumb. Because walls are seldom exactly plumb, you may have to make some adjustments so the cabinet will hang correctly. Bumps or high spots can sometimes be sanded; low points will need to be shimmed. When all is in order, tighten the screws and recheck with the level.

Some cabinets include "scribing strips" along the sides—extra material you can shave down to achieve a tight fit. To scribe a cabinet, first position it; then run masking tape, if desired, down the side to be scribed. Setting the points of a compass with pencil to the widest gap between the scribing strip and wall, run the compass down the wall next to the strip,

A Selection of Cabinets

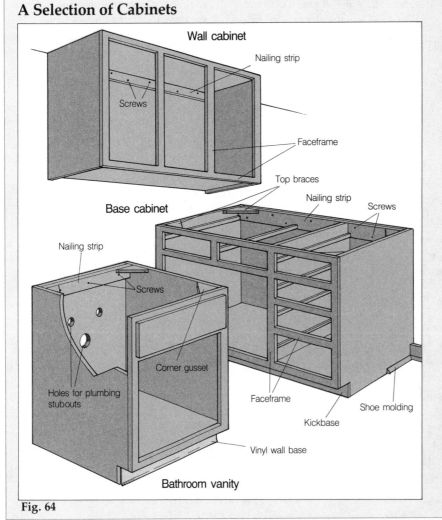

Wall cabinet
Nailing strip
Screws
Faceframe
Top braces
Nailing strip
Screws
Base cabinet
Nailing strip
Screws
Corner gusset
Holes for plumbing stubouts
Faceframe
Kickbase
Shoe molding
Vinyl wall base
Bathroom vanity

Fig. 64

Cabinet Reference Lines

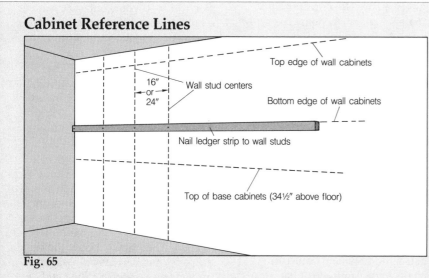

Top edge of wall cabinets

16" or 24"

Wall stud centers

Bottom edge of wall cabinets

Nail ledger strip to wall studs

Top of base cabinets (34½" above floor)

Fig. 65

Scribing a Cabinet

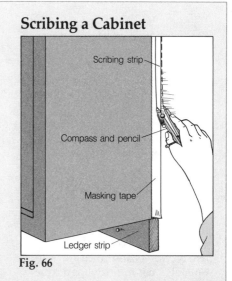

Scribing strip

Compass and pencil

Masking tape

Ledger strip

Fig. 66

as shown in **Fig. 66.** The wall's irregularities will be transferred to the tape or cabinet.

Remove the cabinet from the wall and trim the scribing strip to the line with a saw, block plane, or belt sander. Then reinstall the cabinet.

Adjacent wall units may be joined together on the wall or on the floor; clamp them together with C-clamps, carefully aligning the front edges, and screw together adjacent cabinet sides or faceframes.

Installing base cabinets
Standard dimensions for base cabinets are 24 inches deep by 34½ inches high; the addition of a countertop raises them to 36 inches.

After you remove any baseboard, moldings, or vinyl wall base that might interfere, measure up 34½ inches in several spots; then use the highest mark for your reference point. Draw a level line through the mark and across the wall. If you haven't done so when hanging wall cabinets, locate and mark the wall studs above your reference line.

If you need to cut access holes in a cabinet's back or bottom for plumbing lines or electrical boxes, do so

now. Then, with helpers, move the cabinet into position. Check level and plumb carefully—from side to side and front to back—and shim the unit as necessary between the cabinet base and the floor. If your cabinet includes scribing strips along the sides to allow full alignment with the wall, trim the strips as described for wall cabinets. Both shims and irregularities in the floor and wall can later be hidden by baseboards, moldings, or new flooring.

When the cabinet is aligned, drill pilot holes through the nailing strip at the back of the cabinet into the wall studs. Fasten the unit to the studs with 3-inch woodscrews or drywall screws and finishing washers.

Once installed, base cabinets are fastened together like wall cabinets (see at left). To install countertops, turn to pages 112–113.

Installing a vanity
Vanities come as narrow as 12 inches and as wide as 60 inches. Typical height is 30 inches; if that isn't high enough, look for a kitchen sink unit or plan to add a taller kickbase to the bottom. You can purchase the vanity with or without a countertop and

sink; you can also buy integral countertops and sinks of your choice.

To begin your installation, remove any present baseboard or trim in the area. From the floor, measure up the exact height of your vanity. Measure in several spots and then use the highest for your reference point. Draw a level line through the mark and across the wall or walls (if the vanity will sit in a corner, mark both walls). Next, locate and mark all wall studs above your reference line.

If the vanity has a solid back, measure, mark, and cut holes for the drain and water supply pipes, using a drill or a keyhole or saber saw. With a helper, if necessary, move the unit into place, slipping the back over any plumbing stubouts.

Level the vanity side-to-side and front-to-back, shimming between the unit and the floor as needed. If your vanity has a scribing strip, fit it to the wall as described for wall cabinets. Drill pilot holes through the vanity's nailing strip and into the studs; secure the vanity with woodscrews or drywall screws and finishing washers.

Once the cabinet is secure, install the countertop (see pages 112–113).

Custom Countertops

Ready-made countertops are available in a variety of materials, sizes, and colors. But if you're after a custom look and feel, your countertop will have to be custom-built. In this section, we offer instructions for working with the two most popular kitchen and bathroom countertop surfaces: plastic laminate and ceramic tile.

Plastic laminate countertops

Plastic laminate countertops come in two types—post-formed and self-rimmed. Post-formed tops are premolded, from curved backsplash to bullnosed front, and can be cut to any length. The term self-rimmed, on the other hand, really means custom-made.

Though making your own self-rimmed countertop entails some extra work, it allows you to choose from a broader selection of laminates and to tailor your countertop exactly to your needs.

Here's how to assemble and install a self-rimmed top.

Assembling the countertop.
You'll first need to choose the laminate—1/16 inch is the standard thickness for countertops—and cut the core material from 3/4-inch high-density particleboard or plywood. Build down the edges of the core with 1 by 3 battens (see **Fig. 67**).

An electric router equipped with a laminate-trimming bit is the easiest way to cut and fit the laminate. Because the bit is designed to trim the laminate flush with the edges, you can glue it down with wide overhangs and then trim and fit it with a single pass of the router.

Measure each surface to be laminated and transfer the measurements to the laminate. If you're using a router, allow a 2- or 3-inch overhang on all sides and trim to rough size. Or add 1/4 inch to each dimension as a margin for error, score the cutting line with a sharp utility knife, and then cut the laminate with a fine-toothed saw (face up with a handsaw, face down with a power saw).

Attach the front and side strips to the core before attaching the top sheet. Spread contact cement on both surfaces to be glued and wait for 20 to 30 minutes or until completely dry. (If your contact cement is not latex-base, be sure to provide adequate ventilation and extinguish any pilot lights nearby.)

Checking alignment carefully, attach the edge strips, pressing them against the core. Using a block plane or router, trim the laminate flush with the core's edges and finish with a file held absolutely flat.

Next, glue the top piece and let it dry. Cover it with a piece of heavy brown wrapping paper and lay the glued side of the laminate down on the paper. If dry enough, the glue should not stick to the paper. Align all edges; then slowly begin pulling the paper out, carefully pressing the laminate down with a rolling motion as you do. Be sure to avoid trapping air bubbles under the laminate. (A roller is helpful once the laminate is attached.)

On large surfaces, use two overlapping sheets of paper, working one side at a time. Trim the laminate flush with the edges.

Cut backsplashes and endsplashes from the same core material and laminate them; then butt-join them to the countertop with sealant and screws. Add a trim piece of soft pine along the top edge of the backsplash, as shown, to serve as a scribing strip.

Installing the countertop. Position the countertop on the cabinet. To trim the scribing strip so it follows the exact contours of the wall, see the instructions for scribing cabinets on pages 110–111.

Reposition the top on the cabinet and carefully check it with a level. You may need to add shims around the perimeter and along cross-members of the cabinet top to level the surface.

Fasten the countertop by screwing from below up through the top braces or corner blocks of the cabinet and through any wood shims or blocks. Use screws just long enough to penetrate 1/2 inch into the counter-

A Self-rimmed Countertop

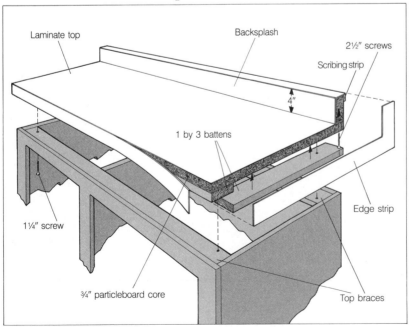

Laminate top

Backsplash

2½" screws

Scribing strip

4"

1 by 3 battens

1¼" screw

Edge strip

¾" particleboard core

Top braces

Fig. 67

top core. Finally, run a bead of silicone sealant along all exposed seams between the countertop and the walls.

Ceramic tile countertops

Wall tiles, lighter and thinner than floor tiles, are the usual choice for countertops and backsplashes. Standard sizes range from 3 by 3 inches to 4½ by 8½ inches, with thicknesses varying from ¼ to ⅜ inch. Type I mastic, water-resistant and easy to use, is the best adhesive for installing countertop tile.

Before laying tile, you'll need to install a ¾-inch exterior plywood base, cut flush with the cabinet top; screw it to the cabinet frame from below. Both the base and the wall surface to be tiled may need priming or sealing; check the label of your adhesive container.

Planning your layout. Decide how you'll trim the countertop edge and sink; for some ideas, see **Fig. 68.** If you choose wood trim, seal the wood and attach it to the cabinet face with its top edge flush with the planned height of the installed tile. This is also the time to install a countertop sink that will be tiled in; for instructions, see page 183.

On the front edge of the plywood base, locate and mark the center line of the sink, if any, or countertop. Lay out the edge tiles starting from that mark. Then carefully position the "field" tiles and any cove tiles, making any adjustments needed to eliminate narrow cuts or awkward fits.

If your tiles don't have lugs molded onto their edges, use plastic spacers to allow for grout joints. Mark reference points from your layout on the plywood; then set the tiles aside.

Setting the tiles. Spread, or "butter," the back of each front edge tile with adhesive and press it into place. If your edge trim consists of two rows of tile, set the lower piece first. Next, butter any back cove tiles and set them against the wall. If

you've installed a sink, lay the sink trim now.

Spread adhesive over a section of the countertop (for information on tools and techniques, see pages 122–123). Lay the field tiles from front to back, cutting tiles as necessary. As you work, check the alignment with a carpenter's square, as shown in **Fig. 69.**

To set the tiles and level their faces, slide a carpet-wrapped wood block over them and tap it lightly with a mallet or hammer.

Finally, set the backsplash, beginning one grout joint space above the cove or countertop tiles. Cover the backsplash area with adhesive; for a better grip, you can also butter the back of each tile.

Unless you're tiling up to a window or a wall cabinet, use bullnose tiles for the last row. If there are electrical switches or receptacles on the wall, cut tiles in two and use tile nippers to nip out a hole.

Grouting and sealing the tiles. Remove any spacers and clean the tile surface and grout joints until they're free of adhesive. Allow mastic adhesive to set for 24 hours; then grout the joints, following the instructions for grouting tile flooring on page 123.

Wait at least 2 weeks for the grout to cure; then apply a sealer recommended by the tile dealer. Finally, caulk all gaps between any fixtures and the tile.

Tile Edge & Sink Treatments

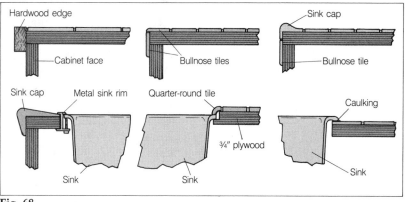

Fig. 68

Setting Countertop Tiles

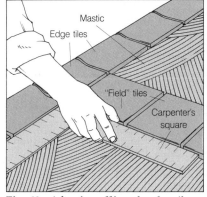

Fig. 69. After installing *the edge tiles, set the "field" tiles, using a carpenter's square to keep them perpendicular to the edge trim.*

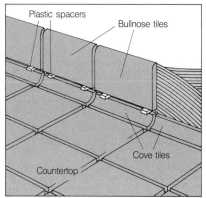

Fig. 70. Align backsplash tiles *with countertop tiles; finish off with bullnose tiles. Plastic spacers allow for grout joints.*

Floors & Stairs

The floors in your house must play a number of important roles: they have to provide strong, sturdy support, look beautiful, wear well, and feel good underfoot.

Flooring has two "sides" to it. The first side is the all-important underpinnings—the subflooring and supports you normally don't see. The second side is the finished flooring—the covering you want to show off, whether it's gleaming hardwood or plush carpeting. If the flooring in your house is wanting in either category, then this chapter is for you.

If you're remodeling a basement or attic, we'll show you how to create a floor for your new living space. And to carry you there, we've included a section on how to build a simple stairway.

We also explain how to install the most popular choices in finished flooring. From the subfloor up, you'll find step-by-step instructions for laying down classic hardwood floors, practical resilient sheet flooring, and gleaming ceramic tile. In addition, you'll learn the basics of installing wall-to-wall carpeting, a sure-fire solution for covering up old flooring and providing soft warmth underfoot.

For any project where you must work with house framing, such as building an attic floor or working on a subfloor, it's important to be familiar with your home's basic structure; for help, turn to pages 74–75.

If you'd like more ideas and information about flooring, see the *Sunset* books *Do-It-Yourself Flooring* and *Remodeling with Tile*.

Basement Floors

To transform a cold or leaky concrete slab into a usable basement floor, you simply build another subfloor directly above it and add new finished flooring over that. First, however, you'll have to seal the old floor, lay down wood "sleepers," and take whatever steps are necessary to guard against moisture.

Sealing the slab. Begin by applying asphalt primer to the slab. If your slab is relatively dry, a single layer of polyethylene film laid atop the primer may be all the moisture protection you'll need. But if you suspect that moisture will be a problem or if the slab is at or below grade, install a "two-membrane" vapor barrier directly over the primed slab for extra protection.

To install a two-membrane barrier, first plug any floor drains. Use a notched trowel to spread a coat of asphalt mastic over the primer; allow it to dry. Then roll out a layer of 15-pound asphalt-saturated felt, butting the edges and ends of each section.

Trowel on a second coat of mastic; then roll out a second layer of asphalt felt so the seams run parallel to, but lie between, the seams of the first layer (see **Fig. 1**).

Laying down sleepers. The best material for sleepers is 2 by 4 lumber, pressure-treated with wood preservatives for pest and moisture resistance. If you've installed a two-membrane moisture barrier, set the sleepers in mastic directly on the asphalt felt. Otherwise, nail them to the slab with concrete nails, spacing the sleepers 16 inches on center. Level the sleepers, if necessary, with shims (see **Fig. 2**).

If you're planning to install a hardwood strip floor, lay the sleepers at a right angle to the direction you'll run the strips. In any case, sleepers should be placed at least ½ inch from any wall to allow for air circulation. Insulation between sleepers isn't strictly necessary when the slab is below grade.

Once the sleepers are in place, spread a vapor barrier of 4-mil polyethylene sheeting on top, overlapping all edges and taping the edges together, as shown in **Fig. 3**.

Laying a plywood subfloor. Though ¾-inch-thick tongue-and-groove strips can be laid directly across the sleepers and vapor barrier, any other type of flooring will require a continuous subfloor. To make one, use ¾-inch exterior plywood— it's much less liable to warp than solid boards.

Cut the first panel of every other row so that end joints will be staggered. Leave about a ¹⁄₁₆-inch gap between panels to allow for expansion; also leave a ¼- to ½-inch gap along walls. Nail the plywood to the sleepers, using 6-penny ring-shank or cement-coated nails (see **Fig. 4**).

For best results, cut at least two openings through the subfloor and vapor barrier close to the walls at the ends of the sleepers in order to vent the space beneath. Cover the openings with warm-air registers or with ventilating louvers.

For more tips on laying down a plywood subfloor, turn to page 117.

Finally, add the finished flooring of your choice (see pages 118–125).

Building a Subfloor with Sleepers

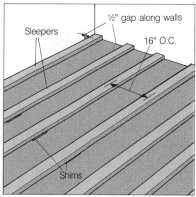

Fig. 1. A two-membrane vapor barrier *helps keep out moisture. Simply build up alternate layers of asphalt mastic and asphalt-saturated felt.*

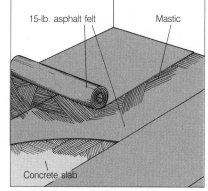

Fig. 2. Pressure-treated sleepers *form a firm base for the new floor; insert shims below the sleepers to level out a wavy or sloping slab.*

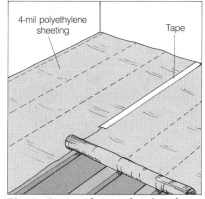

Fig. 3. A second vapor barrier *of 4-mil polyethylene sheeting goes atop the sleepers; overlap the edges and tape them.*

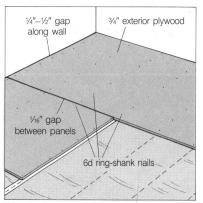

Fig. 4. To lay a plywood subfloor, *stagger the ends of adjacent plywood panels and nail them to the sleepers.*

Attic Floors

If you decide to convert your attic to living space, you may want to frame out new walls and a ceiling, as explained on pages 88–89. But just as important is making sure that the attic floor can take the use planned for it.

The components of a sturdy attic floor are strong, evenly spaced floor joists and a solid subfloor over which you can install your finished floor covering. Before you add the subfloor, you'll need to check the existing joists to determine whether or not they require reinforcement.

To evaluate the joists, check three things: the *spacing* of the joists (they should be 16 or 24 inches apart on center), the joist *dimensions* (2 by 4, 2 by 6, and so forth), and the *span* of the joists between bearing points (the top plates of bearing walls below).

Next, consult your local building code for a span chart that will tell you whether you need to strengthen your existing joists and what lumber to use for the job. The size joists you'll need depends on their lumber species and grade, the span and spacing, and the type of ceiling below.

Directions for reinforcing your existing joists follow. If your present structure is adequate for the new load, you can immediately frame the access opening, if necessary, and lay the subfloor (see below).

Reinforcing attic floor joists

If the original joist spacing is acceptable, you can lay the new joists right next to the old ones, as shown in **Fig. 5.**

Unless your new joists will span the entire distance from outside wall to outside wall, plan to butt them together over an interior bearing wall, as shown. You may need to reroute electrical wires: for guidelines, see pages 149–153.

Cut each new joist to length and then sight along both edges. If there's an edge warp, mark the crown (the convex edge) and plan to place that edge up. Trim the joist ends to the rafter angle, as shown in the inset in **Fig. 5.**

Installing new joists. Lay all the joists in place and check them for level. If you need to adjust level, slip wood shims in between the joist and the bearing surface. Nail the new joists to the old ones with 10-penny nails. Toenail the joists to the top plates of the outside walls and interior bearing wall, using 8-penny nails. If the joists butt together at the center, tie them together with blocking, as shown.

If you're planning an attic partition wall parallel to the joists (see page 89), there should be doubled joists of the correct size directly below where the wall will go.

Framing an access opening. Your remodeled attic may require a new access opening for a stairway from

Adding New Ceiling Joists

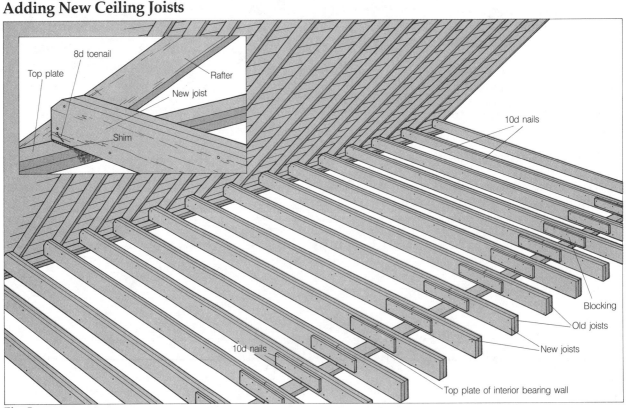

Fig. 5

below. The minimum headroom required above the stairwell is 6½ feet, so plan accordingly. To frame the opening, see pages 126–127.

Installing a plywood subfloor

Floors are generally constructed in layers. The first, known as the subfloor, is usually made from plywood, rated Sheathing, C-plugged, or a similar grade. Next comes a thinner, smoother underlayment, which goes on just before the finished floor covering. Since the underlayment you'll use will depend on your flooring choice, see the appropriate flooring section for more information.

Combination subfloor-underlayment plywood is increasingly popular. Ranging in thickness from $^{19}/_{32}$ to 1⅛ inches, these panels are available with tongue-and-groove edges that eliminate the need for edge support between joists.

Instructions for installing both types of subflooring follow.

Installing plywood panels. Plywood panels are laid perpendicular to joists, with ends centered on the joists. You don't need to support panel edges if the joints of the underlayment above will be staggered or if you plan to install $^{25}/_{32}$-inch wood strip flooring. Otherwise, you'll need to add blocking, cut from the same material as the joists, every 48 inches between joists.

For 16-inch joist spacing, $^{7}/_{16}$-inch plywood is normally the minimum thickness; for 24-inch joist centers, ¾-inch plywood is required.

To install the subfloor, first measure in 49 inches from the inside edge of the rafters at both ends, as shown in **Fig. 6,** and snap a chalkline across the joists. Lay the first row of plywood with the edges flush to this line and the ends centered on joists. Panel ends in adjacent rows must be staggered; begin every second row with a half-sheet (see **Fig. 8**).

When laying out the subfloor, simply tack the panels in place as you go

Laying a Plywood Subfloor: Two Tips

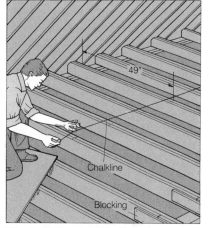

Fig. 6. **To lay out the first row,** *measure in 49 inches from the rafter edges and snap a chalkline between marks.*

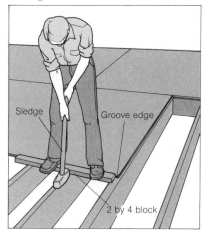

Fig. 7. **Drive tongue-and-groove** *plywood panels together by rapping a scrap block with a sledge.*

A Sample Plywood Layout

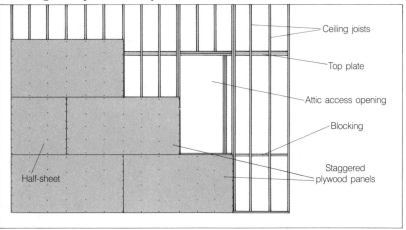

Fig. 8

so you can make adjustments, if necessary. Later, snap a chalkline on the panels to mark the joist centers and finish nailing. Use 6-penny common nails for panels up to ½ inch thick and 8-penny nails for thicker panels. Space nails 6 inches apart at panel ends and 10 inches apart at intermediate joists.

Installing combination subfloor-underlayment panels. Combination panels are laid out in the same manner as standard subfloors, but working with tongue-and-groove edges calls for a little more technique. Begin the first row by positioning the tongue so it faces the out-

side wall. To fit the tongues of the second row into the grooves of the first, you'll need a sledge and a scrap 2 by 4 block. Use the sledge to rap the block all along the groove edge, seating the tongue (see **Fig. 7**).

Use 6-penny ring-shank nails for sheets up to ¾ inch thick and 8-penny nails for thicker sheets. When tacking the panels, don't nail the groove edge or you'll have trouble fitting in the next panel's tongue.

For an even sturdier floor, use both nails and an elastomeric construction adhesive. Gluing enables you to use fewer nails: space them 12 inches apart both at panel ends and at intermediate supports.

Hardwood Strip Flooring

Hardwood flooring, popular for its rich, warm glow, is not difficult for the do-it-yourselfer to install. A good choice is wood strips with tongue-and-groove edges and ends. Available in random lengths, the strips come either finished or unfinished. Though widths and thicknesses vary, the most common size has a face width of 2¼ inches and is ¾ or 25/32 inch thick.

Preparing the subfloor. Subfloor preparation can be more demanding than laying the new flooring. Moisture is the number one enemy of wood floors, so you must ensure that the subfloor is—and will remain—dry. Any crawlspace beneath must also be properly ventilated (total vent area should be at least 1½ percent of the floor area). If the crawlspace has no moisture barrier, cover the ground with roofing felt or 4- to 6-mil polyethylene sheeting.

Though it's possible to lay new wood flooring over an old wood floor that's structurally sound and perfectly level, you may need to remove that flooring to repair the sub-floor or install underlayment. In any case, it's best to lay a new floor right on an existing or new underlayment.

Check the exposed subfloor for loose boards or plywood panels. If planks aren't level and can't be flattened by nailing, either rough-sand the floor or cover it with an underlayment of ⅜- or ½-inch plywood or particleboard. Fasten down ⅜-inch material with 3-penny ring-shank or cement-coated nails, ½-inch material with 4-penny ring-shank or 5-penny cement-coated nails. Space nails 6 inches apart.

Clean the subfloor thoroughly and cover it with a layer of 15-pound asphalt-saturated felt (butt the seams) or soft resin paper (overlap the seams 4 inches). As you lay the felt or paper in place, mark the center of each joist on the covering, as shown in **Fig. 9.**

Planning the new floor. For trouble-free installation, the first row of wood strips you lay must be parallel to a line drawn down the center of the room, perpendicular to the joists. Measure the width of the room in several spots and locate the center line as accurately as possible. Snap a chalkline to mark it.

Next, measuring equal distances from several points along the line, lay out and snap another chalkline about ½ inch from the wall you'll use as a starting point (see **Fig. 10**).

Using Splines

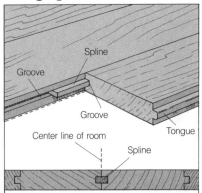

Fig. 12. If you're starting in the center *of an irregularly shaped room, join two strips' grooved sides with a spline.*

For a room that's obviously irregular in shape, locate the center line as accurately as possible and begin laying the first row of flooring from that point. Here, you'll need to use a special wood strip called a spline to join two back-to-back grooved boards along the center line (see **Fig. 12**).

When you're starting from a crooked wall, it may be necessary to trim a few strips so they'll line up properly, yet maintain the ½-inch distance from the wall (see **Fig. 11**). If you're starting from the center of an irregularly shaped room, you'll trim the strips later, when you reach the walls.

Installing the flooring. You can install a floor using basic hand tools,

Planning & Laying Out Wood Strip Flooring

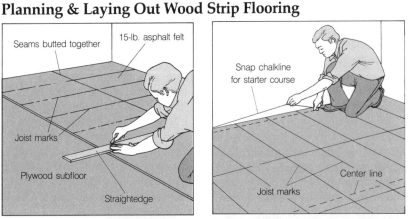

Fig. 9. After locating one joist's center, *measure every 16 (or 24) inches to mark the centers of the other joists.*

Fig. 10. Measuring from the center line, *snap a chalkline for the starter row approximately ½ inch from the wall.*

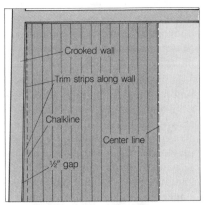

Fig. 11. For a crooked wall, *trim border strips, keeping one edge parallel to the center line, the other ½ inch from the wall.*

Nailing Wood Strip Flooring

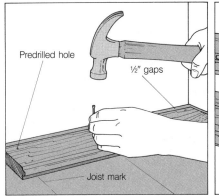

Fig. 13. For the first row of strips, *predrill holes slightly smaller than the diameter of the nails; then face-nail the strips.*

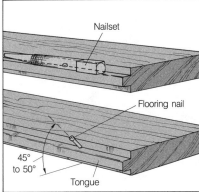

Fig. 14. Blind-nail the next few rows *by hand—start nails with a hammer and then drive them flush with a nailset laid on the tongue.*

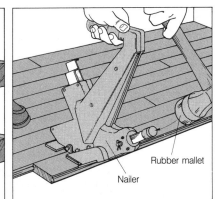

Fig. 15. Once there's working room, *drive nails with a nailer and rubber mallet; the nailer automatically drives nails flush.*

but a nailer—available from most tool rental firms—will speed up the work considerably. Similarly, strips can be neatly cut to length with a back saw and miter box, but a radial-arm or power miter saw saves time and labor.

Tongue-and-groove strip flooring is blind-nailed to the subfloor at an angle through the tongues, where nail heads won't show. To ensure a tight floor, install the strips perpendicular to the joists and nail into the joists whenever possible, using your earlier marks as a guide. Nail approximately every 8 inches.

Laying out boards six or seven rows ahead will help you plan an attractive pattern. Stagger the end joints so none is closer than 6 inches to a joint in an adjoining row. Leave approximately ½ inch between each end-of-row piece and a wall. As a rule, no end piece should be shorter than 8 inches. Also, when laying strips over plywood or particleboard, avoid placing joints directly over subfloor joints.

If you're starting along a wall, face-nail the first row of strips, as shown in **Fig. 13.** To prevent splitting, predrill the boards with holes slightly smaller than the diameter of your nails. Nail where you can cover the nails later with molding.

When beginning at the center of an irregularly shaped room, start off by splining together the two center

boards and blind-nailing through their tongues.

As you lay each strip, move a block of wood along the edge of the piece just laid and rap the block sharply with a mallet or hammer before driving each nail. This will ensure a tight fit between rows. To avoid damaging the tongue, cut a groove in the block or use a short piece of flooring as your block.

Since you won't have enough space to use a nailer until you're several rows from the wall, you'll have to nail the first rows by hand. After the first face-nailed row, predrill nail holes at a 45° to 50° angle to the floor. Take care not to crush the upper edges of the strips. Instead of using your hammer to drive the nails flush, leave the heads exposed; then place a nailset sideways over each nail along the top of the tongue, as shown in **Fig. 14,** and tap it with your hammer. Use the nailset's tip to drive the nail flush.

Once you've nailed the first few rows by hand, you can begin to secure the flooring with a nailer, which automatically drives all nails flush (see **Fig. 15**).

When you reach the last few rows, face-nail again through predrilled holes. The final strip of flooring must be placed to leave a ½-inch gap to the wall. If you're lucky, a standard board will fit. If not, you'll have to rip strips to the proper width.

If your new floor creates a change of level from one room to the next, smooth the transition in doorways with a rounded reducer strip.

Finishing touches. If you've installed prefinished strips that are already stained and varnished, you won't need to sand. For unfinished strips, begin by renting a heavy-duty drum sander; look for one with a tilt-up lever so you can raise the drum off the floor without lifting the machine. Before sanding, drive down any protruding nail heads with a nailset and fill any holes, dents, or gouges with wood putty.

Usually, three sandings, each with a different grade of sandpaper, are needed prior to finishing. For tips, see the *Sunset* book *Do-It-Yourself Flooring* or ask your flooring supplier.

Polyurethane is the most popular floor finish—it offers a hard, plastic-like surface that's easy to care for and impermeable to water, especially when applied in two or three layers. Begin by brushing it on around obstacles and along walls; then roll over the remainder with a long-handled mohair roller. Let it dry (for drying time, check the instructions on the can). Between coats, smooth with a floor buffer equipped with 2/0 steel wool.

Once the surface is finished, you can add new baseboard molding, as described on page 108.

Resilient Sheet Flooring

Resilient flooring is durable and moisture-resistant, low in cost, and easy to install. In addition, it can be fitted easily around existing built-ins, such as kitchen and bathroom cabinets.

You can lay resilient sheet flooring over a level, moisture-proofed concrete slab, over a wood subfloor, or even over old resilient flooring in good condition. It's fastened down with adhesive. Depending on the size and shape of your room and the width of your sheets, you may have to seam sheets together.

In this section, we explain how to install resilient sheet flooring both with and without seams.

Planning & preparation

Before spreading adhesive and laying the flooring, you'll need to make a plan and prepare the surface of your current floor.

Planning the new floor. Take exact measurements of the floor area to be covered; then draw the floor to scale on graph paper. Note the exact location and dimensions of any built-ins or other irregularities in the room. If the room is very irregular, you may even want to make a full-size pattern on paper instead of the scale drawing.

Looking at your plan and the pattern of your flooring material, decide how to best combine sheets to cover the floor, using the minimum amount of material. Do this before purchasing your flooring; remember to add extra for matching patterns at seams and for trimming around edges.

Preparing the subfloor. A new subfloor is the best base for your new flooring. Old resilient floors and wood floors are also good bases, provided they're completely smooth and level. Old resilient sheet or tile flooring must be the solid, not the cushioned, type and should be firmly bonded to the subfloor. Uneven wood floors will need rough-sanding. Both types must be thoroughly cleaned, with any loose tiles or boards secured in place.

Old resilient flooring in poor condition or a ceramic tile or masonry floor should be removed down to the subfloor, if possible. Breaking up and removing mortar or masonry is usually a job for a professional. Old resilient flooring comes up more easily if you score it in manageable pieces and apply heat, such as from a steam iron, over it while prying it loose from its adhesive.

If the subfloor is in poor condition or would be damaged in removing the old flooring, cover it or the flooring with ⅜-inch particleboard or ¼-inch underlayment-grade plywood. Leave a 1/16-inch gap between panels to allow for expansion. Fasten the panels down with 3-penny ring-shank or 4-penny cement-coated nails spaced 3 inches apart along the edges and 6 inches apart across the face of each panel. If the surface isn't perfectly smooth, fill any gaps with patching plaster and smooth with a belt sander.

Before laying your floor, carefully remove any baseboards or shoe molding from walls or built-ins.

Installing sheet flooring

The most critical step in laying sheet flooring, whether you have seams or not, is making the first cuts accurately. Double-check your measurements just before cutting.

Installing flooring without seams. Unroll the flooring in a large room. Transfer the floor plan or paper pattern directly onto the top of the flooring, using chalk or a water-soluble felt-tip pen, a carpenter's square, and a long straightedge.

Installing Resilient Flooring with Seams

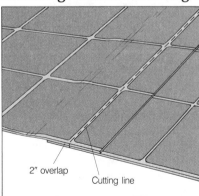

Fig. 16. **Overlap the sheets** *at least 2 inches, aligning the design. Cut along the midpoint of any simulated grout joint.*

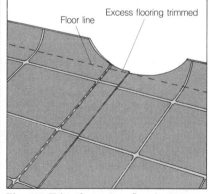

Fig. 17. **Trim the excess flooring** *overlapping the wall in a half-moon shape so the ends butt against the wall.*

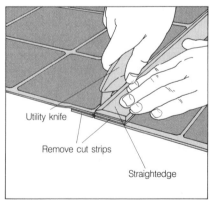

Fig. 18. **Cut down** *through both sheets along a straightedge, using a utility knife; remove both cut strips.*

Trimming Resilient Flooring

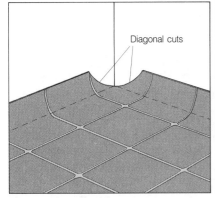

Fig. 19. At an inside corner, *cut away the excess flooring with diagonal cuts until the flooring lies flat.*

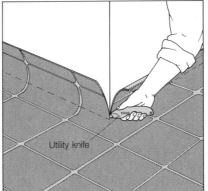

Fig. 20. At an outside corner, *cut straight down to the point where wall and floor meet.*

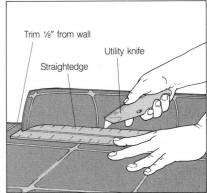

Fig. 21. Trim the flooring, *leaving a ⅛-inch gap between the edge of the flooring and the wall.*

With a linoleum or utility knife or heavy-duty scissors, cut the flooring roughly 3 inches oversize on all sides, to allow for later adjustment and trimming.

Next, spread adhesive over the entire subfloor or, depending on the type of adhesive, spread it in sections as you unroll the flooring onto the subfloor. Always check the adhesive's "open time"—the time you have to work with it.

Lay the longest edge of the rolled-up flooring against the longest wall of the room, letting the 3-inch excess curl up the wall. Position that floor edge exactly; then slowly roll the flooring across the area. Set the flooring firmly into the adhesive as you proceed. When you've positioned the flooring to your satisfaction, press out the air bubbles, starting in the center of the room and working out. Use a rolling pin or a rented floor roller.

Installing flooring with seams.

Transfer your plan or pattern to the flooring as described above. On flooring with a decorative pattern, be sure to leave the margins needed to match the pattern at the seams on the adjoining sheets. If your flooring has a simulated grout or mortar joint, plan to cut the seam along the midpoint of that joint.

Cut the piece that requires the most intricate fitting first. Spread adhesive on the subfloor, stopping 8 or

9 inches from where the seam will be. Then position the sheet.

Cut the second sheet so it will overlap the first by at least 2 inches; be sure the design is perfectly aligned, as shown in **Fig. 16.** Again, spread the adhesive to within 8 or 9 inches of the seam and position the sheet.

When the flooring is in position, trim away excess material at each end of the seam in a half-moon shape so the ends butt against the wall (see **Fig. 17**).

Using a steel straightedge and a sharp utility knife, make a straight cut down through both sheets of flooring. Remove the cut strips. Lift up the flooring and spread adhesive under the seam.

Clean the area around the seam, using the appropriate solvent for your adhesive. Finally, fuse the two pieces with a recommended seam sealer.

Trimming to fit.
You'll need to make a series of relief cuts at all inside and outside corners to allow the flooring to lie flat on the floor.

At inside corners, gradually trim away the excess with diagonal cuts until the flooring lies flat (see **Fig. 19**). At outside corners, simply cut straight down the lapped-up flooring from the top to the point where wall and floor meet, as shown in **Fig. 20.**

To remove the lapped-up material along the walls, press the flooring

into a right angle where floor and wall join, using a straight 18- to 24-inch piece of 2 by 4.

Then lay a heavy metal straightedge along the wall and trim the flooring with a utility knife (see **Fig. 21**), leaving a gap of about ⅛ inch between the wall and the edge of the flooring. (This allows the material to expand without buckling; the baseboard and/or shoe molding will cover the gap.) If you're planning to attach vinyl wall base (see below), be sure the base will overlap the edge of the flooring at least ¼ inch.

The most effective way to hide an exposed edge around a doorway is to cut away just enough of the bottom of the door casing to permit the flooring to slide underneath.

Finishing touches.
When the new floor has been cleaned and is flat and well settled, replace any baseboards that have been removed. Then reattach any shoe molding, leaving a 1/16-inch gap between the flooring and the bottom of the molding. Always drive nails through the molding into the baseboard, not into the flooring.

Vinyl wall base, an alternative to baseboards and molding, is fastened directly to the wall or built-ins with adhesive; the lower edge rests on, but is not attached to, the flooring.

The last step is to finish your new floor with the wax or other treatment recommended by the manufacturer.

Ceramic Tile Flooring

Good looks and easy upkeep make ceramic tile floors a good choice for many areas of your house. But be aware that laying a tile floor requires extra care to achieve a professional look; also, the grout takes at least 2 weeks to cure completely, during which time you'll be unable to use the room.

Glazed tiles, Type I mastic adhesive, and cement-base grout are usually the best materials for the home remodeler to use.

Preparing the subfloor. If at all possible, remove any old flooring before installing new ceramic tiles. Not only does this allow you to examine the subfloor and make any necessary repairs, but it also should make the new floor level with floors in adjacent rooms.

But if your old flooring—whether it's resilient (solid, not cushioned), ceramic tile, wood, or masonry—is level and in good repair, you can successfully cover it with tile. Your tile dealer can recommend the best adhesive and method of application for your particular situation.

To prepare a plywood or wood board subfloor, first make certain that all panels or boards are securely attached. Then drive any protruding nails flush with the surface.

If your board subfloor is uneven or if the plywood subfloor is in poor condition, you'll have to install a new layer over the old before laying the tile. Use exterior or underlayment-grade plywood at least ⅜ inch thick and leave a 1/16-inch gap between adjacent panels.

Fasten the panels with 6-penny ring-shank nails spaced 6 inches apart. Where possible, drive them into the floor joists.

Regardless of your subfloor material, you may need to use a sealer before applying the tile adhesive. Check your product for instructions.

Establishing working lines. The key to laying straight rows of tile is to establish proper working lines. You can begin either at the center of the room or at a wall.

If two adjoining walls meet at an exact right angle, plan to start laying tiles along one wall. This method allows you to cut fewer border tiles and to work without stepping on rows you've previously set.

To check for square corners and straight walls, fit a tile tightly into each corner. Stretch a chalkline along the wall between the outside corners of each pair of tiles. Pull each line tight and snap it. Variations in the distance between the chalklines and walls will reveal any irregularities in the walls. You can ignore variations as slight as the width of a grout joint. With a carpenter's square, check the intersections of lines in each corner of the room.

Assuming that your walls are reasonably straight, you can begin laying tile at any straight wall adjoining a square corner. Snap a new chalkline parallel to the original line and approximately two grout joint widths closer to the center of the room, to allow for the grout on both sides of the border tile (see **Fig. 22**). Snap a similar line, at a right angle to the first, along the adjoining wall. These are your working lines.

If you can't find a square corner or if your tile has a definite pattern, begin at the center of the room. Locate the center point on each of two opposite walls and snap a chalkline between the two points.

Then find the centers of the other two walls and stretch your chalkline at right angles to the first line; snap the line only after you've used a carpenter's square to determine that the two lines cross at a precise right angle. You'll be working the room in quarters with this approach.

Whether you begin at a wall or in the center, it's best to make a dry run before you actually set the tiles in adhesive. Lay the tiles out on the lines, allowing proper spacing for grout joints. In deciding on the best layout,

Laying Out & Cutting Ceramic Tiles

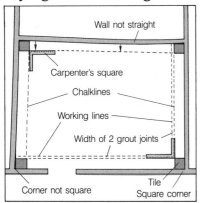

Wall not straight
Carpenter's square
Chalklines
Working lines
Width of 2 grout joints
Corner not square
Tile
Square corner

Fig. 22. Put tiles *in each corner; snap chalklines. Two grout joints away, snap lines on either side of a square corner.*

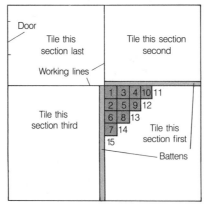

Door
Tile this section last
Working lines
Tile this section third
Tile this section second

1	3	4	10	11
2	5	9	12	
6	8	13		
7	14			
15				

Tile this section first
Battens

Fig. 23. To set tiles *from the center outward, tile a quarter of the room at a time, using battens as guides.*

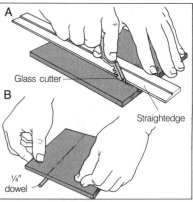

A
Glass cutter
B
Straightedge
¼" dowel

Fig. 24. To cut a tile, *score it with a glass cutter (A); then press it evenly over a dowel to break it apart (B).*

Setting Ceramic Floor Tiles

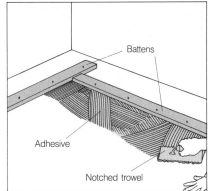

Fig. 25. Nail battens *at right angles, flush with the working lines. With a notched trowel, spread adhesive along one batten.*

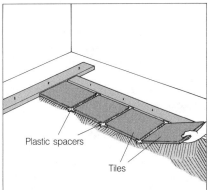

Fig. 26. Beginning at one corner *formed by the battens, set the tiles, using spacers to maintain the width of grout joints.*

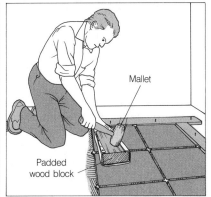

Fig. 27. Start each row *at the same end as the first. To set the tiles, slide a padded block over them while tapping it with a mallet.*

try to keep the number of tiles you'll have to cut to a minimum. If your pattern is very complex, you may want to use a paper plan as a guide and number each tile according to the order in which it's laid.

Adjust the lines as necessary to avoid ending up with a sliver of tile on either end.

Then nail battens flush with the working lines; if you're beginning at the center of the room, nail battens along the working lines that outline the quarter of the room farthest from the door, as shown in **Fig. 23.** (If you're working over a masonry base, you'll have to use the chalklines as your guide.)

Setting the tiles. Using a notched trowel, spread a strip of adhesive alongside one of the battens, as shown in **Fig. 25** (border tiles are set last); cover about a square yard at first or the area you can comfortably tile before the adhesive starts to set.

With a gentle twisting motion, place the first tile in the corner formed by the two battens. Using the same motion, place a second tile beside the first. To establish the proper width for the grout joint, use molded plastic spacers, available at tile supply outlets (see **Fig. 26**). Continue laying tiles along the batten until the row is complete. Start each new row at the same end as the first. If you're working from the center, follow the sequence shown in **Fig. 23.**

As you lay the tiles, slide a carpet-wrapped wood block over them; tap it with a mallet or hammer to "beat in" the tiles, as shown in **Fig. 27.** Keep checking with a carpenter's square or straightedge to make sure each course is straight. Wiggle any stray tiles back into position while the adhesive is still flexible. If you're starting from the center, move the battens as necessary to outline the quarter you're working on. Tile along the walls last.

When you're ready to install border tiles, carefully remove the battens along the walls. Measure the remaining spaces individually, subtract the width of two grout joints, and mark each border tile for any cuts.

You can cut tile with a tile cutter rented from your tile supplier; or you can score it with a glass cutter and straightedge, as shown in **Fig. 24,** and then press it down evenly over a ¼-inch dowel until it breaks cleanly. To cut curved or irregular shapes, use a tile nipper after first scoring the cutting lines with a glass cutter.

After all the tiles are placed, remove any spacers and clean the tile surface so it's completely free of adhesive. Before applying the grout, allow the tiles to set properly—about 24 hours for mastic adhesives.

Applying grout. Grout can be applied liberally around glazed tiles. Grouting unglazed tiles requires more care, as the grout may stain the

tile's surface. Be sure to read the manufacturer's recommendations.

To grout glazed tiles, spread grout across the surface of the tiles with a rubber-faced float or a squeegee. Force the grout into the joints so they're completely filled; make sure no air pockets remain. Working diagonally across the tiles, scrape off excess grout with the float.

Soak a sponge in clear water and wring it out. Wipe the tiles with a circular motion, removing any remaining grout, until the joints are smooth and level with the tiles. Rinsing and wringing out the sponge frequently, go over the surfaces as often as necessary.

When the tiles are clean, let the grout dry for about 30 minutes. By then, any film of grout left on the tile will have formed a light haze; immediately polish it off with a soft cloth. Smooth the grout joints with a jointer, striking tool, or toothbrush.

Finishing touches. Most grouts take at least 2 weeks to cure. You'll need to damp-cure a cement-base grout by covering the newly installed floor with plastic. Leave the plastic in place for 24 hours; then remove it and allow the grout to cure thoroughly. Stay off the tile until it has cured.

Once the grout has fully cured, seal it and the tile with a sealer recommended by your tile supplier.

Wall-to-Wall Carpeting

Today's synthetic carpeting is long-wearing, good-looking, and available in a full range of colors and sizes. It's sold either with or without backing.

Synthetic carpeting without backing is called *conventional*; installed under tension with stretchers, it's secured around the perimeter of the room with tackless strips and binder bars (see **Fig. 28**). Usually, a separate pad is required.

The other type of synthetic carpeting has a rubber pad bonded to it. Known as *cushion-backed*, it's easier to install than conventional carpeting, but it doesn't last as long. The cuts are made in the same way as for conventional carpeting, but instead of tackless strips and binder bars, the carpeting is secured with adhesive or double-faced tape.

The instructions that follow are for laying conventional carpeting. You'll need tackless strips, binder bars for doorways and wherever else the carpet ends, and enough padding to cover the area. You'll also need a few special tools: a knee-kicker, a power stretcher, a row-running knife, and perhaps a seaming iron and wall trimmer. All these tools can be rented.

No underlayment is necessary if you're laying carpeting over a flat, smooth plywood subfloor.

Planning guidelines. Prepare a scale drawing of the area to be carpeted, noting exact measurements and marking doorways and other obstacles. Then fit the planned carpet layout to your sketch, placing seams where they'll be the least visible and running the pile in the direction from which you'll view it most often. Remember that the pile of all pieces must run in the same direction.

Placing tackless strips. Begin your installation by laying tackless strips around the perimeter of the room (except in front of openings); make sure the tacks' points face the wall. Use heavy-duty shears to cut the strips to length.

Allow a gap between strip and wall about two-thirds the thickness of the carpet. A makeshift wood or cardboard spacer helps keep the distance consistent. Nail the strips to a wood subfloor. If the subfloor is concrete, buy strips with masonry nails; if you're carpeting over tile, attach the strips with contact cement.

Attach binder bars in doorways and wherever else carpeting meets an opening. In a doorway, position the bar so it will be directly under the door when it's closed. If the door opens away from the carpeted area, notch the binder bar to accommodate the door's stop molding.

Laying the padding. Unroll the padding and cut it so it covers as much floor area as possible. If the padding has a wafflelike print on one side, place that side up. The padding should overlap the tackless strips slightly.

If your subfloor is concrete, be certain it's dry and coat it with a sealer before laying padding. For either concrete or ceramic tile, use the adhesive recommended by your carpet dealer to secure the padding. Otherwise, working along the edges of the tackless strips, staple the padding to the floor every 6 to 8 inches.

When all the padding is securely in place, use a sharp utility knife to trim off the overlap along the inside of the tackless strips, leaving a gap of ⅛ to ¼ inch between pad and strip.

Making the rough cuts. Using your scale drawing, roll out the carpeting and measure for the cuts you have to make. Be sure to allow at least a 3-inch overlap around the edges of the room.

Snap a chalkline; then, using a straightedge and a row-running or utility knife, cut through the backing only. Cut loop-pile carpeting from the front—between the rows of loops. If you're using cut-pile carpeting, cut it from the back.

Seaming. Place the carpeting in the room, overlapping any pieces to be seamed by 1 inch; check to see if the top piece is straight. Using the edge of the top piece for a guide, cut the underlying carpet with a row-running knife (see **Fig. 29**).

A special hot-melt carpet seam tape and seaming iron will make the most durable and least noticeable seam in synthetic fiber carpeting.

Slip a length of hot-melt seam tape, adhesive side up, halfway under one carpet edge, as shown in **Fig. 30**. Holding back one edge of the

A Close-up of Conventional Carpeting

New carpeting

Padding

Subfloor

Binder bar

Tackless strips

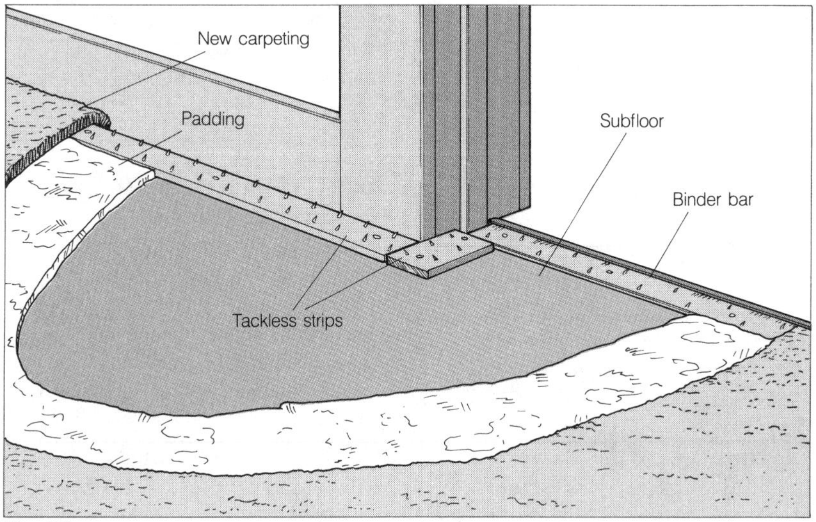

Fig. 28

How to Make a Smooth Seam

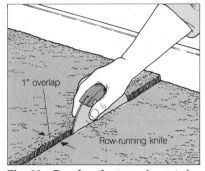

Fig. 29. Overlap the two pieces *to be joined; then cut through the bottom piece, using the top edge as a guide.*

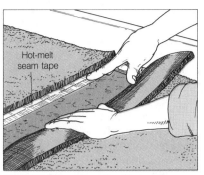

Fig. 30. Slip a length *of hot-melt seam tape, adhesive side up, halfway under the edge of one carpet piece.*

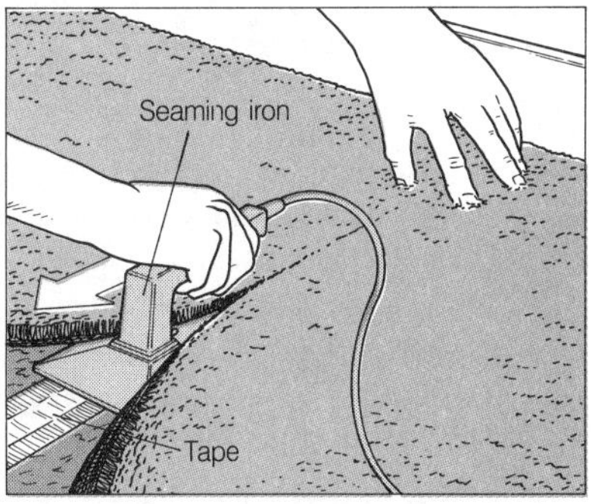

Fig. 31. Draw a seaming iron *slowly along the tape, pressing the carpet edges down into the heated adhesive as you go.*

carpet, slip the preheated seaming iron under the other carpet edge and hold it on the tape for about 30 seconds. Then draw the iron slowly along the tape as you press the carpet edges down into the heated adhesive (see **Fig. 31**).

Let the seam set before stretching the carpet.

Stretching the carpet. Walk around the perimeter of the room and use your feet to shift the carpet so it lies smoothly. Trim away any excessive overlap with a utility knife—the carpet should overlap the tackless strips by only an inch or so.

Make relief cuts at each corner so the carpeting rests flat on the floor; also cut around register grates and other obstacles.

To stretch the carpet, you'll need both a knee-kicker to produce the slack necessary to slip the carpet up and over the tackless strips and a power stretcher to pull the carpet across the room so it can be secured on the strips.

To use the knee-kicker, place its head about an inch from the tackless strip. When you bump the pad with your knee, the head will move forward and catch the carpet backing on the pins of the tackless strip, holding the carpeting in place. Use the knee-kicker at a slight angle.

Equipped with a series of handle extensions, the power stretcher can be braced against an opposite wall. When the stretcher is in place, you

achieve the "stretch" by lowering a lever that moves the head forward with steady pressure.

Follow the sequence outlined in **Fig. 32** to secure the carpeting around the room.

Finishing the job. If possible, use a wall trimmer designed specifically for making the final cuts around the room; otherwise, use a utility knife. Leave just enough carpeting to be

folded over the tackless strip and down into the gap between the strip and wall.

Using a trowel or wide-bladed putty knife, force the edge of the carpeting down into the gap.

Where you've used binder bars, trim the carpet to fit; then take a block of wood and a hammer and rap the top edge of the binder bar to bend it tightly over the edge of the carpet.

The Carpet-stretching Sequence

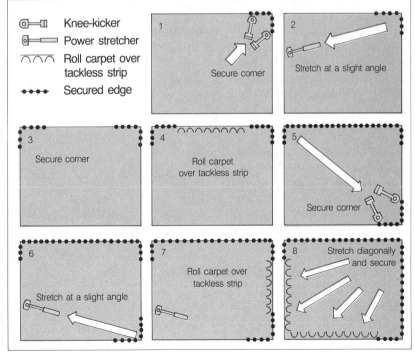

Fig. 32

Stairways

When you expand upward or downward in your home—as when finishing an attic or basement for more living space—you may have to add a stairway. The type described here is "rough," suitable for outdoor, attic, and basement applications. A do-it-yourselfer can build such a stairway, but major stairways in interior living spaces are best left to professionals.

The key to success with a rough stairway is to follow certain basic rules, measure carefully, and plan each detail in advance.

Planning a stairway

Three calculations are critical to your stairway's plan: the stairway's angle, riser height, and tread depth. You must also consider headroom, stair width, and handrail height. A layout of ideal stairway proportions is shown in **Fig. 33**.

Calculating layout. The angle of a stairway is a function of its riser-tread relationship. If the angle is too steep, the stairs will be a strain to climb.

Normally, the sum of the riser height and the tread depth should be 17 to 18 inches. The ideal riser height is 7 inches (many building codes specify a maximum of 7½ inches).

To find the number of steps you'll need, measure the vertical distance in inches from finished floor to finished floor; divide that figure by the ideal riser height, 7 inches. If your answer ends in a fraction, as it probably will, drop the fraction and divide the whole number into the vertical distance. The resulting figure is the exact measurement for each riser.

Next, to find the exact ideal depth of your treads, subtract the exact riser height from the ideal sum for both risers and treads—17½ inches. (For safety, treads must measure at least 10 inches.)

To determine whether that ideal figure will work for you, calculate the total run, or horizontal distance between top and bottom risers, and compare it with the space you have available. To figure out the run, multiply your exact tread depth by the number of risers, minus one.

If this theoretical run won't fit your space, simply adjust the riser-tread relationship, increasing one dimension and decreasing the other, until you achieve a total run that will fit. If a straight run just won't fit, you may have to change to a U- or L-shaped design.

Headroom, width, and rails. To avoid hitting your head or ducking every time you ascend or descend your stairs, you must allow for adequate headroom. Most codes require a minimum headroom of 6½ feet, measured from the front edge of the tread to any overhead obstruction. About 7½ feet is preferable, however, to avoid a cramped feeling.

The width of the stair is less important and will be dictated largely by the space available; but it should allow two people to pass on the stairs. Building codes usually specify a minimum of 30 inches; a width of 36 to 42 inches is preferable.

Handrails 30 to 36 inches high (measured from the tread's nosing to the top of the rail) are comfortable

and safe for a person of average stature; 34 inches is a good height above floors and landings. This, too, may be covered by local codes.

Choosing materials. Because it provides the greatest strength, the best stringer design is the single-piece stringer with sawtooth cutouts for the steps. You'll need two or three pieces of 2 by 12 lumber long enough to reach from the top landing to the bottom flooring.

For risers and treads, select a knot-free grade of lumber not less than 1 inch thick. It's common to use 2-by boards for treads and 1-by boards for risers. Or buy precut treads and risers.

Building guidelines

Before building the stairs themselves, you'll have to frame a rough opening, or well, in the floor or ceiling to accommodate the stairway. Frame the opening with trimmers, headers, and tail joists. If the opening is over 4 feet wide, use double headers, as shown in **Fig. 34**. Joist hangers should be used to attach headers over 6 feet long to the trimmers, and tail joists over 12 feet long to the headers.

Stringers. To lay out the sawtooth cuts on a stringer, you'll need a car-

Ideal Stairway Proportions

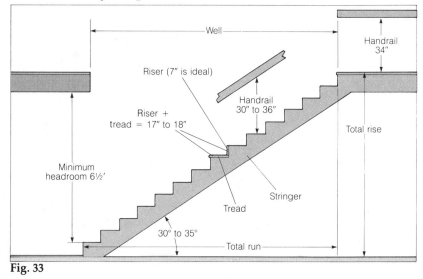

Fig. 33

penter's square. Mark the dimension of the risers on the square's tongue and that of the treads on the square's body. Then line up the marks with the top edge of the 2 by 12 stringer and trace the outline of the risers and treads onto it (see **Fig. 35**).

Cut out the notches with a handsaw or circular saw, always finishing with a handsaw. Because the tread thickness will add to the first step's height, measure the exact thickness of a tread and cut this amount off the bottom of the stringer (the edge that will sit on the finished floor).

Once your pattern is cut, check the alignment; if it's satisfactory, use it as a guide to mark the second stringer. If your stairway will be 36 inches wide or more (30 inches if your treads are 1⅛ inches thick or less), you'll need to add a third stringer in the middle.

Generally, nailing the top of the stringer to the rough opening's trimmers or headers is sufficient, but for a stronger connection add an extra header board, metal joist hangers, or a plywood ledger. At the bottom, either toenail the stringers to the floor or notch them for a 2 by 4 ledger. Fasten the ledger to the flooring.

If any of the stringers will be "closed," that is, attached to a wall, first nail a 1 by 12 plate to wall studs. It will act both as trim and as a nailing surface for the main stringer.

Framing an Opening

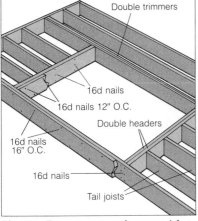

Fig. 34. Frame an opening *over 4 feet wide with double headers.*

Risers and treads. When measuring and cutting risers and treads, remember that the bottom edge of a riser overlaps the back of a tread, and the forward edge of a tread overlaps the riser below it; be sure to allow for those overlaps. Also, giving each tread a 1⅛-inch rounded nosing, or projection, beyond the front of the riser makes the stairway safer.

To begin, nail the first riser to the stringers with 8-penny finishing nails; then add the tread, using 12-penny nails. Fasten the bottom edge of the riser to the back of the tread with 8-penny box nails. Continue in the same fashion until all risers and treads are attached. Gluing the treads and risers to the stringers as you nail helps minimize squeaks.

Handrails. Whether you use a simple length of 2 by 4 or purchase a ready-made decorative handrail, fasten it securely on the wall side by screwing or bolting commercial brackets to studs at every third stud.

For the open sides of stairways, bolt sturdy support posts not less than 2 inches square directly to the stringer. Cap rails for rough stairways are usually 2 by 4s or 2 by 6s nailed to the top of each support post.

Laying Out a Stringer

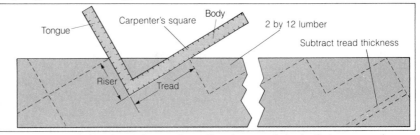

Fig. 35. To mark a stringer for cutting, *align the square's marks that correspond to riser height and tread depth with the 2 by 12's edge; then trace along the square.*

The Finished Rough Stairway

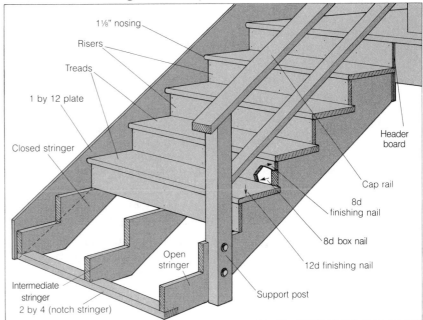

Fig. 36. Glue and nail the risers and treads *to the stringers; then add sturdy support posts and a cap rail.*

Windows & Doors

When you add a handsome bay window or a set of small-paned French doors opening onto a patio, you not only make your interior more dramatic, but you also bring in light and open up space by extending the inside to the out-of-doors. Few home remodeling projects yield so much for so little.

In this chapter, we present a wide variety of window and door options—from basic doors to expansive sliding panels, and from simple fixed-glass windows to spacious popouts. There's even information on choosing and installing a skylight. We also explain, using step-by-step instructions, how to cut and frame a new opening for a window or door, as well as how to install windows and doors of all types.

Perhaps your plans call for closing off an existing doorway or window opening. If so, you'll learn what's involved in eliminating such an opening.

Since you'll be cutting into house framing members when you make rough window or door openings, it's especially important to be familiar with the basic structure of your house. For general information, turn to pages 74–75; or consult the *Sunset* book *Basic Carpentry Illustrated*.

For a complete description of windows and skylights and details on their construction and installation, see *Sunset's Windows & Skylights*.

Cutting In a Doorway

Often, remodeling plans call for changing the location of a doorway or adding one where none existed earlier.

Before choosing the exact location, check the wall carefully. If it's a bearing wall (see page 83) or if it conceals any complex heating, plumbing, or electrical systems, you may need to call in a professional.

Because cutting into any wall is messy work, protect the floor and any furnishings and wear a painter's mask, safety glasses, and gloves.

If you need to eliminate an existing doorway, see page 135.

Locating the opening. Before starting work, determine the type of door you want and check the manufacturer's "rough opening" dimensions—the exact wall opening required for the door and jambs after the new rough framing members are in place. Or simply add ½ inch all around the opening for shimming (adjusting level and plumb).

The simplest way to frame a doorway is to remove the wall covering from floor to ceiling between two studs (which will become the king studs for the new doorway) and to use at least one of the king studs at the outside of the opening.

For this reason, find the existing studs, using one of the methods described on page 95, and adjust the location of the doorway accordingly. Then, using a carpenter's level, draw the outline of the opening on the wall.

Removing wall coverings and studs. Starting at a joint, use a pry bar to carefully remove any base molding. If your wall covering is gypsum wallboard, cut along the outline you drew, using a reciprocating or keyhole saw and being careful to sever only the wallboard, not the framing beneath it. Pry the wallboard away from the framing, keeping it intact, if possible (you may need some pieces for patching once you've installed the door).

To remove plaster-and-lath wall covering, carefully chisel through the plaster with a cold chisel and soft-headed steel hammer to expose the lath; then cut through the lath, using a keyhole, reciprocating, or saber saw, and pry it loose.

Before cutting the studs within the opening to the height required for the header (for a nonbearing or partition wall, you can use a single 2 by 4 laid flat), double-check the dimensions of the rough opening, being sure to add the rough framing depth needed.

Using a combination square, mark the studs to be cut on their faces and on one side; then sever them carefully with a reciprocating or crosscut saw. Pry the cut studs loose from the sole plate, leaving the top portions of the studs (called cripple studs) in place, as shown in **Fig. 1.**

Rough-framing the opening. Measure and cut the header and nail it to the bottoms of the cripple studs with 16-penny nails. Then toenail it to the king studs with 8-penny nails.

Measure and cut two trimmer studs and nail one to each king stud with 10-penny nails in a staggered pattern. You'll probably need to adjust the width of the opening by adding a pair of trimmers on one side, as shown in **Fig. 3.** Nail them to the header and sole plate.

Finally, cut through the sole plate—taking care not to damage any flooring beneath it—to match the width of the rough opening. Pry the sole plate away from the subflooring or flooring.

To install a door frame and hang the door within the rough framing, turn to pages 130–131.

How to Cut & Frame a Doorway

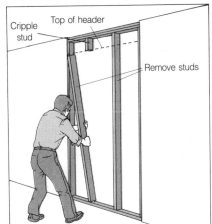

Fig. 1. **Mark and cut** *the studs even with the top of the header, leaving the top portions (now cripple studs) in place.*

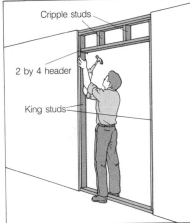

Fig. 2. **Nail the new header** *into the bottoms of the cripple studs; then toenail it to the king studs.*

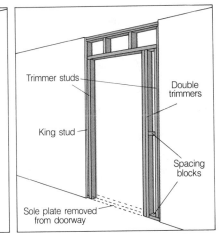

Fig. 3. **Nail trimmer studs** *to the king studs, adding two more trimmers if needed. Remove the sole plate.*

Hanging a Door

With the exception of bifold, sliding, or pocket doors, any door you install will have to be hung on side hinges within a frame. This process requires some patience—and probably a helper—to accurately center the finished frame within the rough frame and the door on its hinges within the finished frame. Every element must align in order for the latch and strike plate to meet and the door to swing smoothly and evenly, with adequate clearance on all sides.

Since most remodeling plans call for interior rather than exterior door installation, the doors will probably be *hollow-core* doors, which are built from thin veneers—often ⅛-inch plywood—over a gridlike core. For greater soundproofing between rooms, *solid-core* doors are also available. Standard door height is 6 feet 8 inches; interior doors are typically 2 feet 6 inches wide and 1⅜ inches thick.

You can either use a custom-built door for which you install jambs, door, lockset, and casing or buy a prehung unit. Below are instructions for hanging both types.

Hanging a custom-built door

Though more difficult to install, a custom-built door allows you to "design" your door to complement your planned interior. The basic steps of installation include framing the door, hanging the door on its hinges, installing the lockset, and adding the casing.

Installing the door frame. You'll need to construct a finished frame to cover the rough frame you've built (see **Fig. 4**). The finished door frame consists of two side jambs and a head jamb. You can buy standard jambs at lumberyards: the width of the jamb should be the same as the thickness of your finished wall.

The width of your frame is dependent on the length of the head jamb. To determine that length, add up the width of the door to be installed, a ¹⁄₁₆-inch clearance between the door and each side jamb (⅛ inch in all), and the depth of the side jambs' routed grooves. Cut the head jamb to that length; then assemble the frame with glue and box nails.

Prop the jamb assembly up in the opening. If your floor covering isn't yet in place, insert scraps of the flooring material or small blocks of the same thickness below the side jambs. Next, check the level of the head jamb. If it's uneven, trim the ends of the side jambs as needed.

Center the frame in the opening, from front to back and from side to side, by wedging shims temporarily between the head jamb and header.

Beginning next to the lower hinge location (see "Adding hinges," at right), drive two shims snugly between the side jamb and the trimmer stud, driving one shim from each side. Nail through the jamb and

shims partway into the stud with two 8-penny finishing nails.

Insert shims next to the upper hinge location, check the jamb for plumb, and nail partway. Then shim, plumb, and nail halfway between the top and bottom hinge positions.

Then shim on the opposite side, locating the middle shims behind the strike plate; don't nail where you'll need to notch or bore for the plate.

Check the frame once more for plumb. Then drive the nails home and set their heads with a nailset.

Adding hinges. For an interior door, hinges are normally positioned about 7 inches from the top of the door and 11 inches from the bottom; choose 3½-inch-long butt hinges.

To lay out hinge locations, prop the door up within the frame, raising it on blocks to the correct height above the floor (the diameter of a 4-penny nail will give you the correct spacing, which is measured from the top). Mark the hinge locations simultaneously on the door and jamb.

Anatomy of a Door Frame

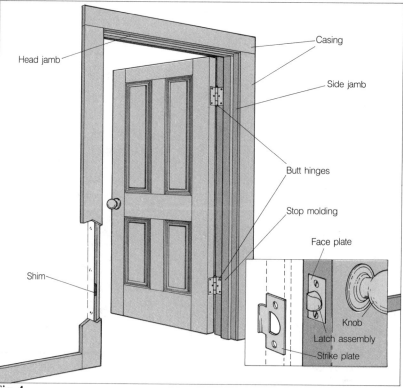

Head jamb · Casing · Side jamb · Butt hinges · Stop molding · Face plate · Knob · Latch assembly · Strike plate · Shim

Fig. 4

Remove the door and cut mortises for the hinges in the door, using a sharp chisel or an electric router and template, as shown in **Figs. 5** and **6**. Be sure to leave ¼ inch between the hinge's edge and the back of the door. The hinge must sit flush with the door. Attach the hinges to the door; mortise the door jamb for the corresponding hinge leaves and attach them to the jamb.

Position the door. Place the pin in the top hinge first, then in the bottom one. If the door binds slightly either at the top or at the bottom of the lock side, insert cardboard shims behind the hinge leaves (shim the lower hinge if the door sticks at the top, the upper hinge if the door sticks at the bottom).

If the door is too tight at both the top and the bottom of the lock side, increase the clearance between the door and strike plate jamb by shimming each hinge leaf at the end farthest from the pin (see **Fig. 7**). Too loose? Shim near the pin to decrease the clearance between the door and the strike plate jamb. If your door is much too tight on any side, sand or plane it along that side until it fits.

Installing the lockset. A purchased lockset will come with detailed instructions for installation and should include a template to help you position the holes in the door for the lock and latch. Plan to

place the lock cylinder and the attached knob 36 to 38 inches above the floor.

Mark for the holes and drill them with either a hand brace with an expansion and auger bit or an electric drill fitted with a hole saw and spade bit. Cut a mortise for the latch's face plate.

Install the cylinder and knob, as well as the latch and face plate; then close the door and mark where the latch contacts the jamb. Cut a mortise in the jamb for the strike plate and a hole for the latch bolt. Then attach the strike plate.

Attaching the casing. The door casing, or trim, may be either standard lumber or contoured molding. If you choose lumber, you can butt or miter the joints at the top; with molding, you'll have to miter them. (To install casing, see pages 108–109.)

Adding stop molding. Unless your door frame includes them, you'll need to add narrow strips of stop molding inside each jamb to prevent the door from closing too far.

Beginning on the hinge-side jamb, nail a length of molding from the floor to the head jamb; use a 4-penny finishing nail every 12 inches, spacing the molding ¹⁄₁₆ inch from the door face so the door won't bind. Nail molding on the opposite side and at the top so it's flush with the

Shimming the Hinge Leaf

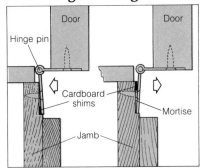

Fig. 7. **The clearance** *between the door and strike plate jamb can be increased (A) or decreased (B) by shimming between the opposite jamb and hinge leaf.*

door. If the door binds, bevel the inside edge on the hinge side to help it clear the molding.

Installing a prehung door

It's a lot easier to install a prehung door, since it's already hinged to the jambs and usually includes a lockset, either installed or to be inserted in predrilled holes. The strike plate will be notched into the jamb, and often even the stop molding and casing are included in the unit.

To install the unit, first remove any bracing, blocking, or stop molding tacked to it. Position the unit in the rough opening and, if necessary, raise the side jambs to the correct level with blocks. Shim the jambs level and plumb as described for a custom-built door (see facing page). If the casing is attached to the face side, insert shims from the back only.

Fasten the unit to the rough door framing by driving 8-penny finishing nails through the jambs and shims. Fasten the attached casing to the rough door framing near the outside edge with 8-penny finishing nails spaced every 16 inches.

Check the door for adequate clearance and smooth operation. Adjust it in the same way as for a custom-built door. If the unit doesn't include a lockset, install one now.

Add casing to the back side of the door. Finally, nail the stop molding to the jambs as described above.

Two Ways to Cut a Hinge Mortise

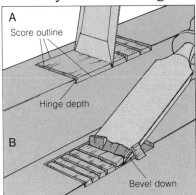

Fig. 5. **Using a chisel,** *score the hinge outlines; then make parallel cuts (A). Chip out the waste wood, bevel down (B).*

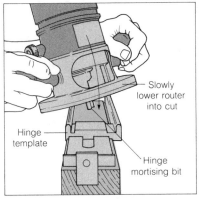

Fig. 6. **To rout a mortise,** *use a mortising or straight bit and a template; plunge cut with the motor running.*

French & Sliding Doors

One popular remodeling project is a new door leading onto a deck, patio, or garden. Two types of doors—French and sliding—are the traditional choices for connecting indoor and outdoor living spaces.

French doors

A French door is a hinged wood door with either one large tempered-glass panel or a number of smaller panes of glass divided by muntins. Such doors often come in pairs, with an inactive door held stationary by slide bolts at top and bottom and an active door closing and locking against it (see **Fig. 8**).

Though you install exterior French doors in much the same way as interior hinged doors (see pages 130–131), you must add a threshold and sill, and you may have to take special precautions to weatherize the unit.

Before choosing your door, decide how much work you want to do. You can purchase the parts separately, to be cut and assembled on site; you can buy a prehung door, hinged to a frame with exterior trim in place; or you can buy a factory-assembled unit, completely weather-stripped and finished on the exterior, with threshold and sill included.

Once the rough opening is prepared (see page 129) and the door unit assembled, installation of each type is similar. You fit the door and frame unit into the rough opening, shim it, and firmly screw or nail it to the wall framing.

You may need to add a sloping sill and a threshold at the base of the jambs. The sill must be installed flush with the finished floor, so you may have to notch the subfloor and possibly the framing below. You can also buy a combination threshold-and-sill unit.

The factory-assembled unit requires much less adjusting than the other types, and once it's attached in place, it's weathertight. The others require that you protect the finish and certain key spots from the weather.

Weatherizing the finish and joints. The exterior finish keeps water from reaching the wood surfaces so the door won't swell and bind, and the joints between the rails and stiles won't break down.

To minimize maintenance of the exterior finish, you may want to consider a door with vinyl or aluminum cladding. However, color choices for cladding are limited, and it's difficult to change the color. A painted door offers more choices but requires a lot more maintenance. Whatever finish

A French Door Unit

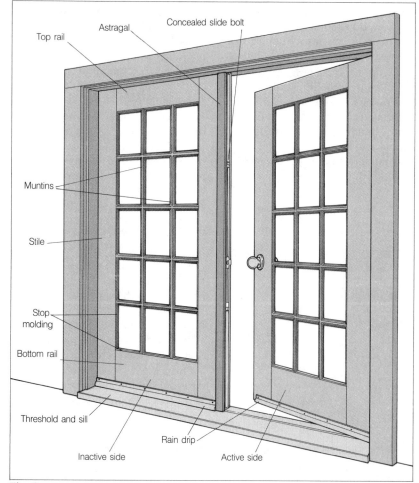

Top rail
Astragal
Concealed slide bolt
Muntins
Stile
Stop molding
Bottom rail
Threshold and sill
Rain drip
Inactive side
Active side

Fig. 8

Weatherizing the Door

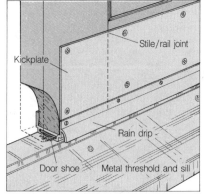

Stile/rail joint
Kickplate
Rain drip
Door shoe
Metal threshold and sill

Fig. 9. To weatherize *the bottom of a French door, add a kickplate and a door shoe with rain drip (offset to allow for the astragal).*

you choose, it must cover the top, bottom, and side edges of the door, as well as the exposed face.

To maintain a tight seal at glass-wood joints, be sure that all stop moldings around the glass are set in a heavy bead of caulking.

Weatherizing the door bottom. If you've decided to paint the entire door, paint the door bottom at the same time as the rest of the door and with as many coats—at least three. A door shoe with a rain drip (see **Fig. 9**) is an excellent way to weather-strip the door bottom and to keep water trapped below the door from being drawn up into the stiles and rail.

Weatherizing the bottom rail and stile joints. To reinforce and water-proof the joints between the bottom rail and the stiles, you may want to install a kickplate. Available at hardware stores, kickplates are set in caulking and screwed to the outside face of the door, covering the bottom rail and stile joints.

Sliding doors

If you don't have room for a hinged door or you're afraid your door will swell shut, then you should opt for a sliding door, such as the one shown in **Fig. 10**.

Factory-assembled sliding door units consist of two-door panels of tempered glass in a wood or aluminum frame. The units are a minimum of 5 feet wide, with one active side that slides past a stationary, inactive side. Installation procedures are the same for both wood and aluminum sliders.

Choosing your unit. Aluminum units have the advantage of being prefinished, requiring no painting. Because they don't swell and shrink the way wood doors may, they require a lot less maintenance.

Select a frame built with a thermal break, which separates the exterior aluminum from the interior aluminum. This prevents heat loss and ensures that water vapor in the house won't condense on the aluminum, corroding it and running off onto the floor.

Wood sliding doors can be finished to match your interior decor; they're usually primed or clad on the exterior and are also weather-stripped. Because they touch the jamb on only one side and rest on adjustable rollers, they're less likely to swell shut than hinged French doors. No thermal break is necessary, and water does not condense on a wood frame.

Aluminum- or vinyl-clad units that eliminate painting and minimize upkeep are also available.

If you're replacing an existing aluminum sliding door, you'll find that many wood sliding doors are designed for that purpose, requiring minimal alteration of the existing wall opening.

Installation. You install a sliding door unit much as you would a factory-assembled French door unit. Once the rough opening is prepared, you slip in the unit, align and adjust it plumb and level, and then screw or nail it to the wall framing. Finally, you adjust the slider rollers to ensure smooth movement.

Sliding door locks. Unlike French doors, sliding doors have stiles that are too thin to accommodate standard deadbolts. However, for extra security, many units now come equipped with small slide bolts that are screwed to the frame of the door. These slide into holes in the head or sill of the unit, preventing the active door from being pried off its track.

A Sliding Door Unit

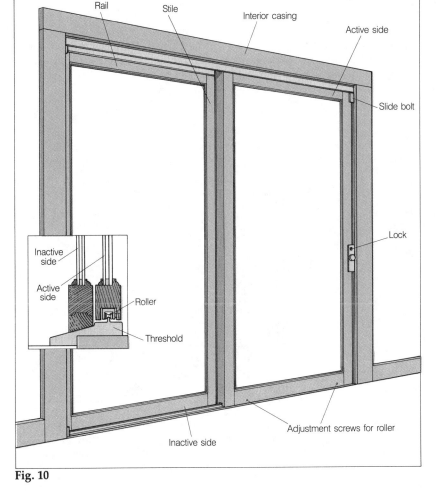

Rail — Stile — Interior casing — Active side — Slide bolt — Lock — Adjustment screws for roller — Inactive side — Inactive side — Active side — Roller — Threshold

Fig. 10

Framing a Window

A window added to a room brings light, air, and a new sense of spaciousness to almost any area. If your home's siding is wood, you can tackle this project using basic carpentry skills. The steps for cutting and framing a window are much the same as for a doorway (see page 129), unless the wall is bearing or balloon-framed (see pages 74–75); if so, note the special instructions below.

Locating the opening. Before you start, figure the width of the rough opening you need: check the window manufacturer's specifications or simply add 3/8-inch shimming space to each side of the actual width of the window unit you plan to use. Mark that width on the wall where you'd like the window.

Next, locate the studs (for help, see page 95). If possible, move the window slightly to the left or right so you can use at least one existing stud as a king stud at the edge of the opening. Also, check for any wires, ducts, or pipes that cross your opening and either reroute them or relocate the opening.

Once you've determined the opening's exact location, remove the interior wall covering.

Marking the studs. To lay out the top of your opening, measure the height of existing doors and windows; then add on a 3/8-inch shimming space and the height of your header. (Unless your local building codes demand something heavier, the header for a nonbearing wall can be a single 2 by 4 or 2 by 6 laid flat. For header sizes for a bearing wall, consult your code.)

Using a combination square, mark the total height on the king studs flanking the opening. Similarly mark all studs within the opening, on the edge and one side.

To find the bottom edge of the rough opening, measure down from your top marks the length of the rough opening (or the window unit plus 3/4 inch), adding the header height and 1 1/2 inches more for the rough sill. Mark the studs.

Supporting the structure. If your wall is bearing or balloon-framed, you must support the ceiling and structure over the opening before you can begin cutting.

For a bearing wall, build a temporary wall slightly longer than the width of the opening and about 4 feet away from the existing wall (see page 84). Raise the wall into position. While a helper holds the wall plumb, drive shims between the top plate and the ceiling joists above until the top plate is tight against the ceiling.

To support the studs above the opening in a balloon-framed house, place a 2 by 8 board against the ceiling and attach it to the studs with lag screws, as shown in **Fig. 11.** Wedge 4 by 4 posts between the board and the floor.

Framing the new opening. With a reciprocating saw or handsaw, carefully cut the studs within the opening (the remaining stud pieces at the top and bottom become the cripple studs). Cut and fasten two additional cripple studs to the king studs at the bottom (see **Fig. 12**). Next, cut a rough sill to the length between the king studs and nail it to the tops of the cripple studs with two 16-penny nails in each.

Have a helper position the top of the header against the upper cripple studs. Toenail the cripple studs to the header with 8-penny nails; then toenail the header to the king studs.

Finally, cut two trimmer studs to the height of the rough opening and nail them to the king studs with 10-penny nails. To adjust the opening's width, add a doubled trimmer on one side.

Opening up the outside. On a clear day, drill a hole through the wall from inside at each corner of the rough opening. Stick a long nail through each hole so you can find the corners outside.

From outside, mark the rough opening with a pencil and level. Then, using a reciprocating or circular saw, cut through the siding and sheathing along those lines, laying the cut material aside.

Supporting & Framing an Opening

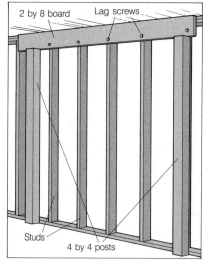

Fig. 11. **To support** *a balloon-framed wall, place a 2 by 8 against the ceiling, screw it to studs, and wedge supports between it and the floor.*

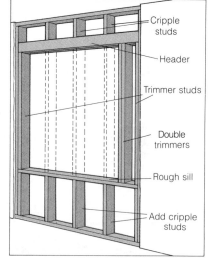

Fig. 12. **Framing a new opening** *means cutting away existing studs and adding cripple studs, a rough sill, a header, and trimmers as needed.*

Prehung Windows

You have several types of windows to choose from when you're installing a new window. Fixed-glass, or "picture," windows are stationary units mounted within a frame; to install this type, see page 136. A popular movable window is the double-hung unit, shown in **Fig. 13;** it has two sashes that move up and down within grooves in the frame. Other movable units include sliding and casement windows.

Most movable windows are available as prehung units, which makes installation easy. The unit arrives with its sash or sashes already installed in the frame, all hardware on, and often with the exterior casing attached. All you need to add is the interior casing. Before doing any work, check your local building code for any flashing required.

Working from the outside, place the unit in the rough opening. With a helper, center, level, and plumb the window as you would a prehung door (see page 131). Depending on the type of window, you fasten it by nailing through a flange into the exterior sheathing, by screwing the jambs to the rough framing, or by nailing through the preassembled exterior trim.

Then caulk the joints between the siding and the window. Finally, install the interior casing (see page 109) and patch the wall coverings as needed.

Anatomy of a Window

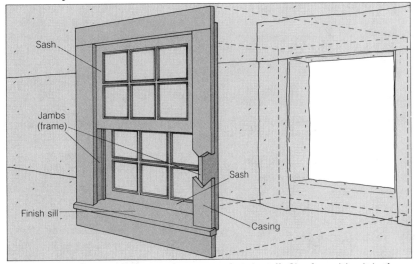

Sash

Jambs (frame)

Finish sill

Sash

Casing

Fig. 13. A prehung window unit *comes ready to install. Simply position it in the rough opening, level and plumb the jambs, and fasten the unit to the framing through the jambs or casing.*

CLOSING OFF DOORWAYS & WINDOWS

Though covering up existing doorways and windows in the course of remodeling is easier than cutting in new ones, it may be difficult to match existing interior wall coverings and exterior surfaces. For this reason, you may want to combine this kind of remodeling with an all-over change of paint, wallpaper, or masonry. For help with replacing wall coverings, see pages 92–101.

Eliminating an interior doorway. First, remove the casing on both sides of the wall. Carefully take the door off its hinges or guide track and pry any remaining jambs or tracks away, leaving the rough framing exposed. Remove all exposed nails and fastenings.

To make the sole plate, cut a length of 2 by 4 lumber to fit the bottom of the rough opening; nail it to the floor with 10-penny nails.

Next, cut new studs to fill the opening, positioning them every 16 inches on center. Toenail the studs to the new sole plate and to the header with 8-penny nails. If required by code, install fire blocks between the studs.

Stripping the wall covering back far enough to give yourself a firm nailing surface and an even edge will help when patching in new materials. As a last step, match or replace the baseboard molding.

Covering up a window. As with eliminating a door, your first step is to remove all casings. When you lift out the sash or frame, use extra care—you may be able to use that unit elsewhere.

To close up the opening, follow the procedures outlined for door openings, omitting the sole plate. Fill in the opening with studs centered every 16 inches and finish the job by adding interior and exterior covering materials that match the existing ones.

Fixed-glass Windows

As their name implies, fixed-glass windows have no movable parts. Traditional "picture" windows have a single large pane for an unbroken view, but you can also purchase fixed windows with removable muntins.

You can buy a window with a ready-made aluminum sash and mount it in a new or existing frame. Or you can have a glass dealer cut glass to your frame size and then mount it in a frame yourself. If you're building a new frame, you'll need to install the completed window unit in the rough opening.

Recycling an existing frame. To reuse a casement window's frame, first remove the sash, molding, and hardware. For a double-hung window, pry off the inside stop molding and remove the lower sash and balance. Then pull out the parting strips separating the sashes and remove the upper sash and balance.

If you're planning to repaint any part of the old frame, you'll save

work by doing the preparatory steps now.

To mount a new aluminum-sash window or plate glass in the frame, see at right.

Building a new frame. To build a simple, solid window frame, choose clear, knot-free lumber—pine is a good choice. Consider 1-by lumber (¾ inch thick) to be the minimum thickness; for a large window, use 2-by lumber. The width of the lumber should match the thickness of your wall, including its siding and inside wall covering.

A window frame is basically a simple box. But the bottom piece, or sill, should be sloped (14° is standard) to allow water to run off outside. You can buy premade sills or build your own. If you choose to make your own, cut a thin groove under the outside lip to serve as a "drip edge."

Lay out dadoes near the tops of the side jambs, as shown in **Fig. 14,** and cut them with a table saw and dado head or with an electric router. Also dado the bottoms of the jambs or angle the jamb ends to match the sill's slope.

Assemble the frame with box nails and waterproof glue. Add an

aluminum-sash window or plate glass (see below) and install the unit in the opening in the same way as for a prehung window (see page 135).

Mounting an aluminum-sash window. To secure an aluminum-sash window in a frame, you'll need to nail stop molding all around, both inside and out (see **Fig. 15**). Using finishing nails, nail one set of stops to the jambs. Following the manufacturer's directions, caulk along the stops and frame with a nonhardening glazing compound to the joint. Set the window in position, add another bead of glazing compound around the opposing perimeter, and carefully nail a second set of stops in place. (The interior stool can serve as a bottom stop.)

Installing plate glass. Ask your glass dealer for recommendations on glass type and thickness and have the glass cut to fit your frame exactly. The glass should "float" in a layer of glazing compound; use small glazier's clips, rubber seals or gaskets, or metal or plastic moldings to space the glass away from the stops and frame (see the inset in **Fig. 15**). If you wish, have the dealer mount the glass in the frame for you.

Installing a Fixed-glass Window

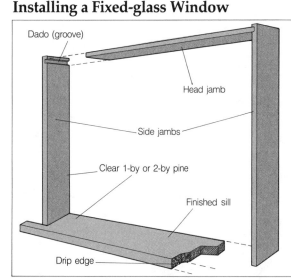

Fig. 14. **To construct a new window frame,** *use solid lumber. Fit the head jamb into dadoes cut in the side jambs. Slope the sill; to make a "drip edge," cut a small groove under the outside lip.*

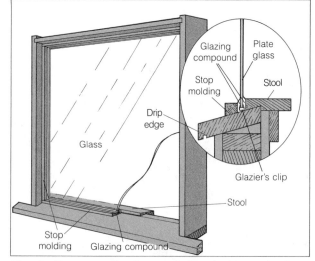

Fig. 15. **Secure an aluminum window** *in the completed frame with stop molding; then caulk along the molding and frame. Or mount plate glass cut to fit the frame, using glazier's clips and glazing compound (see inset).*

Greenhouse Windows

The popularity of greenhouse windows is well deserved, for they're both highly versatile and simple to install. In a north wall or in one close to a neighbor's structure, they "reach out" to capture light for a longer period of time. A small, cramped room can gain a new lease on life with a strategically placed greenhouse unit. And such a unit can even help conserve energy when placed in a south wall and properly insulated.

Most prefabricated greenhouse windows are 12 to 16 inches deep and are designed to fit standard window sizes. All preassembled units include glazing (either plastic or glass), framing, and adjustable shelving, and most have vents. Though plastic glazing is shatter-resistant, glass is more durable and less prone to scratching.

The structural components also offer a choice: aluminum sections are lightweight and maintenance-free; wood-framed units, though bulkier, offer more finishing possibilities. Other options to consider include weather stripping along the vents, screens, and double glazing.

Installing the window

Installation techniques differ depending on local building codes, the exterior siding of your house, the type of window unit, and whether or not you're replacing an existing window or framing a rough opening where no window—or one of a different size—had been before.

The simplest situation is replacing a same-size window on a home with smooth, flat wood siding. You simply remove the old window's sashes, stops, and exterior trim, and attach the unit directly to the siding. For beveled or shingled siding, you'll have to use furring strips. If the size of your unit differs from the existing window size, you'll need to strip the window down to the rough opening and extend or reduce its size as needed, using the techniques described for framing windows on page 134. To cut and frame a completely new opening, also see page 134.

Before purchasing your unit, it's a good idea to study various manufacturers' specifications and installation instructions.

Adding furring strips. If your home's siding is beveled or shingled, you must cut back a strip of siding all around and add 1 by 4 furring strips outside, around the rough frame and projecting slightly beyond the flange area of the new unit, as shown in **Fig. 16.** (For masonry, masonry veneer, or stucco exteriors, follow the manufacturer's instructions or consult a contractor.)

To attach the strips, cut the siding back to the underlying sheathing all around the window opening so the furring can lie flat.

Apply a generous bed of caulking to the sheathing or paper. Then nail the furring to the sheathing. The nails should be long enough to extend into the studs or header to a depth equal to twice the thickness of the furring.

Mounting the unit. Most units and situations call for the same simple mounting procedure. With helpers holding the unit in place, level the window in the opening. Temporarily nail it in place and check the level again. Attach the unit with screws long enough to pass through the mounting flange and penetrate to a depth of at least an inch into the studs and header.

Finishing details. For units wider than 5 feet, it's best to add triangular brackets between the base and wall. If you've used furring strips, caulk the seams between the flange and furring and between the furring and siding. If you like, you can cover the bottom shelf of the unit with tile or finish it to match an adjacent countertop or other room surface. Finally, you may need to replace or fashion interior casing around the window.

A Preassembled Greenhouse Window

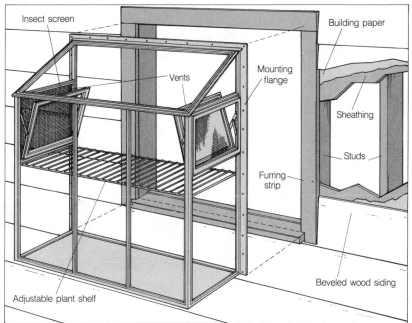

Fig. 16. To mount a unit on uneven siding, *apply furring strips around the opening. Then nail through the flanges, furring strips, and sheathing into the studs. Caulking seals all seams.*

Installing a Bay Window

In the classic Victorian bay window design, the entire house wall projects outward, containing three windows. But today, bay windows can be purchased in kits and installed in the same type of rough opening as a conventional window. (To frame a rough opening, see page 134.) Some manufacturers even supply a precut roof and support brackets.

First steps. Assemble your window, following the manufacturer's instructions. Then check to see if you'll have to cut back the house siding to allow for the window's trim. If so, mark the window outline on the siding and cut along your lines with a circular saw, setting the blade to cut through the siding only. Inside, you may also need to open up the interior wall below the window opening.

Mounting the unit. To position the window, you'll need helpers—one for every 3 feet of window width—and some sawhorses. Lift the unit, resting its bottom platform, or seat board, on the rough sill (see **Fig. 17**); then swing it up so its outside trim meets the sheathing. Center the

jambs between the trimmer studs of your rough window opening, holding the unit in place with sawhorses.

Next, use a carpenter's level to determine which end of the seat board is higher; nail that end to the rough sill. Leaving the level on the seat board, drive shims between the sill and seat board until the seat board is level; place the shims over the cripple studs, as shown in **Fig. 18**. Nail through the seat board and shims into the rough sill.

Holding the level on the face of one jamb, drive shims about 12 inches apart until the jamb is straight and plumb. Then, with the level on the jamb's interior edge, move the top of the window in and out until the jamb is plumb in that direction, too. Nail through the jamb and shims into the trimmer stud. Repeat this process on the other side.

Fill any spaces between the jambs and framing with insulation. Finally, install a drip cap around the top edge of the window and add any other exterior trim provided with the unit.

Installing support brackets. To support the window, you'll need an external bracket under each of the two main mullions. If there isn't a cripple stud under each mullion, toenail one to the sill and sole plate.

Outside, position a support bracket under each mullion. Fasten

the brackets as directed by the manufacturer.

If the manufacturer requires any brackets or supports between the head board and studs above the window, install these next.

Building a roof. The procedure described below is for the precut roof that comes with some kits, but this method can be applied to most others.

First, set the center section of the roof sheathing on top of the window and draw a line on the siding along the edge of the sheathing. Then set the end sections of sheathing in place and mark again. Remove the sheathing; saw through the siding along the lines and pry it off.

Nail the hip and end rafters at each end. Then, using 6-penny common nails spaced every 6 inches, fasten the end sheathing sections to the rafters and to the top of the window. Cover the top of the head board with insulation; then nail the center sheathing in place (see **Fig. 19**).

Add flashing, if required, and then finish the roof of the bay to match your house; or have a professional cover it with copper. For more information on roofing, see the *Sunset* book *Roofing & Siding*.

Finally, caulk the joints between the window and roof, and between the window and siding.

Adding a Bay Window

Fig. 17. **To mount the window unit,** *rest the seat board on the rough sill; then tilt the top into position. Sawhorses help keep the unit in place.*

Fig. 18. **Check the seat board for level,** *driving shims as needed between the seat board and rough sill. Align the side jambs in the same way.*

Fig. 19. **To build the roof,** *add hip and end rafters at each end; nail sheathing to the rafters and drip cap. Flashing and finished roofing complete the job.*

Popouts

Pushing out a wall with a custom popout may be all that's required to house new storage cabinets in your kitchen, an extra closet in the bedroom, or even a tub or shower in a bathroom. And in the process of gaining space, you can also flood an entire room with sunshine and admit a previously cut-off view.

Can you add a popout to your home? Probably. Most houses can handle a 3- or 4-foot extension that utilizes materials similar to those in the rest of the house. The easiest place to put a popout is where an opening already exists, but other locations are possible. Just remember, before you remove a large section of a wall, be sure the remaining sections will provide enough shear strength. If you're considering adding a popout in a bearing wall (see page 83), you'll have to take extra precautions.

Consult local building codes and a structural engineer to determine exact limitations and specifications.

Though you could extend your present foundation to support the popout, a *cantilevered* projection saves on concrete costs and creates a custom-built, "floating" look. Here are three techniques for cantilevering. All are illustrated in **Fig. 20.**

Balance beam construction
In this method, the most common, the cantilever's floor joists or support beams extend from well back under the main house, crossing the foundation wall and extending as far out as needed (or as can be structurally tolerated). This distributes the weight evenly on both sides of the foundation wall.

A balance beam cantilever is especially practical if your floor joists run in the direction you wish to extend. However, you can also add joists at right angles to the existing ones. (Both situations are shown in the inset drawing in **Fig. 20.**)

When adding joists, remember this rule: extend the new joists under the house at least twice as far as they protrude beyond the foundation.

Compression
A cantilevered popout can also be propped up from below with rigid *compression* members (usually triangular wooden brackets), which transfer the cantilever's weight back to the foundation at an angle.

Compression is most often used when the popout starts above floor level, as with a bay window (see facing page).

Shear wall
Here a "skin"—usually plywood—is part of the popout's vertical side walls. When it's nailed to the house along one edge, it helps transfer the popout's weight to the foundation below. Shear wall construction is typically used in conjunction with either a balance beam or compression design. A structural engineer can help you determine your exact needs.

Cantilevers: Three Basic Types

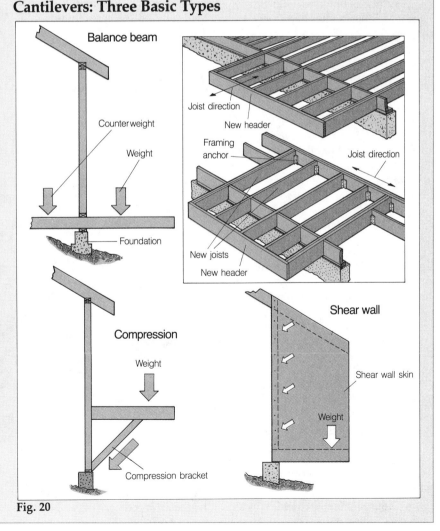

Fig. 20

Skylights

Need a long, dark hallway brightened? More natural light to illuminate workspaces in kitchen or study? Whatever your needs, skylights can work wonders in your home—and their installation is probably within your abilities as a home remodeler.

A skylight designed for installation by the do-it-yourselfer usually consists of a preframed plastic window you buy and attach to your roof surface. It may also include some kind of shutter or light diffuser added at ceiling level for light control. If there's a space between your roof and the ceiling, you'll need a light shaft.

The instructions that follow assume a moderately sloped roof (no more than a 6-inch rise for every 12 horizontal inches) covered with asphalt or wood and a ceiling without exposed rafters. If your roof is flat or your rafters are exposed, your task may be even simpler. But if your roofing material is tile or slate, or your skylight more than 48 inches square, it's best to call in a contractor. For more information, see the *Sunset* book *Windows & Skylights*.

Choosing a skylight

You can choose from a wide assortment of rectangular, square, triangular, and even round skylights that are manufactured to fit standard 16- or 24-inch rafter spacings. Most have acrylic plastic domes that are clear and colorless (for maximum light transmission and solar heat gain), translucent white (for soft, diffused light), or a neutral gray or other tint (to reduce light and heat but allow for a view skyward).

Double-glazed skylights are available to prevent heat loss as well as condensation on the inside of the skylight. Some skylights can be opened for ventilation.

If your roof is covered with thick wood shakes or the roof slope is greater than 3 in 12, your skylight should be mounted on a curb, or box frame, that sits on the opening. It then must be flashed to prevent leaks. The other option is a self-flashing skylight, designed for roofs that are shingled with thinner materials and that have less slope. The curb and flashing are integral with the unit.

Installing a skylight

In brief, the installation process involves cutting an opening in the roof, framing it, and then going inside to cut the corresponding ceiling opening and finish the shaft between the two holes. You may also need to build a curb. The most critical jobs are reframing the openings wherever roof rafters or ceiling joists must be cut and sealing the opening in the roof sufficiently to prevent water from leaking through the opening.

Work of this type is governed by local codes, so be sure to check with your building department before you begin. You may need a building permit.

CAUTION: Work on the roof only when the weather is dry and be sure you have the proper ladder.

Preparing the opening. Working from the attic or crawlspace and ideally utilizing existing rafters for the two sides, lay out the opening you plan to cut (it should correspond to the inner dimensions of the skylight). Add 3 inches to the "top" and "bottom" to allow for rough framing; then drive nails at the corners, positioning them against the inner faces of the rafters to be spanned.

Next, go up on the roof and, guided by the nails you've driven, peel back or remove the finished roofing materials 12 to 16 inches beyond the perimeter of the opening.

Anatomy of a Skylight

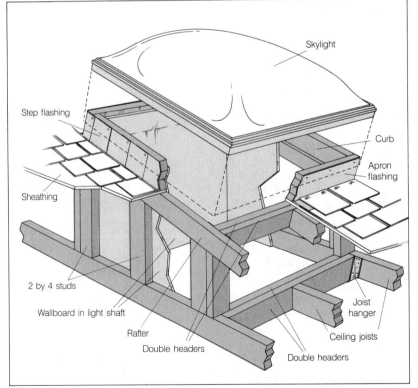

Fig. 21. After the opening is cut and framed *and flashing is applied, the skylight is installed over the curb. A wallboard-lined light shaft connects the skylight to the opening below.*

If possible, save those materials for later reapplication.

After removing the roofing materials down to the felt, draw the outline of the opening with a straightedge, again using the nails to guide you. To check that your outline is exactly square or rectangular, measure diagonally from nail to nail: the distances should be identical. Cut the felt along the lines.

Early on a perfectly clear day, cut through the sheathing along the lines, using a circular or saber saw. If it's necessary to saw through rafters, support them first by nailing a 2 by 4, on each side of the opening, to the rafter and corresponding ceiling joist below. Then make the cuts.

Framing the opening. Where you've cut through a rafter, you'll need to brace it top and bottom with double headers the same dimension as the rafter. (Single headers are sufficient if no rafters are cut.)

Nail double joist hangers to the rafters, place a header into each pair of hangers, and nail it to the rafter. Add the second header, nailing it to the first header. Cover the headers with 3-inch-wide strips of sheathing (see **Fig. 22**) and 6-inch-wide strips of roofing felt.

Building a curb. If you need to build a curb for the skylight, use well-seasoned 2 by 4 or 2 by 6 lumber. Make sure the curb's inside dimensions are the same as those of the roof opening so the curb will sit flush with the framing.

Next, apply a generous coat of roofing cement around the hole, embed the curb into it, and toenail the curb to the roof, as shown in **Fig. 23**.

Reapply roofing materials along the lower edge of the skylight opening so that apron flashing can be installed over it.

Flashing the curb. The role of flashing is to form a watertight seal around any insert into the roof—therefore, this stage is critical. Unless your unit is self-flashing, you'll be installing purchased metal flashing around all four sides of the curb (see **Fig. 24**).

Embed the flashing in a generous base of roofing cement; then fasten it to the curb with galvanized nails. Along the sloping sides of the curb, embed step flashing in cement over roofing felt with each course of shingles or shakes.

Finally, reapply the finished roofing materials to within ½ inch of the base of the curb at the top.

Positioning the skylight. Following the manufacturer's instructions, install the skylight on the curb, using sealant between the curb and skylight and around all nail holes.

Finishing the interior. Finishing a skylight installation requires cutting the ceiling opening and building a light shaft from it to the roof opening.

From the attic or crawlspace, drop a plumb bob from each corner of the skylight opening to the ceiling below and mark the four spots by driving nails through the ceiling below.

In the room, draw the outline carefully, using the nails as a guide, and cut the ceiling opening, using a keyhole, reciprocating, or saber saw. Frame the edges of the opening with double headers to support any cut ceiling joists and to provide a base onto which to nail wallboard.

To make the shaft, nail 2 by 4 studs between the openings, spacing them every 16 inches; double the studs at each corner. Insulate between the studs, if desired, and then cover them with ½-inch wallboard cut to fit the shaft (to apply wallboard, see pages 92–94). Finish the wallboard either in a color that matches your room or in white, which best reflects the light.

Installing a Skylight

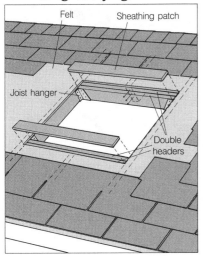

Fig. 22. Add strips of sheathing *to the double headers framing the top and bottom of the opening.*

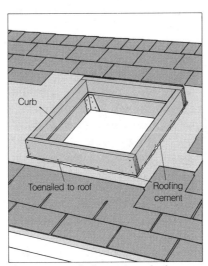

Fig. 23. Attach the curb *to the frame with roofing cement and nails. The curb should be flush with the framing.*

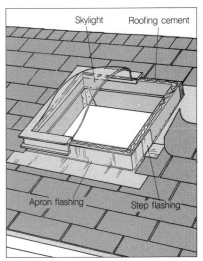

Fig. 24. For a watertight seal, *install step and apron flashing. Apply roofing cement to the curb; add the skylight.*

Electrical Basics

Whether you're replacing a dining room light fixture or wiring a newly remodeled room, this chapter can help. We begin by reviewing the basics—how to select electrical materials and how to work with wire. Then we take you through a variety of wiring projects, from extending an existing circuit to installing all-new service entrance equipment. Our instructions include techniques for use where wall and ceiling coverings are in place, as well as where framing is exposed.

In addition to good technique, it's important to have a clear understanding of how your electrical improvement will fit with the existing wiring in your house. Before you begin work, look through the entire chapter to get an overview of all the factors involved. For a quick course on electrical terms and systems, turn to pages 76–77.

Is doing your own electrical work a good idea? A check with your local building department may reveal that your jurisdiction has restrictions on what kinds of wiring a homeowner can do. For instance, you may be able to do all the wiring up to the point at which the circuit is connected to the service panel, but the final hookup may have to be done by a licensed electrician. In any case, it's best to consult a professional if things crop up that you don't understand.

And finally, if you need additional information on electrical wiring, see the *Sunset* book *Basic Home Wiring Illustrated*.

Basic Materials

On the shelves of most hardware and electrical supply stores you'll find a seemingly limitless array of electrical materials and gadgets. In this section we'll explain what materials you'll need for most interior wiring projects.

Electrical wire

To do electrical work in your home, you can use either a combination of single conductors or a multiconductor cable. Though wiring sizes and methods are traditionally based on single conductors, today most people find cable more convenient to use.

A *single conductor* is simply an individual wire. Four common single conductors are type T (for dry locations only), type TW (moisture-resistant), type THW (heat- and moisture-resistant), and type THWN (similar to THW but with a nylon jacket).

Typically, *cable* combines a neutral wire, a grounding wire, and one or two hot wires inside a plastic or metal covering.

Several types of cable (see **Fig. 1**) are available for various uses. Nonmetallic sheathed cable—type NM—is the most convenient choice for most interior projects. Type UF is approved for wet locations and direct burial. SE cable is the choice for wiring service entrance panels, and some large appliances. Durable AC (armored) cable is still used for some interior jobs but is expensive. Some cable is flat, some round.

Wire colors. All wires are color-coded: white or gray insulation, or thermoplastic, indicates a neutral wire; green (or a bare wire) means a grounding wire; and all other colors (black, red, blue, etc.) are used to identify hot wires. When a white (neutral) wire is used as a hot wire, it should be taped or painted black for easy identification.

Note: In our drawings, hot wires are colored thick black or gold, neutral wires are thick white, and grounding wires are narrow black.

Wire sizes. American Wire Gauge (AWG) numbers indicate the diameter of metal conductors, not including the insulation. The larger the wire's diameter, the larger its ampacity (current-carrying capacity)—and the lower its gauge number.

Fig. 2 lists the ampacity of copper conductors and cable as specified by the National Electrical Code. If you opt for aluminum or copper-clad aluminum wire, you'll need a larger wire size to conduct the same amount of electricity.

Multiconductor Cables

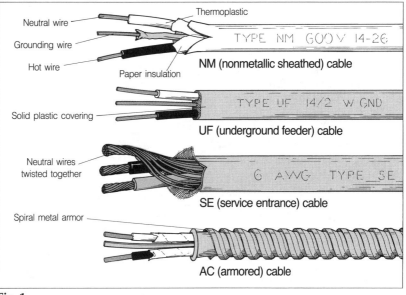

Fig. 1

Size & Rating of Single Copper Conductors & Cable

AWG Numbers (wire size)	Insulation type	Rating (amps)
14	T, TW, THW, THWN, NM, UF	15
12	T, TW, THW, THWN, NM, UF	20
10	T, TW, THW, THWN, NM, UF	30
8	T, TW, UF, NM	40
8	THW, THWN	50
6	T, TW, NM, UF	55
6	THW, THWN	65
4	T, TW, NM, UF	70
4	THW*, THWN*	85
2	T, TW, NM, UF	95
2	THW*, THWN*	115
1	THW*, THWN*	130
2/0	THW*, THWN*	175
*Exception—when used as service entrance conductor:		
4	THW, THWN, SE	100
2	THW, THWN, SE	125
1	THW, THWN, SE	150
2/0	THW, THWN, SE	200

Fig. 2

... *basic materials*

Cable is identified by both the size and number of conductors it contains. For example, NM cable with two #12 wires (one hot and one neutral) and a grounding wire is called "12-2 with ground."

Housing boxes

Housing boxes (see **Fig. 3**) provide connection points inside walls or ceilings, either for splicing wires or for mounting such devices as receptacles, switches, and light fixtures. Boxes come in both metal and nonmetallic versions. Metal boxes are stronger, but unlike nonmetallic ones, they require grounding.

Rectangular boxes that hold only receptacles and switches are called *switch boxes*. Some metal types have removable sides and can be ganged together to form a box large enough to hold more than one device.

Outlet boxes are used to mount devices and light fixtures. When an outlet box contains only wire splices—no devices—it's topped with a plain cover and referred to as a junction box. Outlet boxes used in ceilings are typically ceiling or pancake boxes.

For mounting purposes, housing boxes fall into two main categories— *new-work* and *cut-in*, or old-work. New-work boxes are for use in situations where there's no wall covering to contend with; they're nailed directly to exposed studs or joists. If wall or ceiling materials are already in place, use cut-in boxes, which have brackets or spring ears designed expressly for remodeling work. These are positioned in spaces between studs or joists. Most boxes are designed for mounting in wall-

Number of Conductors per Box

Type of box	Size	Number of conductors*			
		#14	#12	#10	#8
Round or octagonal (outlet)	4″ × 1¼″	6	5	5	4
	4″ × 1½″	7	6	6	5
	4″ × 2⅛″	10	9	8	7
Square (outlet)	4″ × 1¼″	9	8	7	6
	4″ × 1½″	10	9	8	7
	4″ × 2⅛″	15	13	12	10
	4¹¹⁄₁₆″ × 1¼″	12	11	10	8
	4¹¹⁄₁₆″ × 1½″	14	13	11	9
Rectangular (switch)	3″ × 2″ × 2¼″	5	4	4	3
	3″ × 2″ × 2½″	6	5	5	4
	3″ × 2″ × 2¾″	7	6	5	4
	3″ × 2″ × 3½″	9	8	7	6

Fig. 4 *Count all grounding wires as one conductor. Count each hickey, grounding clamp, fixture stud, receptacle, and switch as one conductor. Count each wire entering and leaving box without a splice as one conductor. Pigtails are not counted at all.

A Selection of Housing Boxes

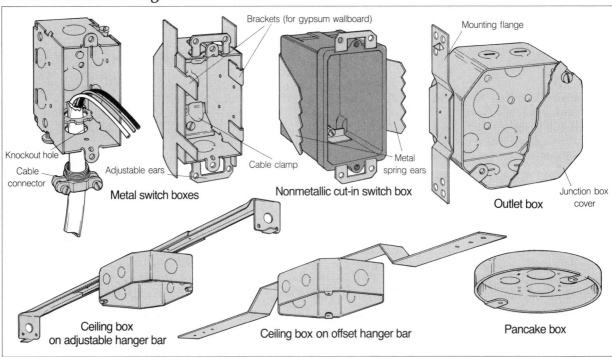

Knockout hole
Cable connector
Adjustable ears
Metal switch boxes

Brackets (for gypsum wallboard)
Cable clamp
Metal spring ears
Nonmetallic cut-in switch box

Mounting flange
Outlet box
Junction box cover

Ceiling box on adjustable hanger bar

Ceiling box on offset hanger bar

Pancake box

Fig. 3

board; *plain boxes* (see page 152) are the choice for plaster or wood walls.

To secure cable, boxes may have built-in cable clamps, or you may have to use separate cable connectors.

The volume of any box determines how many wires may be brought into it. For guidelines, see **Fig 4**.

Receptacles

The National Electrical Code requires that all new receptacles for 15- or 20-amp, 120-volt branch circuits (most of the circuits in your home) be of the grounding type shown in **Fig. 5**. All receptacles are rated according to the specific amperage and voltage they are suited for. Receptacles marked CO-ALR can be used with either copper or aluminum wire; unmarked receptacles and those marked CU-AL may be used with copper wire only.

Standard duplex receptacles have a pair of both hot (brass) and neutral (white or silver) screw terminals, plus a green grounding terminal.

Backwired receptacles feature push-in terminals, as shown in the inset, allowing simple connections.

By removing the break-off fin on any receptacle, you can operate the two outlets independently.

To eliminate the possibility of plugging a 120-volt appliance into a 240-volt receptacle, higher-voltage circuits use special receptacles (shown in **Fig. 6**).

Switches

Like receptacles, all switches are rated for a specific amperage and voltage. Switches marked CO-ALR can be used with either copper or aluminum wire; unmarked switches and those marked CU-AL may be used with copper wire only.

A *single-pole* switch controls a light or receptacle from one location only. It's identified by two hot terminals of the same color and the words ON and OFF on the toggle (see **Fig. 7**).

Three-way switches operate in pairs to control a light or receptacle from two locations. These switches have

three terminals (two of one color, a third—the common terminal—of another color) and a plain toggle.

A *four-way* switch is used with a pair of three-way switches to control a device from more than two locations.

A *dimmer* switch allows you to regulate the brightness of a light. Special dimmer switches are required for fluorescent lights.

Types of Switches

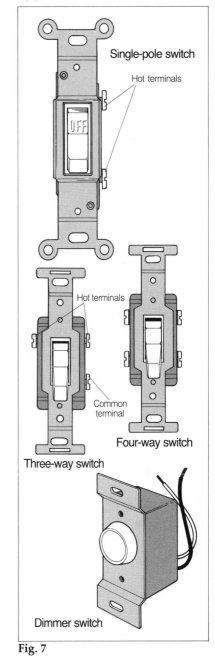

Single-pole switch

Hot terminals

Hot terminals

Common terminal

Three-way switch

Four-way switch

Dimmer switch

Fig. 7

Duplex Receptacle

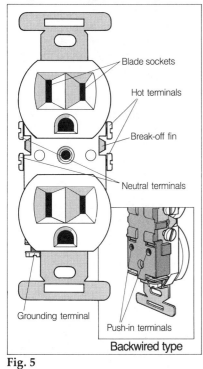

Blade sockets

Hot terminals

Break-off fin

Neutral terminals

Grounding terminal

Push-in terminals

Backwired type

Fig. 5

Special Receptacles

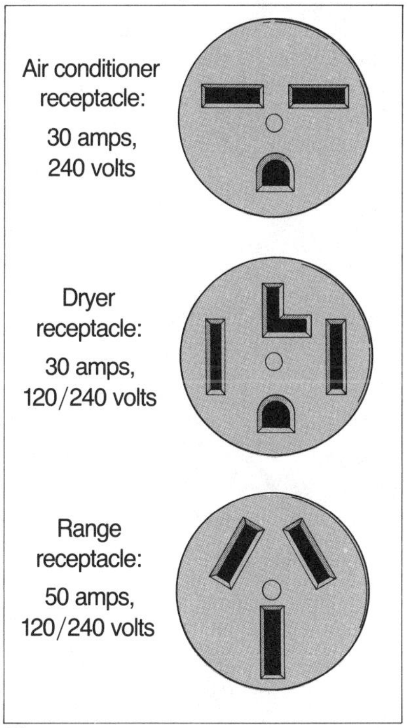

Air conditioner receptacle: 30 amps, 240 volts

Dryer receptacle: 30 amps, 120/240 volts

Range receptacle: 50 amps, 120/240 volts

Fig. 6

Wiring Know-how

In this section we'll give you a brief run-through of basic techniques for working with wire—stripping wires and cable, attaching them to your new devices, and splicing wires together.

Stripping cable & wires

As shown on page 143, multi-conductor cable consists of insulated and bare wires bundled together and wrapped in an outer sheath. Before you can connect a cable to a device or join it to another cable, you must cut open and remove the outer sheath, cut away all paper insulation, string, or other separation materials, and strip the insulation from the ends of the wires.

Removing the outer sheath. To lay open flat cable, such as two-conductor NM, use a cable ripper (see **Fig. 8A**) or a pocket knife. If you're working with round, three-conductor cable, use a pocket or utility knife so you can follow the rotation of the wires without cutting into their insulation.

Once you've exposed the internal wires, cut off the outer sheath and any separation materials with diagonal cutters or utility scissors.

Stripping wires. Stripping wires simply means removing the insulation from the ends of the individual wires. For #14, #12, or #10 wires, use a wire stripper. First, set the adjustment screw for the correct wire size, or gauge. Then follow the steps shown in **Fig. 9**. After you've practiced the movement several times, it will become quite easy.

Strip larger wires—#8 to #2/0—with a pocket knife, using the knife as if you were sharpening a pencil. Be sure to cut away from your body.

Be careful not to nick a wire when you're stripping it—the nicked wire will tend to break. If you do damage a wire, it's best to cut that part off and then redo the stripping.

Joining wires to terminals

Your new switch or receptacle may have traditional screw terminals only or may be backwired for wire connections as well. Both arrangements work fine, though backwiring is a bit faster. Here's how to make the hookup to both types.

Screw terminals. When joining wire to a screw terminal, strip about ½ to ¾ inch of insulation off the wire end. Using needle-nose pliers, form a half-loop in the bare wire, as shown in **Fig. 10A**. Hook the wire *clockwise* around the screw terminal; then tighten the screw. As the screw is tightened, the loop will close. If you're using aluminum wire, wrap it ⅔ to ¾ of a turn around the screw.

Make sure that only a minimum (no more than 1/16 inch) of bare wire extends out beyond the screw head. On the other hand, don't let the insulation extend into the clamped area. Never place more than one wire under a screw terminal: use a pigtail splice (see facing page) instead.

Backwiring. To backwire a switch or receptacle, you make the wire-to-

Ripping Cable

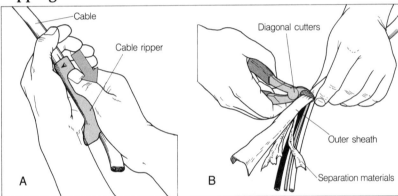

Fig. 8. To expose the wires in flat cable, *first pull a cable ripper down the cable to score the outer sheath (A). Then peel open the sheath, bend it back, and, using diagonal cutters, cut it off (B) along with all separation materials.*

Stripping Wire

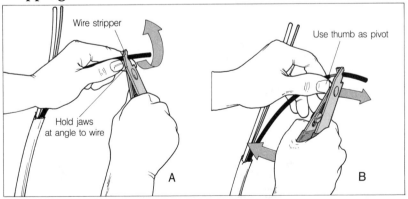

Fig. 9. To strip insulation from wire ends, *hold the wire firmly in your left hand while gripping the wire stripper at an angle (A). Pivoting the stripper so the right wrist moves left and the stripper jaws move right, slide the insulation off (B).*

terminal connection by simply poking a straight wire into a hole. Using the strip gauge that's molded into the back of the device as a guide, strip a wire and poke it into the appropriate terminal (see **Fig. 11**). A jaw inside the terminal allows the wire to enter but prevents you from withdrawing it unless you insert a small screwdriver into a special slot next to the hole. Finally, be sure to tighten down the unused screw terminals. This will help prevent any loose metal from ending up in the box.

Note: Backwiring is suitable for copper wire only.

Splicing wires

Wires are spliced, or joined together, with solderless connectors called *wire nuts*. The size wire nut you need depends on the number and size of the wires you'll be joining. Each manufacturer has its own color code to distinguish the various sizes. The packaging or bin labels will tell you what wires each size wire nut will take.

To put on a wire nut, first strip about 1 inch of insulation from the wire ends and twist the ends clockwise 1½ turns, as shown in **Fig. 12**; next, snip ⅜ to ½ inch off the tips of the twisted wires with pliers or diagonal cutters. Finally, screw the wire nut clockwise onto the wires.

A *pigtail* splice is simply three or more wires spliced together with a wire nut; one of the wires—the pigtail—links the incoming and outgoing wires to a terminal or housing box (see **Fig. 13**). A pigtail running from grounding wires is often called a *grounding jumper*.

Note: If you must splice aluminum to copper wire, use a two-compartment connector made especially for this purpose.

Making Screw Terminal Connections

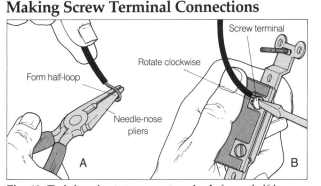

Fig. 10. To join wire to a screw terminal, *form a half-loop in the stripped wire (A) with needle-nose pliers; then hook the wire clockwise around the correct terminal and tighten the screw (B).*

Using Wire Nuts

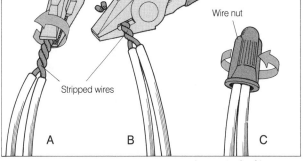

Fig. 12. To ensure a neat splice, *strip about 1 inch of insulation from each wire and twist the ends clockwise 1½ turns (A). Next, snip ⅜ to ½ inch off the ends (B). Finally, screw the wire nut clockwise onto the wires (C).*

Backwiring a Device

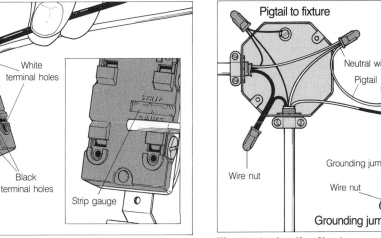

Fig. 11. When backwiring, *use the molded strip gauge (see inset) to measure the amount of insulation to be stripped. Then push the neutral (white) wire into a hole identified as white and the hot (black) wire into a hole identified as black.*

Making Pigtail Splices

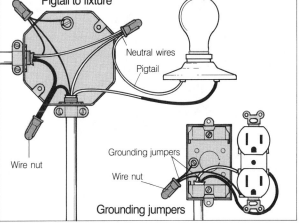

Fig. 13. A pigtail splice *is any group of three or more wires joined with a wire nut. The pigtail (top) connects a fixture to incoming and outgoing wires; grounding jumpers (bottom) link both a receptacle and box to the cable's grounding wire.*

Working with electricity can be dangerous unless you adhere strictly to certain rules. The number one rule is this: *never work on any electrically live circuit, receptacle, switch, or fixture.* Your life may depend on it. Below, we'll discuss how to shut down both individual circuits and your entire system.

In addition, remember that water and electricity don't mix. *Never* work on wiring when you're wet or standing in a damp spot. Lay down dry boards if the floor or ground is wet.

Be sure you thoroughly understand how your particular home is wired before you work on your electrical system. If you don't understand something or encounter problems, call in a professional.

Disconnecting a circuit

Before starting any work on a circuit, you must disconnect it at its source (the service entrance panel or a separate subpanel). This may be located outside your home below the electric meter or on an inside wall right behind the meter. If your circuits are protected by fuses, simply removing the appropriate fuse will disconnect the circuit from incoming current. If your service entrance panel or subpanel is equipped with circuit breakers, you can disconnect a circuit by switching its breaker to the OFF position.

To make sure that you disconnect the correct circuit, turn on a light or appliance somewhere along the circuit before you remove any fuses or turn off any breakers. The device will go out when you've removed the correct fuse or turned off the correct breaker.

If you have any doubt about which fuse or breaker affects the circuit you'll be working on, shut off *all* current coming into your home at the main disconnect, as explained in the following section. So that no one will

replace the fuse or reset the circuit breaker while you're working, tape a note to the panel. Then either carry the removed fuse with you or tape the appropriate breaker securely in the OFF position.

Shutting off the main power supply

Most service entrance panels have a main disconnect, which allows you to disconnect your entire electrical supply instantly. This feature is important in an emergency or when you're working on wiring inside the panel. Here's how to disconnect each type.

■ **Lever disconnect:** Pull the lever to the OFF position.

■ **Pull-out fuse block:** Pull firmly on the handgrip to remove the block(s).

■ **Single main circuit breaker:** Push the main breaker handle to the OFF position.

■ **Multiple circuit breakers:** Under the "rule of six" of the National Electrical Code, some homes are not required to have a single main disconnect. In such cases, *all* the breakers in the main section (not more than six) constitute the main and all must be switched to the OFF position.

Remember that the utility company lines inside your panel are still hot, even after you've turned off the main disconnect.

Four Types of Disconnects

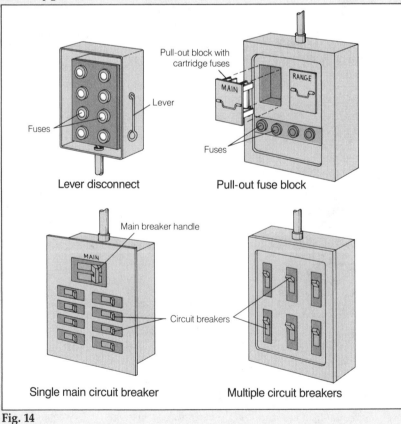

Lever disconnect

Pull-out fuse block

Single main circuit breaker

Multiple circuit breakers

Fig. 14

Extending an Existing Circuit

Your remodeling plans may call for adding a new receptacle, switch, or light fixture to an already existing circuit. In this section we present techniques for extending a circuit with nonmetallic sheathed cable (type NM) in situations where wall, ceiling, and floor coverings are already in place. When you're ready to connect your new device, turn to pages 158–165.

Selecting a power source

A circuit can be tapped wherever there's an accessible receptacle, switch, fixture, or junction box. The only exceptions are when you have a switch box without a neutral wire or a switch-controlled fixture at the end of a circuit.

Because of code restrictions, however, you must tap the correct *type* of circuit. And you must determine that the circuit doesn't already carry the maximum electrical load allowed. For help, see "Mapping Your Circuits," page 157.

Before deciding where to tap the circuit, also consider how you'll route wire to the new switch, receptacle, or fixture. Look for the easiest paths behind walls, above ceilings, and under floors.

The box tapped must be large enough to accommodate the new wires (see page 144) and must have a knockout hole through which you can thread the new cable. If the source is accessible but the box isn't right, replace it.

Preparing for a new box

Cut-in housing boxes for remodeling mount easily where wall or ceiling materials are already in place. Most boxes are designed to be mounted in wallboard. If your wall is plaster or wood, choose the so-called plain box (see page 152).

If you're putting a new box in a room that already has boxes, try to place it at the same distance from the floor as the old ones. Otherwise, place a new receptacle box 12 to 18 inches off the floor and a switch box 48 inches high. Mount a fixture box wherever you want the light.

Selecting a box location. To locate a box in a wall or ceiling, you'll need to locate the positions not only of studs and joists but also of any obstructions, such as pipes or wires.

CAUTION: Be sure to shut off power to all circuits that might be wired behind the wall or ceiling.

Drill a small test hole where you want the box. Then bend a 9-inch length of stiff wire to a 90° angle at the center, push one end of the wire through the hole, and turn it (see **Fig. 15**). If it bumps into something, move over a few inches and try again until you find an empty space.

When locating a box on a plaster-and-lath wall, chip away enough plaster around the test hole to expose a full width of lath. Plan to center the box on the lath.

Cutting the hole. Trace the box's outline on the wall or ceiling, omitting any protruding brackets from your outline.

For a tidy cut in *gypsum wallboard*, use a wallboard or keyhole saw.

To cut a *plaster-and-wood-lath wall*, first apply wide masking tape outside the box outline, as shown in **Fig. 16.** Score the outline several times with a utility knife; then drill two pilot holes in opposite corners. Cut slowly in the direction of the arrows as shown in **Fig. 17,** using a keyhole or saber saw. When cutting a ceiling hole, brace the ceiling as you cut.

To cut into a *plaster-and-metal-lath wall*, tape outside the outline, drill starter holes, and then chisel away

Cutting Box Holes in Plaster-and-Wood-Lath Walls

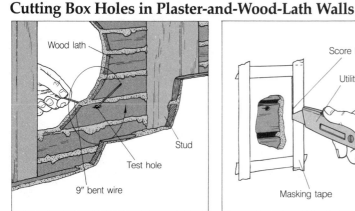

Fig. 15. To find a good box location, *drill a small test hole. Insert a piece of wire and rotate it to make sure there's an open space.*

[labels: Wood lath, Stud, Test hole, 9" bent wire]

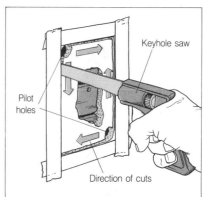

Fig. 16. After centering the box on one lath, *trace its outline; apply tape around the outline and score it with a knife.*

[labels: Score box outline, Utility knife, Masking tape]

Fig. 17. Starting from pilot holes *drilled in opposite corners, cut through the plaster and lath, using a keyhole saw (as shown) or a saber saw.*

[labels: Keyhole saw, Pilot holes, Direction of cuts]

...*extending an existing circuit*

the plaster. Cut the metal lath with a mini hacksaw or saber saw.

Clean cuts are easy in *wood paneling:* simply drill starter holes and cut with a keyhole or saber saw.

Routing cable

After cutting the hole but before mounting the box, you must run cable from the power source to the new box location. Access from an unfinished basement, an unfloored attic, or an adjacent garage can make your work much easier. Getting cable into walls, ceilings, or floors that have coverings on both sides requires some special tricks.

Routing cable where there's access. Where you have access from a basement or crawlspace or from an attic, plan to run cable along joists or beams, or through holes drilled in them (see pages 155–156). From these areas you can "fish" cable through walls that are covered on both sides.

After cutting the box hole, drill a small guide hole down through the floor or up through the ceiling to mark the location. Then, from the basement or attic, drill a ¾-inch hole next to your guide hole up through the sole plate or down through the top plates.

Now you'll need some fishing gear. For short distances, you can use a straightened coat hanger or a piece of #12 wire with one end bent into a hook. But the best tool, especially for longer runs, is a steel fish tape on a 25- or 50-foot reel.

Run fish tape or wire in through the box hole and down (or up) through the drilled hole. Attach the cable to the tape or wire (to estimate cable length, see page 155) and draw it back through the box hole.

For distances of more than a foot or two, you'll need a partner and probably two fish tapes. To make sure your path is clear, have your helper hold a flashlight in the box hole while you peer through the drilled hole. If you can't see the light

Fishing a Short Run with Access from Below

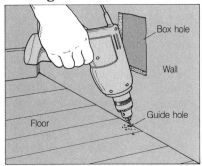

Fig. 18. To run cable from below *drill a small guide hole down through the floor to mark the box location.*

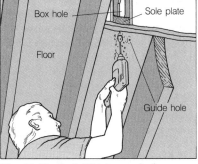

Fig. 19. Next, drill a larger hole *up through the sole plate from below, using the guide hole for reference.*

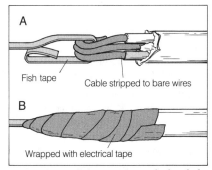

Fig. 20. Run fish tape *from the box hole through the drilled hole. Attach the cable (use method A or B) and draw it up.*

Fishing a Long Run with Access from Above

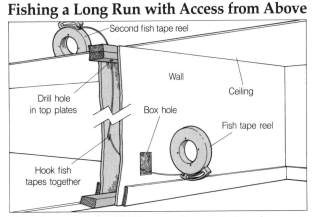

Fig. 21. Fish one tape in through the box hole *and a second tape down through a hole in the top plates. Then hook the two tapes together inside the wall.*

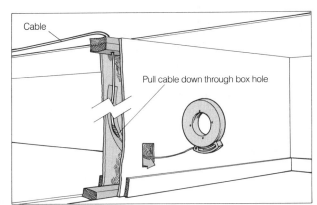

Fig. 22. Pull the hooked tapes up *through the wall; detach the second tape. Attach cable to the first tape and work it back down through the box hole as shown.*

beam, a fire block or some other obstruction is in the way. Either drill through the block or cut away the wall covering and notch the block.

Running cable when there's no access. If you don't have access, you'll probably need to cut away some wall, ceiling, or floor coverings. Wallboard is relatively easy to cut away and replace (for techniques, see pages 87 and 92–94). But some other materials, such as ceramic tile or some types of plaster, are more difficult to patch and should be left alone when possible.

Shown on this page are several ways to route cable. Cable installed less than 1¼ inches from a finished surface should be protected by a

Routing Cable along a Wall

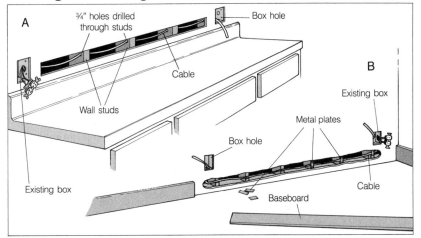

Fig. 23. To route cable, *either cut away the wallboard and drill holes through the studs (A) or run it along notched studs and cover it with metal plates behind the baseboard (B).*

Routing Cable for Back-to-Back Devices

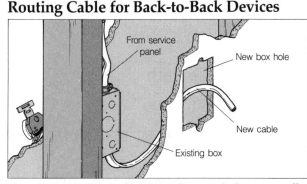

Fig. 24. To wire a new box opposite an existing one, *pull the existing device temporarily from its box and route cable through a knockout hole in that box directly to the new box hole.*

Routing Cable around a Doorway

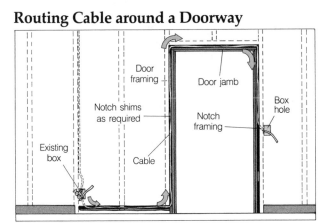

Fig. 25. To circumnavigate a doorway, *remove the door casing and baseboard; then run cable between the door jamb and rough framing from the existing box to the new box hole.*

Routing Cable for a Light Fixture & Switch

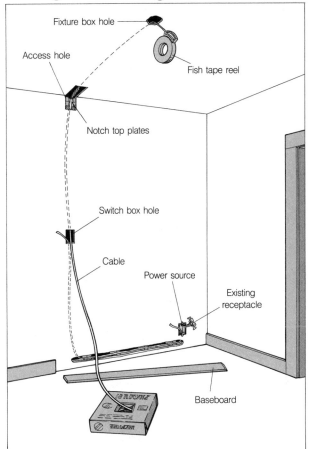

Fig. 26. Run one cable *from the power source to the switch box hole, another to the access hole. Fishing from the fixture box hole, attach the second cable; pull it out the fixture box hole.*

...*extending an existing circuit*

¹⁄₁₆-inch metal plate where it passes through wood.

Mounting the new box

When the hole is cut and the cable routed, the only remaining jobs are mounting the box, making the wiring connections, and doing any patch-up work.

Before mounting the box, insert the cable through the correct-size knockout hole. (To remove a knockout, hold a screwdriver on it and strike the screwdriver with a hammer.)

Cable must be secured to a metal box either with built-in cable clamps or with separate metal cable connectors (see page 144). NM cable need not be clamped to a nonmetallic box if it's stapled with electrical staples to a stud or joist within 8 inches of the box; however, if you can't staple, you'll have to choose a box with built-in clamps. Always leave 6 to 8 inches of cable extending into the box for connections.

How you mount the new box will depend on its type. Several examples are shown in **Fig. 27** and on page 144.

Plain box. Check the box for proper fit in the hole. If necessary, adjust the box's detachable ears forward or backward so the front edge of the box will be flush with the finished wall. On plaster-and-lath walls, clear away enough plaster to accommodate the ears. Mark screw placements on the lath at the top and bottom of the hole. Remove the box and drill pilot holes in the lath for screws. Then attach the box.

On paneled walls, just screw the ears to the wall surface. The cover plate will hide the ears and screws.

Switch box with brackets. Fit and align the box as described above. Put the two brackets in the wall, one on either side of where the box will be, and pull the bracket sides toward you so they're snug against the back

of the wall. Insert the box, bend the tabs over the sides, and secure them with pliers.

Cut-in box. Once this box is mounted, it can't be removed, so try out the fit—without the metal spring ears—and have the cables in place before you install it. Tighten the screw at the back of the box.

Ceiling box with flange. From the attic, check the fit of the box in the hole; then nail or screw the flange to the side of the joist.

Ceiling box on hanger bar. Like the flange box, a hanger bar is installed from above. Adjust the hanger's width; then screw it to the sides of two joists.

Ceiling box on offset hanger bar. This box works well where you don't have access from above. Trace the

hanger's outline on the ceiling material, remove this strip, and screw the hanger to the bottoms of two joists.

Pancake box. Simply screw this box to the bottom of a joist or hang it from a hanger bar.

Tapping into the circuit

You can tap power at fixture, receptacle, or switch boxes, as shown in **Fig. 28.** A fourth option is a junction box, where wires are simply joined.

CAUTION: Before wiring into any existing device, disconnect the proper circuit by removing the fuse or switching off the circuit breaker.

Peel back the outer sheath from the new cable; then cut off the sheath and any separation materials. To strip the insulation off the ends of individual wires and splice them to the old wires, see pages 146–147.

Mounting Three Types of Boxes

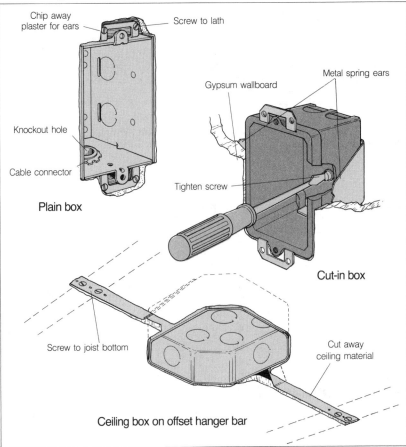

Chip away plaster for ears
Screw to lath
Knockout hole
Cable connector
Plain box
Metal spring ears
Gypsum wallboard
Tighten screw
Cut-in box
Screw to joist bottom
Cut away ceiling material
Ceiling box on offset hanger bar

Fig. 27

Wiring into the Power Source

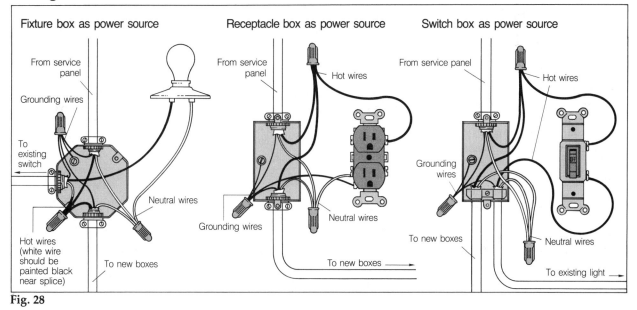

Fig. 28

EXTENDING KNOB-AND-TUBE WIRING

If you live in an older home, you may discover that it has knob-and-tube wiring, separate hot and neutral wires threaded through porcelain knobs and tubes. One recommended way to extend a knob-and-tube circuit is with NM cable and single copper TW wires, as shown in **Fig. 29.**

The TW wires—one hot, one neutral—which run inside flexible tubing, or "loom," must be connected to the cable wires with wire nuts on one end and soldered to the old copper knob-and-tube wiring at the other end. To do this, strip 2 inches of insulation from the knob-and-tube wire you want to splice and 1½ inches from the end of the TW wire. Sand the wire ends with emery paper until shiny. Twist the bare end of the TW wire tightly around the bare knob-and-tube wire, forming a coil ¾ inch long, and snip off the end of the TW wire.

Heat the coil with a 250-watt solder gun; then touch the tip of a roll of rosin-core solder to the coil. You'll know that the coil has reached the proper temperature when the solder flows readily into the spaces within the coil and does not flow out again. Fill all the spaces.

When the liquefied solder has re-hardened and the coil is cool, wrap the coil and the bare portion of the knob-and-tube wire with electrical tape; seal it by wrapping it in the opposite direction with more tape.

Tying into a Knob-and-Tube Circuit

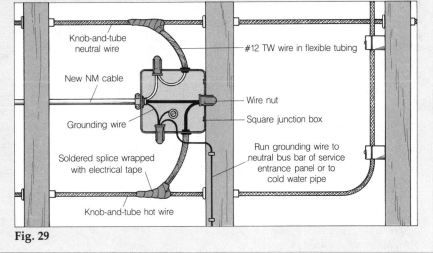

Fig. 29

Adding a New Circuit

Adding a new circuit to your service entrance panel or to a subpanel is often the answer when an existing circuit can't handle a new load. Before you add a circuit, though, you must calculate your total house load, including the new load, to make sure you will still be within your service rating. For help, see "Mapping Your Circuits," page 157.

Don't think that just because your service entrance panel or subpanel is completely full of fuses or circuit breakers you can't add any new circuits. If your panel uses breakers, one option is to replace one 120-volt breaker with a 120-volt, two-circuit breaker specially designed to fit in the same space. Another option is to add a new subpanel or even new service entrance equipment (see pages 166–167 and 169).

The techniques covered in this section are geared toward new construction, where house framing is exposed. For situations where wall, ceiling, and floor coverings are in place, see pages 149–153. When you're ready to hook up your new devices, turn to pages 158–165.

Planning your new circuit

Before you begin, you'll need to know the right type and size of branch circuit for your remodel. We'll help you sort it all out below. In addition, keep in mind that some rooms have very specific rules for the number and placement of electrical devices. Consult your local building department.

Circuit types. Branch circuits fall into three basic categories: 120 volt, 120/240 volt, and 240 volt. You may also wish to run a multiwire circuit, a variation of a 120/240-volt circuit.

Most circuits in your home are 120-volt circuits, either 15-amp

general-purpose or 20-amp small-appliance versions. These require the basic hot, neutral, and grounding wires.

Some appliances, such as a clothes dryer or range, require the input of both 120 and 240 volts. These circuits require two hot wires along with the neutral wire and, in some cases, a grounding wire (see pages 160–162).

Electric water heaters and central air conditioners are examples of appliances that require a straight 240-volt circuit. A strictly 240-volt circuit consists of two hot wires (one from each hot bus bar) and a grounding wire. The complete loop is formed by the two hot wires; thus, no neutral is needed.

Multiwire, or "split-circuit," wiring is a special use of a 120/240-volt circuit. The 120/240-volt cable runs to a junction box, where it's split into two 120-volt circuits, as shown in **Fig. 30**. This method is handy when you want to run a single cable instead of two separate 120-volt cables.

Sizing your branch circuits.

Here's how to choose the proper conductor size for a branch circuit.

■ **Standard 120-volt branch circuits:** For 15-amp general-purpose circuits, #14 copper wire is the rule, though

electricians often run #12 for extra insurance. Choose #12 wire for 20-amp small-appliance circuits.

■ **Major appliance circuits:** When planning for a major appliance, check the appliance installation information and your local code for guidelines. Here are some typical circuit and conductor sizes:

Dishwasher: 20-amp, 120-volt, #12 copper wire.

Garbage disposer: 20-amp, 120-volt, #12 copper wire.

Electric dryer: 30-amp, 120/240-volt, #10 copper wire.

Range or oven/cooktop combination: 50-amp, 120/240-volt, #6 copper wire.

Water heater: 125 percent of nameplate amp rating, 240-volt.

For matching wire size to any amp load, see **Fig. 2** on page 143.

Mounting new boxes

First, you'll need to decide what boxes you need and where you want them. Put your plans on paper: on page 157 you'll find instructions for drawing a circuit map of your house.

Keep receptacles 12 to 18 inches above the floor. Where wall cov-

Multiwire, or "Split-circuit," Wiring

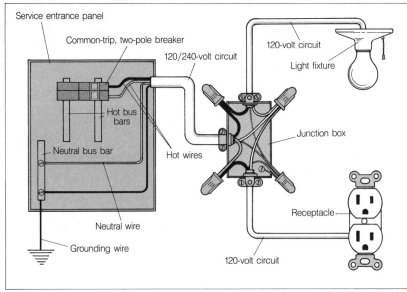

Fig. 30

erings aren't yet in place, locate either the top or bottom of a switch box 48 inches from the floor; that way, if you'll be installing wallboard horizontally, you'll only need to cut into one piece instead of two.

Be sure to avoid placing a switch box on the hinge side of a door. Remember that every box must be accessible.

Whether a new-work box is metal or nonmetallic, it should be simple to mount, using either an internal screw, an external nail or flange, or a hanger bar. For more on box options, see page 144.

Mount boxes so they'll be flush with the finished wall or ceiling. How can you do this if the wall or ceiling covering isn't yet in place? Tack a scrap of your finish material to the stud or joist next to your box and use it to align the front edge of the box.

Routing cable: new construction

In new construction, all basic wiring—or "roughing-in"—is completed before wall, ceiling, and floor coverings are in place. We'll present techniques for this situation in this section. If your access route passes through finished walls, ceilings, or floors, see pages 150–151.

Nonmetallic sheathed cable (type NM) is used for most new work. Whenever possible, plan to run cable along the surface of structural members (studs, joists, rafters, etc.). Where you must route it at an angle to the members, drill holes and run the cable through the members (see **Fig. 31**).

Drilling holes. Use the smallest size drill bit that's practical when boring through joists or studs. To

avoid weakening the wood members excessively, drill in the center of the board. If your hole is less than 1¼ inches from the edge of the board, tack a ¹⁄₁₆-inch metal plate over the edge as shown.

Estimating cable length. Make a rough sketch of your cable route, including critical dimensions such as the height of boxes from the floor and the distance between boxes. Total all the dimensions. Then, for box-to-box runs, add 4 feet (2 feet for each box) for mistakes, box connections, and unforeseen obstacles. When cable goes to a box from either a service entrance panel or subpanel, add 6 feet (4 for the panel and 2 for the box).

Supporting cable. In exposed (new) wiring, cable must be secured with electrical staples every 4½ feet and within 12 inches of each metal

Routing Cable: Two Examples

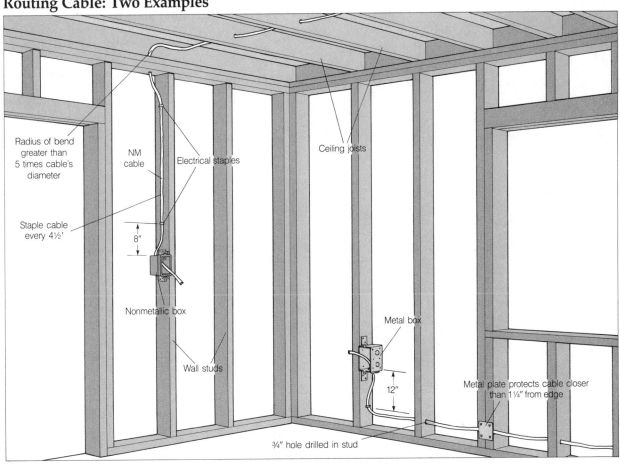

Radius of bend greater than 5 times cable's diameter

NM cable

Electrical staples

Ceiling joists

Staple cable every 4½'

8"

Nonmetallic box

Metal box

Wall studs

12"

Metal plate protects cable closer than 1¼" from edge

¾" hole drilled in stud

Fig. 31

box and 8 inches of each nonmetallic box (see **Fig. 31**). Staples are not required when cable is fished behind existing walls, ceilings, or floors. Drive the staples in with a hammer, but be careful—it's very easy to damage the cable at this point.

Routing cable in an unfinished basement.

When run under the floor at an angle to floor joists, NM cable with two conductors in sizes smaller than #6 or with three conductors in sizes smaller than #8

must be run through holes drilled in the joists, stapled to running boards nailed in place, or supported on the surface of structural members (see **Fig. 32**). Larger NM cable may be stapled directly to the bottoms of joists.

Routing cable in an attic. Cable in an attic can run either atop joists or through holes drilled in joists; accessibility dictates how the cable will run. If a permanent staircase or ladder leads to the attic, cable running at an angle to structural members must be protected by guard strips, as shown in **Fig. 33**.

In an attic reached through a crawl hole with no permanent stairs or ladder, the cable must be protected by guard strips only within 6 feet of the hole. Beyond that distance, cable can lie on top of the ceiling joists. Where cable runs parallel to joists, you can staple it to the joists' sides.

Cable connections. If you're using a metal box, you must secure the cable to it, either with built-in cable clamps (see page 144) or a metal cable connector. (Nonmetallic boxes don't require clamping if the cable is secured within 8 inches of the box.)

After slipping a cable connector onto the end of the cable, if your box requires one, insert the cable through a knockout hole. Leaving at least 6 to 8 inches of cable sticking into the box for wiring your new device, fasten the connector to the box or tighten down on the clamp.

Making branch circuit connections at panels

Where nonmetallic sheathed cable enters a service entrance panel or subpanel, you have some options for making connections. After removing the correct-size knockouts for your cable, you can use either a cable connector or a plastic snap-in clamp to hold the cable. The plastic clamp snaps into the knockout hole to prevent chafing; the cable must then be stapled within 12 inches of the panel. Leave plenty of extra cable extending into the panel: 18 inches isn't too much if the panel is large.

Each 120-volt branch circuit requires three basic connections inside the panel: the hot wire, the neutral wire, and the grounding wire. Both 120/240- and 240-volt circuits include a second hot wire; the 240-volt circuit has no neutral wire. To wire a service entrance panel or subpanel, see pages 167 or 169.

To connect a branch circuit to a circuit breaker type panel, you'll need to know the brand and approximate age of your panel (if possible, get the panel number) in order to buy the right breaker.

Routing NM Cable in a Basement

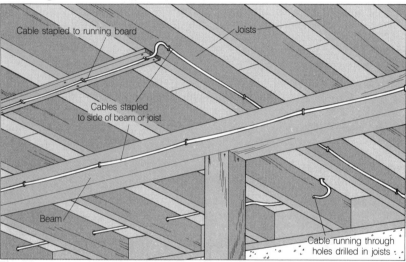

Fig. 32

Routing NM Cable in an Attic

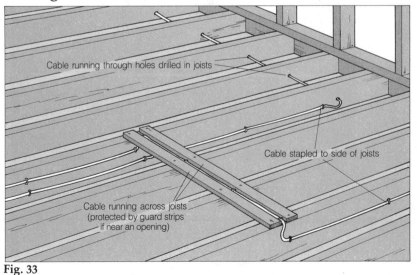

Fig. 33

MAPPING YOUR CIRCUITS

If you're planning a remodel that will affect your home's electrical system, it's important to understand your existing circuitry, as well as its capacity.

Drawing a circuit map

A basic wiring diagram of your entire house is one of the most useful remodeling aids you can have.

Start by giving a number to each fuse or circuit breaker in your service entrance panel and any subpanels. Next, draw a map showing every room in your house, including the attic, basement, and garage. Using the symbols shown in **Fig. 34,** indicate on your map the approximate location of each electrical device.

Chart the 120-volt circuits first. Turn off or remove circuit breaker or fuse number 1. Using a small table lamp or night light, go through the house and check all switches and receptacles; on your map, label those that are now dead with the circuit number 1. Repeat with each circuit.

Then go on to the 240-volt circuits, identified in your panel by a double circuit breaker or a pull-out block with cartridge fuses (see page 148).

Calculating maximum watts

Determining your present usage, or electrical load, is your next step. If you're contemplating an addition to a particular circuit, add up the watts marked on the appliances and/or bulbs fed by that circuit. A 15-amp circuit can handle 1800 watts; a 20-amp circuit is rated for 2400 watts. The number of watts you can add is the difference between these figures and your total. Note that if the load will be *continuous*—switched on for more than 3 hours straight—the circuit rating must be reduced to 80 percent of its normal value.

If you want to add a circuit, you need to know your present house load compared to your service rating. Instead of taking the time to add up wattages throughout your house, you can simply refer to the representative values and formulas established by the National Electrical Code.

If you're confused by the load calculations, call on your building department's electrical inspector. Take along your circuit map, a list of all your major appliances, and a second list of all the boxes and appliances you're planning to add.

Circuit Mapping

Fig. 34

At left is a circuit map of a typical two-bedroom house. Note that the dashed lines indicate which switch controls which fixture; they do not show wire routes.

Electrical symbols

⊗	Light fixture
⊖	Duplex receptacle
⊟	Duplex receptacle, half controlled by switch
S	Single-pole switch
S_3	Three-way switch (two switches control one fixture)
⊖R	Range receptacle
⊖D	Dryer receptacle
⊡	Doorbell
⊖WP	Weatherproof receptacle
----	Switch loop

Circuit identification

1. Range (50 amp)
2. Dryer (30 amp)
3. Kitchen and dining room (20 amp)
4. Kitchen and dining room (20 amp)
5. Washer (20 amp)
6. Dishwasher (20 amp)
7. Bath and hall (15 amp)
8. Bedroom #2 (15 amp)
9. Bedroom #1 (15 amp)
10. Living room (15 amp)
11. Living room (15 amp)
12. Garage (20 amp)

Wiring Switches

Most switches in a home are either single-pole or three-way types. (For a discussion of switch options, see page 145.) When wiring switches, remember that they're hooked up *only* to hot wires.

The switches shown on these pages have no grounding wires because the plastic toggles used on most home switches are shockproof. However, if switches are housed inside metal boxes, as shown below, the boxes *do* need to be grounded. When installing a nonmetallic switch box at the end of a circuit, secure the end of the grounding wire between the switch bracket and the mounting screw.

CAUTION: Before wiring any switch, be sure to disconnect the circuit by removing the fuse or switching the circuit breaker to OFF.

Wiring single-pole switches

Single-pole switches have two screw terminals of the same color (usually brass) for wire connections and a definite vertical orientation. Some models also have terminals for back-wiring (see page 145). Make the hookups as shown on page 147; it makes no difference which hot wire goes to which terminal.

Because of cable-routing logistics, circuit wires may run from the service panel or subpanel through the switch box to the light fixture box, or to the light fixture box first, with a switch loop to the switch box. (In the latter case, identify the white wire as a hot wire by wrapping it with black tape or by painting it black.) Where the switch is in the middle of the circuit, the wires continue on to the next box. All three setups are shown in **Fig. 39.**

Once you've made the connections, fold the wires behind the switch and push the switch into the box. Screw the switch to the box, adjusting the screws until the switch is vertical. If the switch isn't flush with the wall, use the break-off portions of the switch's plaster ears or some washers as shims. Finally, screw on the cover plate.

Wiring three-way switches

These switches have two screw terminals of the same color (brass or silver) and one of a darker color, identified by the word "common." Either end of a three-way switch can go up. It's important to observe, though, which terminal is the common one; it may be located differently from **Fig. 40.** Circuit wires may run first through the fixture box, through one switch box, or through both switch boxes.

To wire a pair of three-way switches, first connect the hot wire from the service entrance panel or subpanel to the common terminal of one switch; then connect the hot wire from the fixture or receptacle to the common terminal of the other switch. Finally, run hot wires from the two remaining terminals on one switch to the two remaining terminals on the other.

Mount the switches and cover plates as directed above.

How to Wire a Single-pole Switch

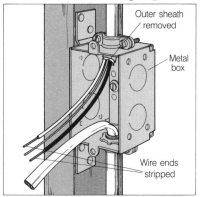

Fig. 35. Remove the outer sheath *of insulation and all separation materials from the cables inside the box; strip the insulation from the wire ends.*

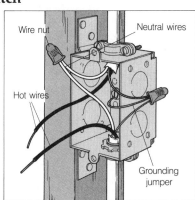

Fig. 36. Join the neutral (white) wires, *if any, and cap with a wire nut. Then join the grounding wires and, for a metal box, add a grounding jumper.*

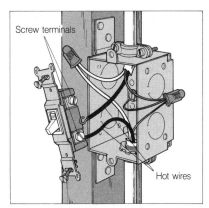

Fig. 37. Connect the hot (black) wires *to the switch's screw terminals. Fold the wires behind the switch and push the switch into the box.*

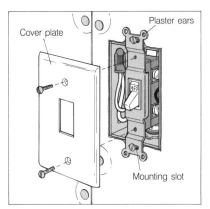

Fig. 38. Screw the switch to the box; *align it by adjusting the screws in the mounting slots. To bring it forward, use the ears as shims. Attach the cover plate.*

Circuit Diagrams: Single-pole Switches

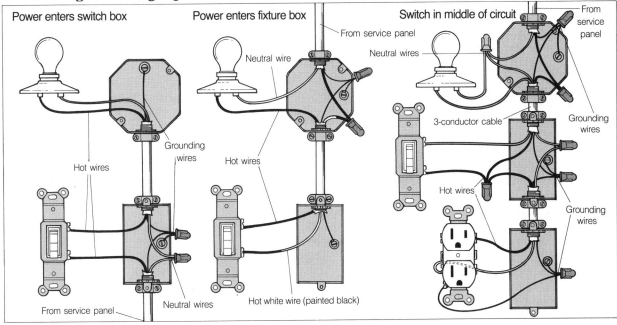

Power enters switch box — Grounding wires, Hot wires, From service panel, Neutral wires

Power enters fixture box — From service panel, Neutral wire, Hot wires, Hot white wire (painted black)

Switch in middle of circuit — From service panel, Neutral wires, 3-conductor cable, Grounding wires, Hot wires, Grounding wires

Fig. 39

Circuit Diagrams: Three-way Switches

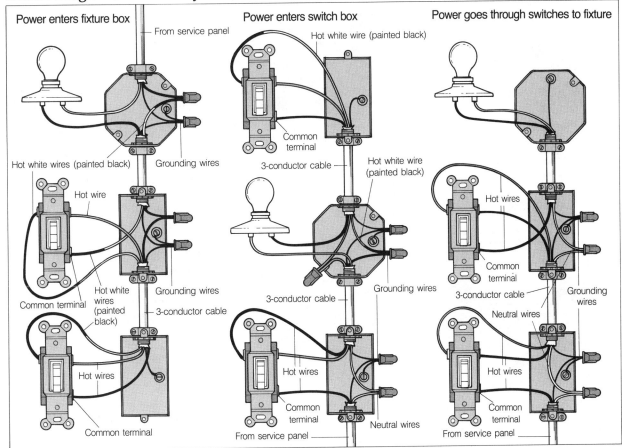

Power enters fixture box — From service panel, Hot white wires (painted black), Grounding wires, Hot wire, Common terminal, Hot white wires (painted black), Grounding wires, 3-conductor cable, Hot wires, Common terminal

Power enters switch box — Hot white wire (painted black), Common terminal, 3-conductor cable, Hot white wire (painted black), 3-conductor cable, Grounding wires, Hot wires, Common terminal, From service panel, Neutral wires

Power goes through switches to fixture — Hot wires, Common terminal, 3-conductor cable, Grounding wires, Neutral wires, Hot wires, Common terminal, From service panel

Fig. 40

Wiring Receptacles

Receptacles are designed for 120-volt, 120/240-volt, or straight 240-volt use. Remember that all receptacles are also rated for a specific amperage; for details, see page 145.

CAUTION: Before wiring any receptacle, be sure to disconnect the circuit by removing the fuse or switching the circuit breaker to OFF. For a 240-volt circuit, you may have to remove two fuses or trip a two-handled breaker.

How to Wire a Receptacle

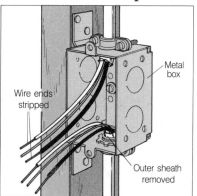

Fig. 41. Remove the outer sheath *of insulation and all separation materials from the cables inside the box; then strip the insulation from the wire ends.*

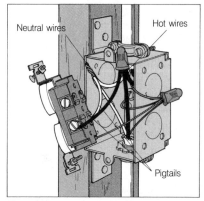

Fig. 43. Join pairs of hot wires and neutral wires *entering and leaving the box. Add a pigtail from each splice to the correct terminal on the receptacle.*

120-volt receptacles

All new receptacles for 15- or 20-amp circuits should be of the grounding type shown in these drawings. If you want to add a receptacle to a circuit that doesn't have a grounding wire, you can either use a grounding type and run a separate grounding wire to a nearby cold water pipe or, in some areas, substitute an old-style non-grounding receptacle. To ground to the water pipe, use bare #12 copper wire and a grounding strap.

Most receptacles have three different-colored screw terminals. The brass ones are hot, the white or silver ones are neutral, and the green one is the grounding terminal. If

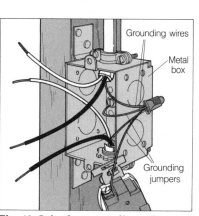

Fig. 42. Join the grounding wires *with a grounding jumper from the receptacle. For a metal box, add a jumper from the box.*

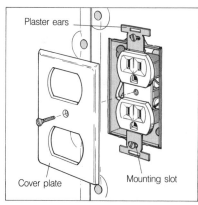

Fig. 44. Screw the receptacle *to the box after first folding back the wires. Make sure the receptacle is straight and flush with the wall. Add the cover plate.*

your receptacle is a backwired type, the hot and neutral terminals will be identified. The grounding wire must still be attached to the green screw terminal.

Fig. 45 shows four common wiring situations. The first, the usual arrangement, is for several receptacles to be wired in parallel, with all outlets always hot. In the second, the receptacle is controlled with a wall switch. In the third, the two outlets of a duplex receptacle operate independently of each other, with one outlet controlled by a switch and the other always hot. (In this case, use pliers to remove the break-off fin that connects the receptacle's two hot terminals.)

The fourth situation allows you to wire a series of receptacles on alternate circuits. In this case, you run a 120/240-volt circuit to the area and only hook up one of the two hot wires to each box. (For more details on this technique, called multiwire, or "split-circuit," wiring, see page 154.)

The drawings on these pages assume your housing boxes are metal; if not, there's no need to ground the boxes, but you'll have to attach a grounding wire to each receptacle.

After you've made the wire attachments, fold the wires back into the box and screw the receptacle to the box. Adjust the screws in the mounting slots until the receptacle is straight. If it isn't flush, shim it out, using the break-off portions of the receptacle's plaster ears or washers. Finally, add the cover plate.

240-volt & 120/240-volt receptacles

Because a straight 240-volt circuit has two hot wires, a grounding wire, and no separate neutral wire, you'll need a two-pole, three-wire receptacle of the correct amperage. Most models feature push-in terminals, as shown in **Fig. 46** on page 162. Using the strip gauge as a guide, strip insulation from the ends of the wires, push the wires into the correct terminals, and tighten the screws.

Circuit Diagrams: 120-volt Receptacles

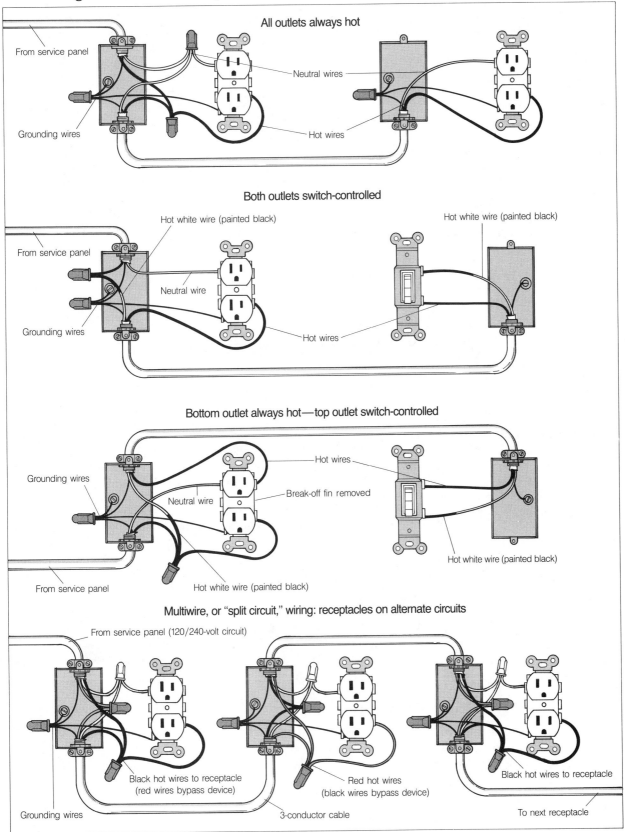

All outlets always hot

From service panel

Neutral wires

Grounding wires

Hot wires

Both outlets switch-controlled

Hot white wire (painted black)

Hot white wire (painted black)

From service panel

Neutral wire

Grounding wires

Hot wires

Bottom outlet always hot—top outlet switch-controlled

Grounding wires

Hot wires

Break-off fin removed

Neutral wire

Hot white wire (painted black)

From service panel

Hot white wire (painted black)

Multiwire, or "split circuit," wiring: receptacles on alternate circuits

From service panel (120/240-volt circuit)

Black hot wires to receptacle
(red wires bypass device)

Red hot wires
(black wires bypass device)

Black hot wires to receptacle

Grounding wires

3-conductor cable

To next receptacle

Fig. 45

... *wiring receptacles*

Circuits rated for 120/240 volts have two hot wires and a neutral wire but, depending on whether the circuit originates at the service entrance panel or at a subpanel, may or may not have a grounding wire.

If the circuit originates at the service entrance panel, some codes permit you to ground the device connected to it through the neutral wire, which lets you use a three-pole, three-wire receptacle. However, if your circuit runs from a subpanel, you must include a separate grounding wire and use a three-pole, four-wire receptacle. **Fig. 46** shows both situations.

Wiring 240- & 120/240-volt Receptacles

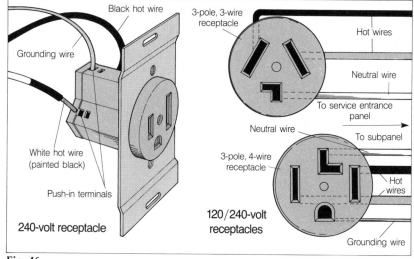

Fig. 46

BUILT-IN PROTECTION: THE GFCI

The ground-fault circuit interrupter (GFCI, or sometimes GFI) is a device designed to protect you from electric shocks.

A GFCI monitors the amount of current going to and from a receptacle or, in some cases, an entire circuit. Whenever the amounts of incoming and outgoing current are not equal—indicating a current leakage (a "ground fault") of 0.005 amperes or greater—the GFCI opens the circuit instantly, cutting off the electricity.

The protection value of a GFCI has made it standard equipment in new construction; the National Electrical Code requires that all bathroom, garage, and outdoor receptacles be equipped with one. You can use a receptacle with a GFCI built right into it, or you can install a GFCI in the service entrance panel or subpanel in place of the circuit breaker protecting that particular circuit.

A receptacle-type GFCI is wired like an ordinary receptacle and provides protection at that individual receptacle. Depending on the model, it may also protect all receptacles downstream (away from the power source), but it will not protect any receptacles upstream (toward the power source).

The circuit breaker type GFCI protects all receptacles hooked up to that branch circuit. To install this kind, first connect the hot (black) circuit wire to the GFCI's black screw and the neutral (white) wire to the white screw (see **Fig. 47**); then attach the GFCI's curly white wire and the circuit's grounding wire to the service panel's neutral bus bar.

The GFCI: Two Types

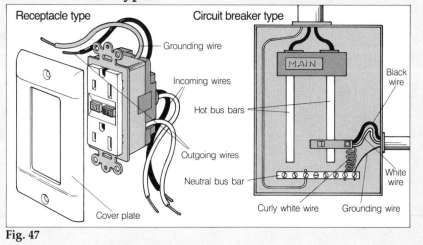

Fig. 47

Installing Light Fixtures

If your plans call for new lighting, you'll choose from surface-mounted, track, or recessed fixtures. (For more details on lighting options, see the planning chapter beginning on page 4.) Instructions for installing each type appear in this section.

CAUTION: Before tackling any lighting job, disconnect the circuit by removing the fuse or switching the circuit breaker to OFF.

Surface-mounted fixtures

Surface-mounted fixtures are either mounted directly to a housing box or suspended from the box by chains or a cord (see **Fig. 48**).

The size and weight of the new fixture determine the mounting method: many ceiling and wall fixtures can be screwed directly to the box's ears. Heavier fixtures, however, may require fastening to the box with a mounting bar, hickey, or reducing nut; any fixture that weighs over 50 pounds must be secured to a joist or beam as well as to the box. New fixtures usually come with their own mounting hardware, which is adaptable to any standard fixture box.

Adding a new fixture. Once you've routed cable and installed the box and switch, mounting the fixture itself is straightforward.

All fixtures with exposed metal parts must be grounded. If you've chosen a metal box, the nipple or screws holding the fixture to the box will ground the fixture. If the box is at the end of the circuit, attach the grounding wire of the cable directly to the box's grounding screw or clip. If more than one cable enters the box, make a grounding jumper (pigtail).

A nonmetallic box doesn't need grounding, but you'll have to ground the fixture. Look for a box with a metal grounding bar (see **Fig. 49**). If the fixture is at the end of

Surface-mounted Fixtures

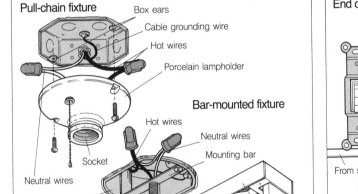

Fig. 48

Circuit Diagrams: Light Fixtures

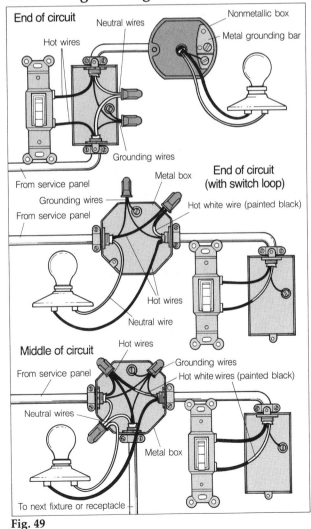

Fig. 49

the circuit, attach the cable grounding wire to the bar. If the fixture is in the middle of the circuit, make a grounding jumper to join the cable grounding wire to the bar.

A cord- or chain-hung fixture also needs a grounding wire run from the light bulb socket to the box. Most new fixtures are prewired with a grounding wire.

To install the fixture, match the box's wires to those of the fixture—black wire to fixture hot wire, white wire to fixture neutral wire. Cap all splices with wire nuts. Mount the fixture with the hardware specified by the manufacturer.

Note: If the fixture is heavy, have a helper hold it while you work; or hang it from the box with a hook made from a wire coat hanger.

Replacing a fixture. Carefully remove the glass shade, if any, from the old fixture. Then unscrew the canopy from the housing box and detach the mounting bar, if there is one. If the existing circuit isn't grounded, you'll need to extend a grounding wire from the box to the nearest cold water pipe, using bare #12 copper wire and a grounding strap.

Match the wires of the new fixture to the wires in the box and cap the connections with wire nuts. Secure the new fixture, using the hardware included with it.

Track systems

Track systems are mounted, either directly or with mounting clips, to the wall or ceiling. Power is provided by using either a wire-in or plug-in connector, as described below. Both types are shown in **Fig. 50.** Tracks are often wired into two separate circuits controlled by two switches.

Attaching the connector. A track system with a wire-in connector is hooked up directly to a housing box. Whether you use an existing box or install a new one, you'll need as many wall switches as your track has circuits. If you're simply replacing a fixture with a single-circuit track system, you can use the existing wall switch.

A plug-in connector, which includes a 12-foot cord and a lamp plug, lets you place a track wherever the cord will reach a receptacle. The connector is mounted flush against the wall or ceiling. Note that plug-in connectors are available only with single-circuit tracks.

Once the power is tapped and any necessary switches installed, attach the connector to the ceiling or wall surface or to the housing box, as shown in **Fig. 50.**

Mounting the track. When attaching a track directly or with mounting clips to the ceiling or wall, you'll use mounting screws or toggle bolts in predrilled holes. To lay out and drill the necessary holes, line up a chalkline or the edge of a yardstick with the center slot of the connector; snap or draw a line to the proposed end of the track.

Setting a length of track beside the line, mark along the line the positions of the knockout holes in the roof of the track. These marks show you where to drill.

If you're using a plug-in connector, it will lie flush against the mounting surface so that you can attach the track directly to the wall or ceiling. Slip the two bare wire ends of the first length of track into the connector's wire receptacles; secure the track to the ceiling or wall with mounting screws or toggle bolts. Attach the remaining lengths of track in the same way.

If you're using a wire-in connector, you'll need special clips to hold the track ¼ to ½ inch away from the mounting surface. Screw or bolt the clips to the ceiling or wall; then slip the first length of track into the connector. Press it, and succeeding lengths, into the clips.

Track Systems

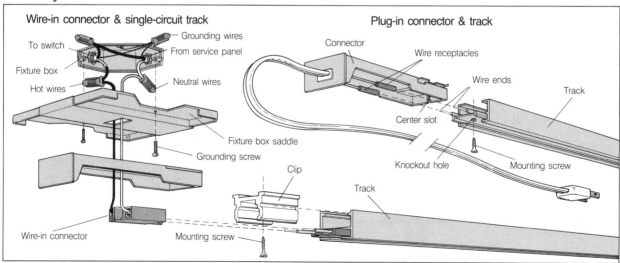

Fig. 50

Recessed fixtures

Common recessed fixtures include incandescent circular or square downlights and larger fluorescent ceiling, or "troffer," panels. To install either type, you'll need to cut a hole in the ceiling between the joists or remove tiles or panels from a suspended ceiling.

Recessed fixtures need several inches of clearance above the finished ceiling, so they're most easily installed below an unfinished attic or crawlspace. Because of the heat generated by many types of downlights, you must remove insulation within 3 inches of the fixture and make sure that no combustible materials are within ½ inch (with the exception of joists or other blocking used for support).

Recessed downlights. There are two types of downlights: one comes prewired and grounded to its own housing box; the other must be wired into a junction box attached to a joist.

Before installing the downlight, you'll need to cut a hole for the fixture housing in the ceiling between two joists. Once you've determined the location, trace the outline of the housing on the ceiling; use a keyhole or saber saw to cut the hole.

■ **Downlight with box.** With this type, the fixture and its box are premounted on a metal frame. You slip the unit through the ceiling hole and clip it to the ceiling's edge, as shown in **Fig. 51B.** Then you snap the fixture into its socket. (If there's no access from above, hook up the wires to the circuit *before* positioning the fixture and frame.)

■ **Downlight without box.** To link this type of fixture to incoming cable, you must select a junction box that can be nailed to a joist, as shown in **Fig. 52.** After clamping and wiring the fixture's cable into the junction box, snap the fixture housing into its socket. Then push the fixture into place and secure it to the ceiling material with clips. The metal-clad cable grounds the fixture to the box.

Recessed ceiling panels. Manufactured ceiling panels are available in a range of sizes. Panels are often designed to fit exactly the space of a panel or tile in a suspended ceiling; the fixture rests on the furring strips or metal channels that support the ceiling material.

In a standard ceiling, you'll have to cut a hole between ceiling joists. Nail 2 by 4s between joists, as shown in **Fig. 53,** spacing them to match the length of your fixture. Use extra blocking parallel to the joists as needed. If your fixture is wider than the space between joists, you'll need to cut away a portion of one joist and install headers to reinforce the gap (see pages 126–127 for more details).

Route electrical cable to the ceiling panel from a junction box, switch box, or adjacent fixture box. (For details, see pages 150–151.) The panel often has its own cover plate, or box, to protect wire splices; if yours doesn't, nail a junction box nearby to house the connections.

If your only access is from below, connect the wiring to the panel before pushing it into the opening. Anchor the panel to the 2 by 4s or joists with nails, screws, or the fixture's mounting hardware.

Downlight with Box

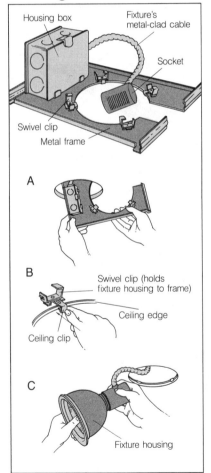

Fig. 51. To mount this recessed downlight, *slip it through a hole cut in the ceiling (A) and clip it to the ceiling's edge (B). The fixture housing then snaps into its socket (C).*

Downlight without Box

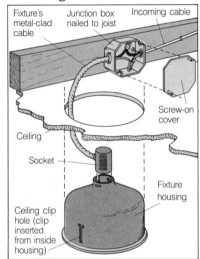

Fig. 52

Recessed Ceiling Panel

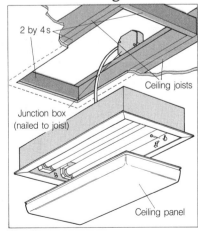

Fig. 53

Wiring a Service Entrance Panel

Older homes with two-wire (120-volt) service of less than 100 amps simply can't support many major electrical additions. To accommodate your remodeling plans, you may need to upgrade your service type or rating. That means replacing the service entrance components, then connecting new and old branch circuits.

If you're simply hooking up a new circuit to your present panel, see the facing page.

Upgrading service entrance equipment

Fig. 54 shows typical overhead and underground service entrance components. When you increase your service rating, you'll probably need to replace all of them. Ask both your utility company representative and your electrical inspector for the right sizes and types of service equipment and conductors for your new rating.

To replace your service entrance equipment, follow these steps:

1. Install new service equipment —panel and, if separate, meter and main disconnect, mast, weatherhead, and service entrance conduit—as close to the present equipment as possible.

2. Ground the new system by running the grounding electrode conductor from the panel's neutral bus bar (see **Fig. 55**) to an approved ground (check local codes). Then be sure to ground the cabinet itself by installing the service bonding screw.

3. Wire the new service entrance conductors to the meter, then from the meter to the new panel's hot bus bars and neutral bus bar, as shown in **Fig. 55**.

4. Have the utility company sever the original service conductors from incoming power.

5. Label all existing and new branch circuits and remove the old circuits.

6. Connect all circuits to the new panel (see facing page).

7. Test the system (see page 168). If possible, have an experienced electrician check your work.

Service Entrance Components

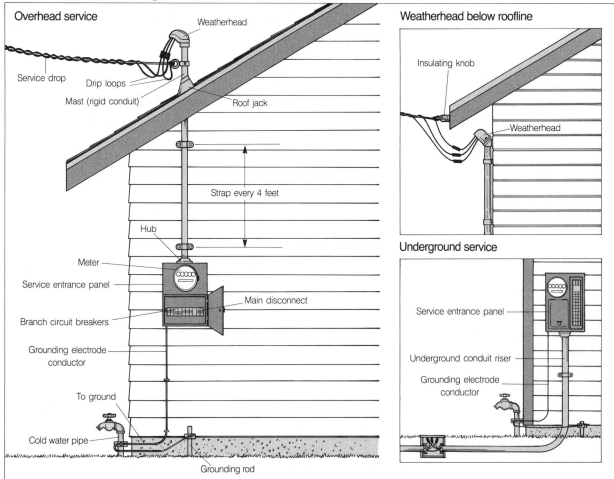

Fig. 54

8. Have the electrical inspector approve the work.

9. Ask the utility company to reinstate power.

10. Remove the old panel, meter (if separate), and other old service equipment.

Making branch circuit connections

Although you may be intimidated by the sheer number of wires inside a service entrance panel, the actual work of connecting branch circuits is straightforward. Here's how to hook up 120-volt, 120/240-volt, and 240-volt circuits. CAUTION: For complete safety, do not work inside the panel until the main disconnect (see page 148) has been turned to the OFF position.

120-volt circuits. To connect a 120-volt circuit at the service panel, first insert a cable through a knockout hole and secure it (see page 156 for details). Then follow these steps:

1. Connect the neutral and grounding wires directly to the neutral bus bar.

2. Connect the hot wire to the circuit breaker or fuse. On a circuit breaker, the connection point is the screw terminal; install the breaker (preferably before the circuit wire is attached) on a hot bus bar by pushing until the clip on the back of the breaker is firmly fastened. For fuse-type panels, the connection point is the screw terminal next to the fuseholder.

3. Balance your total house load so you have approximately the same load on each hot bus bar.

120/240-volt circuits. Connecting these circuits is the same as hooking up 120-volt circuits, except that two hot wires are used along with the neutral and grounding wires. The hot wires connect, through the circuit breakers or fuses, to *each* of the two hot bus bars. With circuit breakers, always use a common-trip, two-pole breaker with one handle when wiring a 120/240-volt circuit. This way, if one hot wire is accidentally grounded, the circuit will be disconnected from both hot bus bars.

240-volt circuits. A straight 240-volt circuit has no neutral wire, simply two hot wires and a grounding wire. In the service entrance panel, connect one hot wire to each of the hot bus bars; connect the grounding wire to the neutral bus bar.

Service Panel Connections

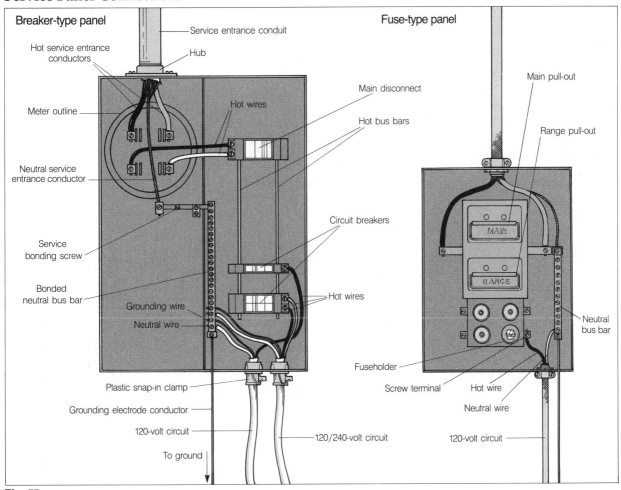

Fig. 55

For safety's sake—and to prevent a lot of extra work later—always test your electrical project as you proceed. Two basic diagnostic tools will help you: the neon voltage tester and the continuity tester (see **Fig. 56**). Here's a description of how to use each tool.

Neon voltage tester
Use this inexpensive tool to determine whether or not a 120-volt circuit is hot. Grasping the tester wires by the insulated areas only, touch one probe to a hot wire or terminal and the other to a neutral wire or terminal. If the tester light goes on, the circuit is hot.

What if you can't tell which wire is the hot one? In this case, touch one probe to the grounding wire or metal box and touch the second probe to the other wires, one at a time. The tester will light when the second probe touches the hot wire.

The tester's probes can also be fitted into the blade sockets of a duplex receptacle to tell whether it's working or not.

CAUTION: When you're using a neon voltage tester, you are near live wires. Use the probes carefully, making sure not to touch any metal parts with your hands.

Continuity tester
The idea of a continuity tester is quite simple: a battery provides the power source, and a light or bell signals when the circuit is complete. Two types are shown in **Fig. 56**. To make the homemade version, tape a doorbell to a 6-volt dry cell battery. Then, with a short piece of wire, connect one battery terminal to a doorbell terminal. Finally, connect another wire about 2 feet long to the other bell terminal.

Use the continuity tester to tell whether or not you have a short circuit and to locate the short. Ideally, circuit testing should be done initially at the rough-wiring stage—before switches, receptacles, or light fixtures are wired. Temporarily make all hot (including switches), neutral, and grounding splices so each circuit is continuous up to the last box; then test the connections. Test again after installing walls, ceilings, and floors.

CAUTION: Before you use the tester, be sure the power is turned to the OFF position.

To test for short circuits, start at the service entrance panel. Test your circuits as follows: hook the alligator clip or bare wire end of your tester to the neutral bus bar; then, one at a time, touch the hot wire of each circuit to the tester (the probe or free battery terminal). The circuits should check out as open (no bell or light). If the light comes on or the bell rings, you have a short in that circuit.

When checking a circuit at a subpanel, you must run the test described above twice. First, hook your clip or wire to the neutral bus bar to check the hot wire/neutral wire circuits. Second, hook your clip or wire to the grounding wire terminal to check your grounding system.

To track down a short, make a careful visual check of your wire splices and look for cut or damaged wire if your wiring is exposed. Be sure that the free device wires at boxes are not inadvertently touching each other or the metal box.

If wiring has already been covered, proceed as follows: undo the wire splices at the next-to-last box on the circuit to open the circuit there. Then test the circuit at the service entrance panel or subpanel. Continue this procedure as necessary, moving closer to the power source each time, until the circuit tests open. You have now isolated the short; it's between the box where the circuit checked out open and the previous box (or at one of those boxes).

Testing Devices

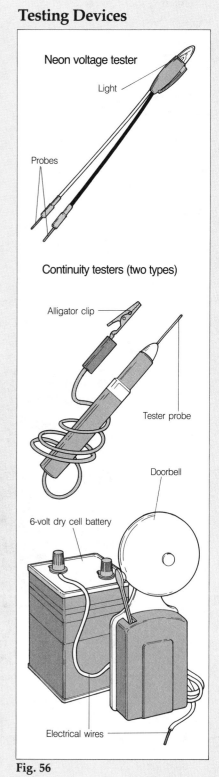

Neon voltage tester
Light
Probes

Continuity testers (two types)

Alligator clip
Tester probe
Doorbell
6-volt dry cell battery
Electrical wires

Fig. 56

Adding a Subpanel

If your service entrance equipment is centrally located, you'll probably want to run all branch circuits directly from it. But if it's in an out-of-the-way spot or if it's completely full of fuses or circuit breakers, adding a subpanel may be your only choice.

By placing the subpanel in or near the remodeled area, you can route new branch circuits directly from the subpanel rather than all the way from the service panel. There's no limit to the number of subpanels you can have, as long as your total house load doesn't exceed your service rating.

CAUTION: For complete safety, do not work inside the panel until incoming power has been turned off.

Mounting the panel. You can mount a subpanel by bolting it directly to a masonry wall, by screwing it to a larger plywood back and fastening the plywood to wall studs, or by recessing the panel in the wall and screwing it to the side of one or both studs.

If you choose the last method and wall coverings are in place, insert all cable through the knockouts in the panel before installing it. Secure the cable with either cable connectors or the plastic snap-in clamps shown on page 167.

Branch circuit connections. Fig. 57 shows a typical subpanel. The hot wires connect to the circuit breakers (or fuses) just as in a service entrance panel (for details, see page 167).

Unlike the neutral bus bar in the service entrance panel, the subpanel's neutral bus bar "floats"—it is *not* grounded with a grounding electrode conductor, and the bonding screw is not installed in the subpanel. The circuit neutral wires are attached to the floating neutral bus bar. Grounding wires in a subpanel are either connected to their own

bonded bus bar or cinched together with a compression lug and bonded (screwed) to the panel (see the inset in **Fig. 57**).

Subfeeds. Think of a subpanel as a branch circuit; like any other branch circuit, the subpanel's ampacity must not be less than that of the circuit breakers or fuses protecting it at the service entrance panel or in the subpanel itself.

The wires leading from the service entrance panel to a subpanel are called subpanel feeders, or just subfeeds. Add up the maximum am-

pacity of all planned branch circuits served by the subpanel; then choose your subfeed wire size from **Fig. 2** on page 143.

At the service entrance panel, the subfeeds connect to a fuse terminal or circuit breaker just like any other 120/240-volt branch circuit (see page 167). In most subpanels, the hot subfeeds attach directly to the hot bus bars, requiring no subpanel main disconnect. Attach the subfeed neutral wire to the subpanel's floating neutral bus bar. Run the grounding wire to the grounding bus bar or compression lug.

Subpanel Wiring

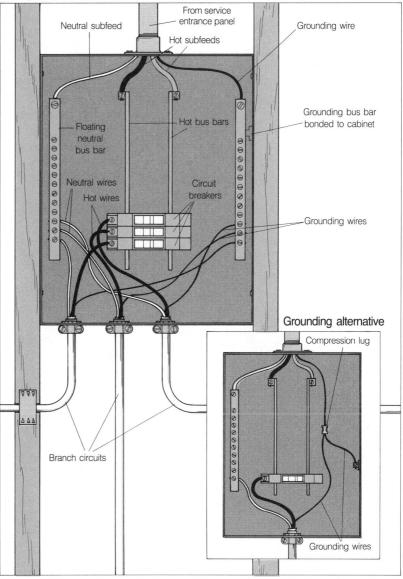

Fig. 57

Plumbing & Heating

Often, remodeling plans include a new bathroom, a remodeled kitchen, or a reshuffled floor plan—changes that can affect two of the basic house systems, plumbing and heating.

A network of pipes that carry water and gas, along with ducts that convey heated air, runs through the walls and floors of your house. How this network operates is described on pages 78–81. Any project that involves rerouting or adding pipes or ducts will require some plumbing or ductwork know-how.

From the basics of working with pipe to the fine points of extending a forced warm air heating system, this chapter shows you how to accomplish the jobs you need to do. The early pages explain pipe-fitting techniques and how to extend plumbing to new locations. Then you'll learn how to replace old sinks, toilets, bathtubs, and faucets with new ones, and how to work with gas lines. You'll also discover how to install a water heater and how to hook up a dishwasher or garbage disposer.

In addition to conventional heating systems that use warm air or water, you'll find basic information on such alternative systems as wood stoves and solar heating.

As with every other aspect of remodeling, you can do as little or as much of the work yourself as makes you comfortable. But don't undertake any job you don't fully understand.

Should you need further information about any aspect of plumbing, turn to the *Sunset* book *Basic Plumbing Illustrated.*

Planning Plumbing Extensions

Though replacing an old plumbing fixture or appliance with a new one at the same location is usually a straightforward job, extending plumbing to a new location takes more skill and planning.

On these pages, we give you some tips on how to plan your plumbing addition, as well as a short course on plumbing codes; for a quick review of a typical plumbing system, turn to pages 78–79.

The planning sequence

The key to a successful plumbing addition is developing a plan that effectively balances design considerations, code requirements, the limitations of your existing system's layout, and, of course, your own plumbing skills.

Checking codes. Almost any plumbing improvement that adds pipe to the system will require advance approval from your local building department and inspection of the work in progress. Find out from the building department what work you may do yourself—some codes require that certain work be done only by licensed plumbers. For some specific information about codes governing pipe sizes, materials, and installation, see page 172.

Mapping your system. A detailed drawing of your present system will give you a clear picture of where it's feasible to tie into supply and drain lines and whether the present drains and vents are adequate for the use you plan. Such a plan will also help you communicate with local building officials and other professionals.

Starting in the basement or crawlspace, locate the main soil stack, branch drains, main drain, and accessible cleanouts; then trace the networks of hot and cold supply pipes as accurately as possible (you'll have to approximate their positions inside walls and floors in many cases). Also, check the attic or roof for the course of the main stack and any secondary vent stacks. Sketch your findings; where possible, note the materials and diameters of all pipes.

Evaluating your existing system. Before you can add new fixtures or pipes, make sure your existing system will be up to the new demands. Are your pipes adequately sized? New fixtures may mean you need larger pipes. Are existing water supply pipes in good condition? Rust stains or corrosion around fittings or rust flecks in faucet strainers may indicate that your supply pipes are due for replacement; low water pressure can be a sign that corrosion may soon clog the pipes.

Finally, is your DWV (drain-waste and vent) system adequate? Sinks, showers, or toilets that drain slowly may signal a problem in the slope, venting, or layout of your system. In addition, consider whether your present water heater can handle an additional shower or sink.

Layout options. To minimize cost and keep the work simple, try to arrange new fixtures so they're as close as possible to the existing pipes—especially the main soil stack. One approach is to connect a fixture directly to the main soil stack, perhaps back-to-back with an existing fixture or group of fixtures, as shown in **Fig. 1A.** But if your new plumbing must serve an area across the house from the existing plumbing, you'll probably need to add a new branch drain (or extend an existing one) and run a new secondary vent stack inside a wall and up through the roof (see **Fig. 1B**). Note: Toilets may not be allowed upstream of fixtures on the same line.

Another approach is to add a fixture or group of fixtures above or below an existing group on the main soil stack, as shown in **Fig. 1C,** but check local codes carefully.

Assessing your skills. Extending supply, drain-waste, and vent pipes to a new fixture group means that you must accurately measure pipe runs, calculate DWV slope, and cut and join pipe and fittings (see pages 173–176). In addition, you'll need general carpentry skills and tools to open walls or floors and notch or drill framing members.

If you're unsure about your ability to do these jobs, consider hiring a professional to check your plans and rough-in the pipes; then you can do

Three Layout Options

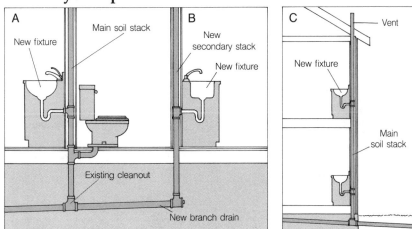

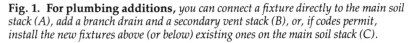

Fig. 1. For plumbing additions, *you can connect a fixture directly to the main soil stack (A), add a branch drain and a secondary vent stack (B), or, if codes permit, install the new fixtures above (or below) existing ones on the main soil stack (C).*

...*planning plumbing extensions*

the final fixture or appliance hook-ups yourself.

Understanding plumbing codes

Plumbing codes specify the materials, pipe sizes, and installation requirements for each plumbing system—water supply, drain-waste, and vent. Make sure the pipe you select is rated specifically for one of those uses.

The standards described here are based on the Uniform Plumbing Code (UPC). But since local codes (which may differ) supercede the UPC, be sure to check with your local building department.

The water supply system. The UPC allows three types of pipe for water supply—galvanized, copper, and plastic. Galvanized and copper pipes are widely accepted, but many local codes prohibit the use of plastic supply lines.

The required diameters for supply pipes are specified clearly in the plumbing code. Typically, the main supply line is a ¾- or 1-inch pipe; risers feeding each group of fixtures are usually ½-inch pipe.

The drain-waste and vent systems. The types of pipe allowed by the UPC for the DWV system include cast iron, galvanized, copper DWV, plastic ABS (acrylonitrile-butadiene-styrene), and plastic PVC (polyvinyl chloride). Codes govern both the size and slope of such pipes. Refer to **Fig. 2** for minimum DWV pipe sizes.

In addition, the plumbing code specifies minimum diameters for drains and vents in relation to the number of *fixture units* (based on the amount of water each fixture uses per minute) sharing a particular line.

Drain lines must slope toward the main house drain at a minimum of ¼ inch for each foot of distance. Vent lines can be either horizontal or slightly sloped for drainage.

Minimum DWV Pipe Sizes

	Drain	Vent
Shower	2″	1¼″
Sink	1½″	1¼″
Toilet	3″	2″
Bathtub	1½″	1¼″
Main stack or drain	3″ to 4″	2″ to 4″

Fig. 2

Critical distance. The maximum distance allowed between a fixture's trap and its vent is called the critical distance. This distance varies with the size of the drainpipe.

For example, for a fixture connected to a 1½-inch drainpipe, the maximum distance to the vent allowed by the UPC is 3½ feet; for a 2-inch pipe, it's 5 feet; for a 3-inch pipe, the maximum distance is 6 feet. (As a drainpipe fills with moving water, it can create a siphon that will pull water out of the fixture trap behind it. Close vents and wide pipes allow air to circulate more easily, reducing this suction effect.)

If your fixture is too far from its vent, you have several choices: increase the size of the drainpipe, move the fixture closer to the existing vent, or add a vent closer to the fixture location.

Critical Distance

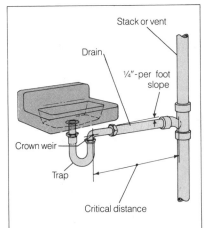

Fig. 3. Critical distance *is the maximum drainpipe length allowed between the fixture trap and the stack or vent.*

Venting options. Fig. 4 shows the four basic venting options, subject to local codes. *Wet venting* is the simplest—several fixtures are vented directly through the soil stack. *Back venting* (reventing) involves running a vent loop from near a fixture back to a main stack above the fixture level.

Individual (secondary) venting means running a new vent stack up through the roof for a fixture distant from the main stack. Finally, *loop venting* allows you to vent an island sink; the loop, which runs up higher than the sink, allows proper air circulation for venting and drainage.

Four Vent Types

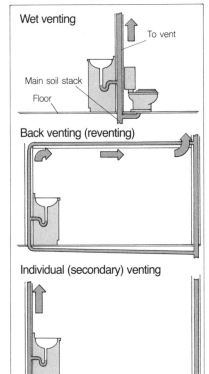

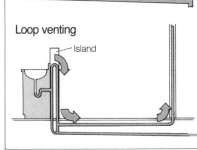

Fig. 4

Working with Pipe

To make almost any plumbing improvement, you'll have to know how to cut and fit pipe. Techniques for working with each of the commonly used types of pipe—plastic, copper, galvanized, and cast iron—differ. In this section, we give you a comparative look at all four types, as well as practical tips on the appropriate pipefitting techniques. To learn about joining two different types of pipe when extending DWV or supply lines, turn to pages 177–179.

CAUTION: Before beginning work on supply pipes of any kind, be sure to turn off the main water supply to the house and drain the lines by opening a faucet at a low point.

Plastic pipe

Plastic pipe can be used for both water supply and DWV systems. Lightweight, low in cost, and easily workable, it's ideal for the do-it-yourselfer. However, its use—especially for water supply—may be restricted by local codes, so be sure to check with your local building department.

Types of plastic pipe. Plastic pipe rated for water supply comes in two types: rigid and flexible. Rigid plastic supply pipe may be PVC (polyvinyl chloride), for cold water, or CPVC (chlorinated polyvinyl chloride), for both hot and cold water. Flexible pipe, which is especially useful because it can follow a winding course without the need for a lot of fittings, may be PE (polyethylene), used for cold water, or PB (polybutylene), used for both hot and cold water. Fittings for flexible pipe are shown in **Fig. 5.**

Two types of rigid plastic pipe are used for DWV systems: ABS (acrylonitrile-butadiene-styrene) and PVC-DWV. Sink traps and their connectors may be made from a third type—PP (polypropylene).

Flexible Pipe Fittings

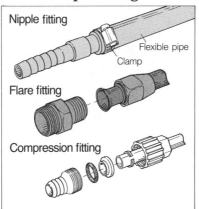

Fig. 5. Flexible pipe *can be joined with nipple, flare, or compression fittings.*

Cutting and joining rigid pipe. You can cut rigid pipe with a hacksaw, a fine-toothed wood saw, a power miter saw, a reciprocating saw, or a pipe cutter (shown on page 174).

The techniques for joining all types of rigid pipe are similar. Lengths are connected using push-on fittings cemented in place with permanent solvent cement. These fittings include elbows and tees that allow changes in pipe direction, reducer fittings that link pipe of different sizes, and threaded transition fittings for linking plastic to other types of pipe. The technique is illustrated in **Fig. 6.**

Before you cut rigid pipe, be sure that measurements are exact and that you've allowed for the distance the pipe will extend into the fitting (measure to the interior shoulder or flange). Then cut the pipe to length and remove any burrs from the cut end with a pocketknife or rasp. Clean the outside of the pipe with sandpaper or a rasp. (Some PVC pipes require removing the gloss from the last inch of the pipe; others require a primer before cementing.)

Be sure you have the right solvent cement for the kind of plastic you're using. It's a good idea to line up the pipe and fittings before cementing and mark their precise alignment—the cement will harden just a few seconds after it's applied, and you won't be able to move the joint. Once you've marked the pieces, brush a heavy coat of cement on the pipe end and inside the fitting. Put the two pieces together immediately and give them a quarter-turn to spread the cement evenly; be sure to line up your marks. Hold the fitting together for a minute. Wait at least an hour before allowing water to run through the pipe.

Using Push-on Fittings

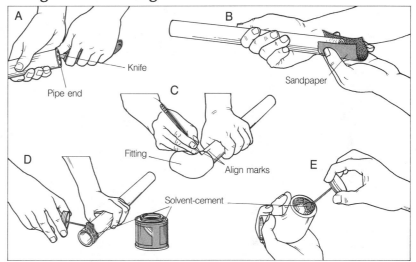

Fig. 6. Remove any burrs *from the pipe's cut end (A) and clean the outside (B). Then line up the pipe and fitting, marking their alignment (C). Finally, apply solvent cement to the pipe end (D) and to the inside of the fitting (E); then join the pieces.*

... *working with pipe*

Cutting and joining flexible pipe.
Flexible supply pipe can be cut with a sharp knife or with a hacksaw or backsaw and miter box. To join lengths of flexible pipe, use one of three types of fittings: nipple, flare, or compression. Flare and compression fittings may be used to join plastic to plastic or as transition fittings to join plastic pipe to copper or galvanized pipe.

Supporting plastic pipe.
Support horizontal runs of plastic supply pipe every 6 to 8 feet. Vertical runs need support every 8 to 10 feet. Use plumber's tape or a variety of special pipe hangers to hang the pipe (ask your supplier for recommendations); make sure that metal hangers don't gouge its vulnerable surface.

For plastic DWV pipe, provide support at every fitting or every 4 feet, whichever is less.

Copper pipe

Copper pipe, also called copper tubing, is used most often for water supply lines, less often for DWV systems. A high-quality choice for either use, it's lightweight, highly resistant to corrosion, and fairly easy to cut and join.

Using a Pipe Cutter

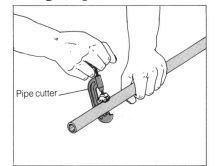

Fig. 7. A pipe cutter *makes straight cuts in copper pipe.*

Types of copper pipe.
Copper supply pipe is available in both hard (rigid) and soft (flexible) forms and in several thicknesses and diameters. Soft supply pipe is more expensive and vulnerable than rigid pipe, but it can be bent around curves without the need for fittings. A special type of copper pipe—copper DWV—is sometimes used for drain-waste and vent systems.

Cutting copper pipe.
Before cutting the pipe, measure carefully, being sure to add the distance the pipe will extend inside the fitting. Cut copper pipe straight, without distorting the end. Using a pipe cutter, twist the cutter's knob while rotating the cutting wheel around the pipe (see **Fig. 7**). Remove any burrs.

Where space is tight and the pipe is already in place, use a compact tubing cutter, a reciprocating saw equipped with a metal blade, or a hacksaw.

Joining copper pipe.
For all types of copper pipe and fittings, soldering, or "sweating," is the most common and durable joining method. You can also join hard supply pipe with compression fittings, soft supply pipe with compression or flare fittings (see **Fig. 8**). As with plastic pipe, you can use reducer fittings to join pipes of different sizes and transition fittings to link copper with plastic or galvanized (with galvanized, use a special dielectric fitting, shown on page 178).

To solder copper pipe, you'll need a small butane or propane torch; some fine steel wool, an emery cloth, or fine sandpaper; a can of soldering flux; and some solid-core wire solder. Before soldering, drain *all* water out of the pipes and polish both the outside of the pipe and the inside of the fitting with the steel wool.

Brush flux around the end of the pipe and inside the fitting. Insert the pipe all the way into the fitting. Heat the pipe and fitting evenly, as shown in **Fig. 9**. Though it takes practice, judging the correct temperature is crucial—both underheated and overheated joints will cause a leaky pipe.

Types of Fittings

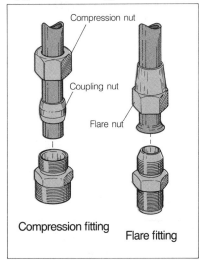

Compression nut

Coupling nut

Flare nut

Compression fitting

Flare fitting

Fig. 8

Joining Copper Pipe

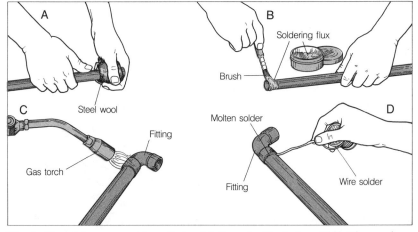

A

B

Soldering flux

Brush

Steel wool

C

Gas torch

Fitting

Molten solder

Fitting

D

Wire solder

Fig. 9. To solder copper pipe, *first polish the end with steel wool (A). Then apply flux (B), position the fitting, and heat (C). Finally, solder all around the fitting (D).*

Galvanized Pipe Techniques

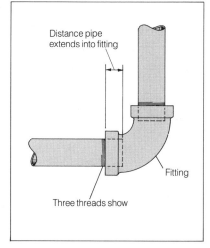

Fig. 10. To measure *galvanized pipe, add the distance between new fittings to the distance the pipe will extend into the fittings.*

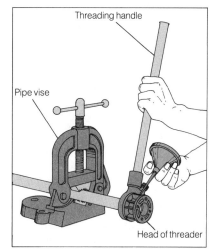

Fig. 11. To thread *the pipe, clamp it down and turn a pipe threader clockwise around the end, applying cutting oil as you work.*

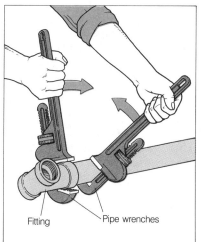

Fig. 12. To tighten *pipe connections, first hand-tighten; then use two pipe wrenches (clockwise) for the final tightening.*

When the flux starts to bubble, remove the flame and touch the solder to the joint edge. If it's the right temperature, the solder will melt and capillary action will pull it between the fitting and pipe. Keep soldering until a line of molten solder shows all the way around the fitting.

CAUTION: Use gloves or a rag to handle newly soldered pipe; it will be very hot. Shield nearby flammable materials with a piece of metal and keep a spray bottle of water handy.

Supporting the pipe. Use plastic or plastic-coated pipe hangers to support horizontal runs of copper pipe every 6 to 8 feet. If you use steel hangers, insulate them from the copper with electrical tape.

Galvanized pipe

If your house is more than 20 years old, chances are you have galvanized water supply pipe and perhaps even galvanized DWV pipe.

The term *galvanized* means that iron or steel pipes and fittings have been coated with zinc to resist corrosion. Nevertheless, galvanized pipe corrodes more quickly than copper or cast iron; it also collects mineral

deposits that can impede water flow.

Galvanized pipe can also be tedious to install because it requires cutting and threading. Replacing short runs of damaged pipe is fairly easy, but if you want to extend your system, consider using copper or plastic instead.

To its credit, galvanized pipe is approved by all codes and is suitable for exposed locations.

Measuring and cutting galvanized pipe. Galvanized pipe is connected to fittings by means of threads. The fittings include elbows, tees, and reducers, all of which can be used to connect galvanized to galvanized, or galvanized to other types of pipe.

To determine how much pipe you need, measure between fittings and add the distance the pipe will extend into them—allow ½ inch for ½- and ¾-inch pipe, ⅝ inch for 1- and 1¼-inch pipe. (A useful rule of thumb says that when the pipe is screwed tight, three threads should be visible outside the fittings, as shown in **Fig. 10.**)

Cut galvanized pipe straight so the threads can be accurately cut in the ends. A rotating pipe cutter with a cutting wheel designed for gal-

vanized pipe does the cleanest job, but you can also use a hacksaw or a reciprocating saw with a metal blade. Remove any burrs from the inside and outside with a reamer or file.

Threading and joining galvanized pipe. On most projects, it's quickest to have the pipes cut to size and threaded by a plumbing supplier. (If you need only short lengths, you can buy nipples—threaded pipe sold in ½- and 1-inch increments up to a foot long.)

To thread pipe yourself, rent a pipe vise and a pipe threader with a cutting head (die) the same size as your pipe. Clamp the pipe in the vise, fit the head of the threader into the threading handle, and slip it over the end of the pipe. Turn the threader handle clockwise, lubricating the area generously with cutting oil (see **Fig. 11**). Stop threading when the pipe emerges from the end of the die. Clean the threads with a stiff wire brush.

Before joining the pipe and fitting, lubricate the pipe threads with pipe joint compound or wrap them with pipe-wrap tape. (Never apply either to the inside threads of the fitting.) Tighten the joint with two pipe wrenches (see **Fig. 12**).

... *working with pipe*

Supporting the pipe. Support horizontal runs of pipe every 6 to 8 feet, vertical runs every 8 to 10 feet, using plumber's tape or other hangers. Mount the pipes firmly.

Cast iron pipe

There's a good chance that the DWV pipe in your house is cast iron; it's strong, resists corrosion, and dampens the sound of running water. But because cast iron is heavy and rigid, you may want to substitute plastic pipe (see pages 173–174) when remodeling, if your building code permits.

Types of cast iron pipe. Older houses often have pipes and fittings with a hub, or bell, at one end and a small spigot at the other. This type, called hub, or bell and spigot (see **Fig. 13**), has joints sealed with oakum and molten lead.

A more modern type is called no-hub, or hubless, and relies on an easy-to-use connector called a no-hub coupling.

Working with hub pipe is a job best left to a professional. No-hub work is far simpler, and most codes allow no-hub and hub pipe to be used interchangeably. The following instructions are for no-hub pipe.

Measuring and cutting cast iron pipe. To determine how much no-hub pipe you need, measure between the edge of one fitting and the cut edge of the adjacent pipe or fitting and subtract ¼ inch for the separator ring.

Cast iron is most easily cut with a DWV pipe cutter; or use a reciprocating saw with a metal blade (see **Fig. 14**). If you're cutting heavy pipe in place, support it securely by wrapping the pipe with plumber's tape, pulling it taut, and nailing it to nearby joists or studs. For a cut near a fitting, leave several inches of old pipe to allow room for the new fitting. Remove any burrs on the outside of the cut end with a wire brush or file.

Joining cast iron pipe. The no-hub coupling can be used to connect a no-hub fitting or a length of no-hub pipe to an existing cast iron pipe.

Two Types of Fittings

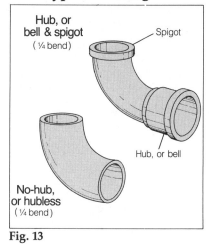

Fig. 13

Loosen the stainless steel band on the coupling and slip the neoprene sleeve and band over the end of the pipe (see **Fig. 15**). Position the new fitting or pipe and tighten the band with a screwdriver or nut driver.

Supporting the pipe. Support horizontal pipe runs at every fitting and every 5 feet, vertical runs every 5 feet. Use plumber's tape or manufactured metal hangers, as shown in **Fig. 16**.

Working with Cast Iron Pipe

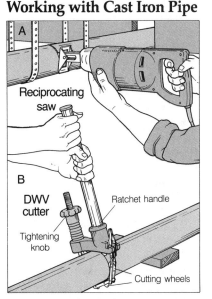

Fig. 14. To cut the pipe, *use a reciprocating saw with a metal blade (A) or a DWV cutter (B). Be sure to support the pipe above and below the cut.*

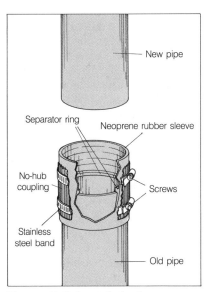

Fig. 15. To join no-hub pipe, *use a no-hub coupling. First, slip on the neoprene sleeve and stainless steel band; then tighten with a screwdriver or nut driver.*

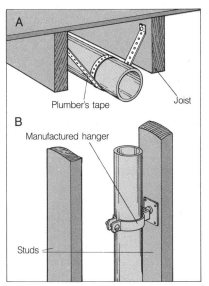

Fig. 16. Support pipe runs *with plumber's tape (A) or manufactured hangers (B); hangers are available for both vertical and horizontal applications.*

Extending Plumbing

Before you can install the new plumbing fixtures called for in your remodeling plans, you'll need to tie into existing DWV and supply lines and route the new pipes through your house.

Locating tie-ins & pipe runs

In the mapping stage, you determined the rough locations of your existing pipes. Now you must pinpoint them exactly. To locate a stack, branch drain, or supply riser, you may have to drill exploratory holes in walls or floors.

Once you've located existing pipe runs, you can plot the new ones and decide where to tie them into your existing system. You'll have to find room for the new pipes where they won't affect the structural integrity of the house or its architectural features. Be sure to look through the information on routing new pipe runs (see page 179) before you draw up your final plans. Also, remember to account for the required ¼-inch-per-foot slope for drainpipes.

To expose the plumbing where you want to tie into it, neatly cut away wall, ceiling, or floor coverings. (Be sure to cut holes large enough to allow you to work comfortably.) In walls where you're making several holes, you may want to strip all the wall covering off the wall. With wallboard, for example, it's often cleaner and easier to replace one large area than to make a number of small patches.

To learn about working with wall and floor coverings, see the chapters "Walls & Ceilings" and "Floors & Stairs."

Tying into DWV lines

Basically, tying into a DWV line entails cutting a section out of the existing pipe, inserting a new fitting (for examples, see **Fig. 17**), and then running pipe to the new fixture location.

Below we describe the various ways to join plastic and cast iron, the most common types of DWV pipe.

Because it's lightweight, easy to work, and economical, rigid plastic pipe (ABS or PVC-DWV) is often the best choice for tying into the old system. Most codes permit its use as a substitute for cast iron or galvanized DWV pipe, except for exterior runs where plastic isn't allowed.

Cutting into existing lines. Before you begin, make sure that the existing pipe is securely supported so it won't vibrate or fall when you cut it. It's best to wrap lengths of plumber's tape around the pipe and nail the tape to nearby studs or joists.

If you're cutting near an existing fitting, leave several inches of the old pipe protruding from the fitting so you'll have enough room to attach the new fitting or coupling.

Position a bucket to catch waste water from the pipe and keep lots of rags handy; be sure to warn others not to use the plumbing.

Joining plastic to cast iron. The key to joining plastic DWV pipe to cast iron is the no-hub coupling (see facing page). To add a plastic tee to an existing cast iron run, for example, it's easiest to glue on spacers (short lengths of plastic pipe) at both ends of the plastic tee, as shown in **Fig. 18**, using solvent cement (see **Fig. 6** on page 173). Then cut out a section of the cast iron pipe that's ¼ inch longer than the combined measurement of the plastic spacers and tee.

Slide no-hub couplings over the ends of the cast iron pipe, insert the new tee with spacers, and finally slide the no-hub couplings into place and tighten them down.

Some codes may require you to use a mission coupling; it's similar to the no-hub, except that one side of the neoprene sleeve is stepped down to accommodate the external diameter of the cast iron pipe, which is slightly smaller than that of the plastic pipe.

Reducer bushings also permit you to step down to smaller-diameter pipes.

Joining plastic to plastic. Inserting a plastic fitting into a run of

DWV Fittings

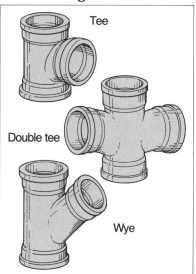

Tee

Double tee

Wye

Fig. 17. Three of the types of DWV fittings *available for making connections between old and new pipe are the tee, double tee, and wye.*

Joining Plastic to Cast Iron

Existing cast iron pipe
No-hub coupling
Plastic spacers
New plastic pipe
Plastic tee
Neoprene sleeve
Stainless steel band
Existing cast iron pipe

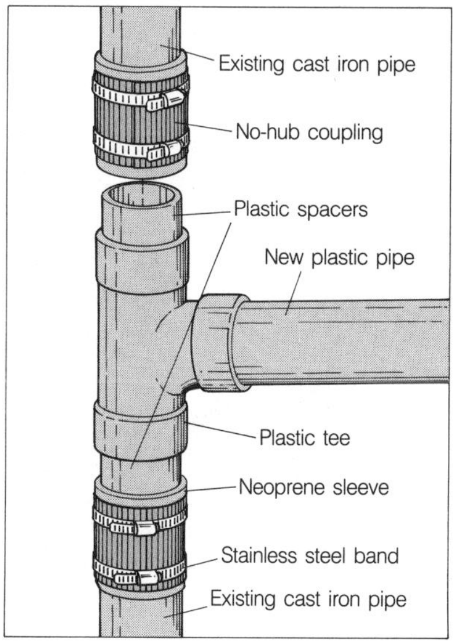

Fig. 18. To connect plastic to cast iron *DWV pipe, use a plastic tee and spacers, joining them to the cast iron pipe with no-hub couplings.*

...extending plumbing

existing plastic pipe is similar to tying into cast iron, except that you can use solvent cement to glue one end of the plastic tee or wye directly to the cut-off end of the existing plastic pipe. Glue a spacer on the other end of the fitting and join that end to the existing pipe with a no-hub coupling or a special glue-on slip fitting.

Joining cast iron to cast iron. When you're required by code to continue using cast iron pipe, use no-hub fittings and no-hub couplings, as described on page 176.

Extending supply lines

To get hot and cold water to new fixtures or appliances, you'll have to tie into the existing water supply lines. Older houses usually have galvanized supply pipe. Newer homes may have copper or, rarely, plastic supply lines. Often, you can save time and money by using transition fittings to change from galvanized supply pipe to easy-to-use copper or plastic lines.

Cutting into supply lines. Choose a location for cutting into your pipe that is close to the new fixture location and provides some working room. If you can, pick a place where there's some play in the old pipe so you'll be able to push, pull, and twist to get the final fit. This is especially important if you have galvanized pipe, which is rigid and requires room for twisting together threaded fittings.

CAUTION: Before doing any work, turn off the water at the main shutoff valve and drain the water from the lines by opening a faucet on the low end.

Cut the old pipes with a hacksaw or reciprocating saw, making sure to brace the pipes. Use a bucket and rags to catch extra water in the line.

An alternative to cutting into the line is to trace the pipe run back to a union fitting (see below) and disassemble the pipe from that point.

Using a union fitting. A union is a fitting that allows like types of pipe to be connected and disconnected easily without turning the pipe itself. Unions allow such appliances as water heaters and water softeners to be easily removed. They also enable you to insert a tee and new line into an old run of threaded pipe without extensive dismantling.

To insert a tee into a run of galvanized pipe, first cut out and re-

Dielectric Union

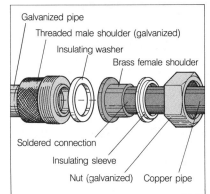

Fig. 21. A dielectric union *joins copper to galvanized pipe. Its nonmetallic washer and sleeve prevent electrolytic corrosion that would result from contact between the two metals.*

move a section of the old pipe between two fittings. Then fill in the space with nipples, a tee for the new line, and finally the union, as shown in **Fig. 20.** Finish up by tightening the union, using a pipe wrench on each half of the union. The new line threads into the third outlet on the tee.

Using transition fittings. Use these fittings to connect unlike types of old and new pipe. Transitions between plastic and galvanized or copper pipe are quite straightforward: threaded plastic fittings allow you to connect plastic directly to galvanized or threaded copper fittings or pipe. But to join copper to galvanized pipe, you must use a special fitting called a dielectric union, shown in **Fig. 21.** It separates the pipes with a nonmetallic washer and sleeve and prevents electrolytic corrosion caused by direct contact between the two metals.

Note: When you solder this union to copper pipe (see pages 174–175), be sure to keep the insulating washers and sleeve away from the heat of the solder.

Dielectric unions must be installed where they can be reached and repaired; they cannot be closed inside walls. Also, a dielectric union on a grounded water pipe will break the electrical circuit.

Extending Galvanized Supply Pipe

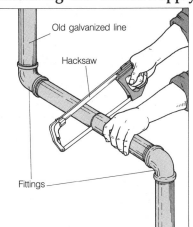

Fig. 19. To remove *a section of old galvanized pipe, saw through it with a hacksaw; then unscrew the old pipe at the fittings.*

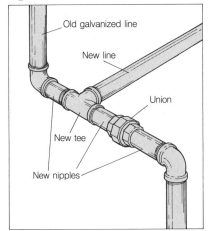

Fig. 20. Replace the old section *of pipe with a galvanized tee, nipples, and a union. Then you can connect the new line to the tee.*

Routing new pipe runs

Once you've completed the tie-ins to the DWV and supply lines, you'll need to run the pipes to the new fixture locations and test them for leaks. (Remember to allow for the ¼-inch-per-foot slope required for drainpipes.) Install the supply pipes after the DWV pipes are in. Their smaller size makes them easier to run, and they won't be in the way of your DWV plumbing.

Horizontal pipe runs. Ideally, you'll be able to run horizontal pipes where there's open access, such as in a crawlspace or basement. In this case, pipes can be suspended below the joists in pipe hangers (see **Fig. 22C**) or with plumber's tape.

If you have a finished basement or your new fixtures will be located on the second floor, you may need to box them in or hide them with a dropped ceiling. If you opt for opening the ceiling or floor, suspend pipes running parallel to the joists inside the spaces between joists.

Routing Horizontal Pipes

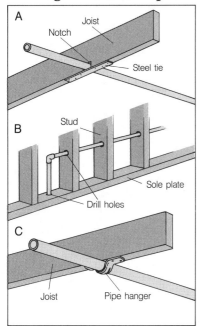

Fig. 22. To route *horizontal pipe runs where pipes run perpendicular, notch (A) or drill holes (B) in the joists or studs. Or suspend pipes in pipe hangers (C).*

For pipes that run perpendicular to joists, you can either notch the joists or drill holes in them. Use the first method if the pipes hit near the joists' tops or bottoms. To preserve the joists' strength, notches must be no deeper than a sixth the width of the joist, and the notch cannot be located in the middle third of the span. Notches should be braced with steel ties or 2 by 2 wood cleats.

If the pipes hit the middle of the joists, drill a hole near each joist's center; the hole's diameter should not exceed a third of the joist's depth.

If you must run pipes through wall studs, take similar precautions when notching or drilling.

If you have a new branch drain that is too thick to fit below the existing floor, you may need to plan for a raised floor or section of floor in the affected area (see **Fig. 23A**).

Vertical pipe runs. A new vent stack and some branch drainpipes that are extra large may require building up a wall to make room for them. A new vent stack may be installed inside an existing wall (a big job), built into a new or beefed up wall, or concealed in a closet or cabinet. In mild climates, a vent stack can run up the outside of the house, but it must usually be enclosed within a box.

You can also "fur out" an existing wall to hide added pipes. Attach new 2 by 4s to the old ones, as shown in **Fig. 23B,** and add new wall coverings.

An oversize wall, called a wet or plumbing wall, can provide the room needed for hefty vent stacks and branch drains. Unlike an ordinary 2 by 4 stud wall, a wet wall has a sole plate and top plate built from 2 by 6 or 2 by 8 lumber, as shown in **Fig. 23C**. Additionally, the studs are usually positioned with their flat sides facing out.

Finishing up. Anchor supply and drainpipe stubouts (the parts protruding through the wall or floor) to the framing. Then test your extensions for leaks. Cap off each pipe,

Concealing Pipes

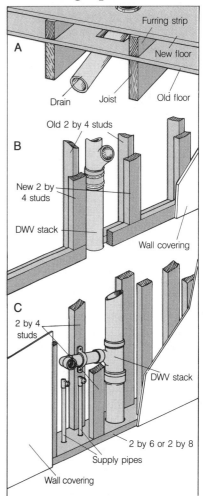

Fig. 23. To conceal *large pipes in existing walls and floors, build a raised floor (A) or build up an existing wall (B). In new construction, build an oversize wet wall from 2 by 6 or 2 by 8 lumber (C).*

turn on the water, and look closely for any sign of leaks.

If a potential leak might spray water where it could do significant damage during the test, you can install a gas pressure gauge (see **Fig. 66** on page 197) and inflate the line to 50 pounds. If the pressure drops, you have a leak. To trace it, apply soapy water to the connections; bubbles mark the leak.

Once the building department has inspected and approved your work, you can repair the wall and floor coverings (see the chapters "Walls & Ceilings" and "Floors & Stairs");

...*extending plumbing*

then install shutoff valves and fixtures, as described in the following sections.

Roughing-in new fixtures

Below are general tips and specifications for roughing-in new fixtures (see also **Fig. 24**). "Fixture templates" that come with many new fixtures also tell you exactly where the supply pipes, drainpipe, and vent for the fixture should be located on the wall or floor. For specific installation instructions, see the appropriate pages in this chapter.

Note: You may be required to install air chambers—short lengths of dead-end pipe that minimize water hammer—at your fixtures.

Sinks. You can usually add a sink without having to enlarge the diameters of your existing DWV lines. The sink can often be wet-vented if it's within the critical distance (see page 172); otherwise, it's usually back-vented.

Supply pipes required: Hot and cold stubouts.

Toilets. A toilet requires its own vent (2-inch minimum) and at least a 3-inch drain. If it's on a branch drain, a toilet can't be upstream from a sink or shower.

Rough-in the closet bend and floor flange first; the floor flange must be positioned at finished floor level.

Supply pipes required: Cold water stubout on wall or floor.

Bathtub and shower. Like sinks, bathtubs and showers can usually be tied into existing DWV lines without overloading them. They're often positioned on branch drains and are usually wet-vented or back-vented; both have a trap below the floor. A shower's faucet body and shower head assembly are installed while the wall is open.

Supply lines required: Hot and cold supply lines and a pipe to the shower head.

Typical Roughing-in Situations

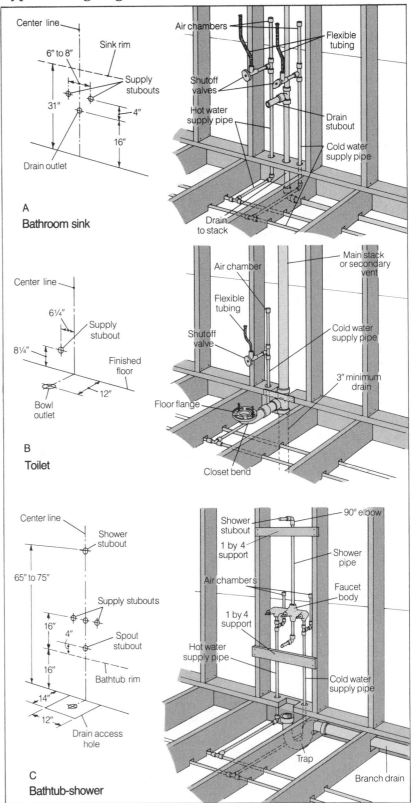

Fig. 24. Use these typical roughing-in measurements *to help you plan a new bathroom sink (A), toilet (B), and bathtub-shower (C). Check your local code and specific fixture dimensions for exact roughing-in dimensions.*

Shutoff valves, installed on water supply lines, allow you to turn off the water to an individual fixture while you repair or replace it. Every sink, toilet, washing machine, hot water heater, and dishwasher should be equipped with one. Sometimes, they're also installed by tubs and showers if the lines are accessible.

On new plumbing runs, install shutoff valves after the supply lines have been tested and inspected and the walls and flooring are finished.

Lengths of flexible tubing save you the trouble of piecing pipe together to join the valve to the fixture.

Types of shutoff valves. To select the correct shutoff valve for a fixture or appliance, you must carefully note the type and size of pipe used for the stubout (the short pipe end protruding from the wall or floor), the type and size of flexible tubing needed to connect the valve to the fixture, and the type of fixture.

Angle shutoff valves are used when the stubout comes from the wall, as for a sink; straight valves are used with pipes that come up from the floor, as for some toilets. Both are illustrated in **Fig. 25.** You may want to use a decorative chrome-plated valve if it will show.

Shutoff valves for water heaters are nondecorative; they're installed on the cold water supply line to the water heater.

Shutoffs for washing machines are usually rugged faucets with threaded nozzles for screwing on the machine's water supply hoses.

Attaching shutoffs to supply lines. If the supply pipe stubouts are capped, turn off the water at the main house valve and drain the lines.

Flexible Tubing

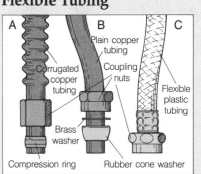

Fig. 26. Three types of flexible tubing include corrugated copper tubing with a compression coupling (A), plain copper tubing with a slip-joint coupling (B), and flexible plastic tubing with a coupling nut (C).

Then remove the caps (catch any remaining water in a bucket). If there are gaps between the supply stubout and the wall covering, hide them with an escutcheon plate.

Attach the appropriate shutoff valve for your stubout. Hand-tighten the connections; finish up with a pair of adjustable wrenches (use the same technique as shown in **Fig. 12** on page 175).

Flexible tubing. Also called flexible connectors, tubing comes in a range of sizes and with a variety of fittings—pick the one that fits both your shutoff valve and your fixture. (Several types of tubing are illustrated in **Fig. 26.**)

Flexible, chrome-plated copper tubing (corrugated or plain) is the standard material for supply tubing. Less durable but easier to use is flexible plastic tubing with threaded coupling nuts that attach to valves with either compression or slip-joint fittings.

When installing tubing, make sure it's well seated and not under stress: vibration and water pressure can loosen the connection and cause a leak.

Installing Two Types of Valves

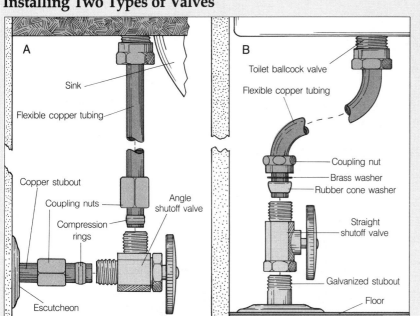

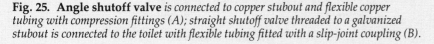

Fig. 25. Angle shutoff valve is connected to copper stubout and flexible copper tubing with compression fittings (A); straight shutoff valve threaded to a galvanized stubout is connected to the toilet with flexible tubing fitted with a slip-joint coupling (B).

Sinks

If your remodeling plans call for a new bathroom or kitchen sink, you'll find a wide array of sinks to choose from. On these pages, we give you an overview of the basic types and cover the fundamentals of removing and installing each type.

Replacing an old sink with a new one is a job you can do without advanced plumbing skills. But if you want to add a new sink or move one to a new location, you'll have to extend the water supply and drain-waste and vent lines. For help, see pages 177–180.

Choosing a sink

Sinks are available in many shapes, sizes, colors, materials, and styles. When you shop, be sure to consider function, durability, and maintenance, as well as aesthetic appeal.

Types of sinks. The four basic types are countertop, wall-hung, pedestal, and integral sink and countertop (see **Fig. 27**).

Countertop sinks are the most common; they fit into a hole cut in a counter or vanity top. Most kitchen sinks are countertop types. *Wall-hung* and *pedestal* bathroom sinks are often found in older homes, though contemporary-style pedestal sinks are increasingly popular today. Wall-hung units come with metal brackets, and sometimes legs, for support. Pedestal sinks, made from vitreous china, are supported on matching pedestal bases. *Integral sinks and countertops* are one-piece molded units that fasten to a vanity top.

Among the materials used for sinks are stainless steel, enameled cast iron, enameled steel, porcelain on steel, brass, and copper. Bathroom sinks may also be made from vitreous china; fiberglass-reinforced plastic, synthetic marble, or acrylic (for integral sink and countertop models); or pottery (for countertop types).

Sink compatibility. When you select your sink, be sure the holes in it will accommodate the type of faucet you plan to install (see page 186).

For example, a kitchen sink will normally have three holes for a simple faucet or four holes to provide an outlet for a sprayer, a hot water dispenser, or an air gap for a dishwasher. A bathroom sink designed for deck-mounted faucets may have no faucet holes at all. Also, the distances between the holes—4, 6, or 8 inches—determine which faucets can be used.

If you're replacing a countertop sink and you want to keep the existing countertop, carefully measure the hole and take the measurements with you when you shop. You may be able to widen the hole to accommodate a larger sink, but you probably won't be able to use a smaller one. Also, be sure the rim of the new sink is compatible with your countertop (see **Fig. 29**).

Preparing for installation

The first step is to disconnect the plumbing of any sink that must be removed. Before installing the new sink, it's usually best to install the new faucet (see page 186) and the sink flange or strainer.

Disconnecting the plumbing. The procedure for disconnecting the plumbing is basically the same for all sink types. If the sink faucet is mounted on the countertop and you don't plan to replace the faucet, it isn't necessary to disconnect the water supply lines. But if the faucet is connected to the sink, you do need to disconnect the lines.

Be sure to turn off the water at the sink shutoff valves or at the main valve before doing any work. Disconnect the supply lines at the shutoff valves, placing a bucket underneath; open the faucets to drain the lines. Then move the bucket under the trap and remove the trap by loosening the coupling nuts. Also disconnect the pop-up, if there is one.

Installing the sink flange or strainer. Kitchen sinks usually have strainers, as shown in **Fig. 35** on page 185; bath sinks have pop-ups and flanges. To install a flange or strainer body, run plumber's putty around the water outlet. Press the flange into the puttied outlet (see

Types of Sinks

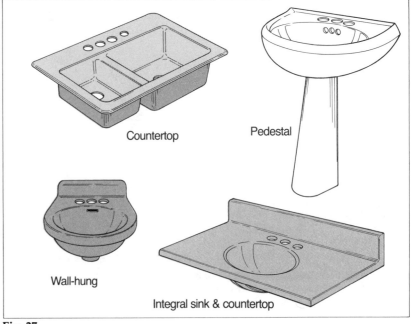

Countertop

Pedestal

Wall-hung

Integral sink & countertop

Fig. 27

Sink Flange Components

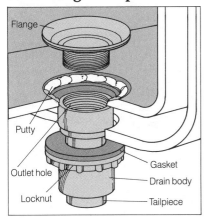

Flange

Putty

Outlet hole

Locknut

Gasket

Drain body

Tailpiece

Fig. 28. To attach the flange, *press it down into the puttied outlet hole and attach the connecting parts from below.*

Fig. 28) and attach the gasket, locknut, and drain body to the bottom of the flange. Add the tailpiece.

Installing a countertop sink

Countertop sinks, whether frame-rimmed, self-rimmed, or unrimmed, fit into a hole specially cut in a countertop. The basic types are shown in **Fig. 29.**

A *frame-rimmed* sink has a surrounding metal rim that holds the sink to the countertop; a *self-rimmed* sink has a molded overlap that sits on top of the finished countertop; an *unrimmed* sink may sit on top of the rough countertop, where it's then tiled in place, or it may be recessed beneath the countertop and held in place with metal mounting clamps.

Before you can install the sink, you'll need to remove the old sink, if there is one, or rough-in the plumbing for a new installation. To remove a self-rimmed sink, force it free from below or by gently prying from above. With frame-rimmed and unrimmed sinks, remove any clamps or lugs from below and lift the sink out. If the sink is tiled down, carefully chisel away the trim tiles one by one, using a soft-headed steel hammer and a cold chisel (be sure to protect your eyes from flying chips); then lift out the sink.

Making a sink cutout. For new installations, or if the old cutout is too small, you'll have to cut a hole in the countertop to fit the new sink. For a frame-rimmed sink, trace the bottom edge of the metal rim onto the exact spot where the sink will fit. Drill pilot holes in each corner and insert the blade of a saber saw into one of the holes to start the cutout. Protect plastic laminate countertops from scratches by covering the bottom of the saw with masking tape.

For unrimmed or self-rimmed sinks, the cutout is smaller than the lip of the sink. Use the sink's edge or the manufacturer's template, if provided, as a guide.

Mounting the sink. For a frame-rimmed sink, apply a bead of plumber's putty or caulk around the lip of the sink. Fasten the frame to the sink, using clamps or bendable tabs as provided by the manufacturer. Lay another bead of putty or caulk around the lip of the cutout and press the sink and frame into place. Fasten the frame from beneath with mounting lugs or clamps and smooth away excess putty on top.

A self-rimmed or unrimmed sink should also be embedded in a bead

of plumber's putty or caulk and anchored with mounting clamps, if provided. For a recessed sink, turning the countertop over, if possible, makes mounting the sink to the underside of the counter much easier.

Installing a wall-hung sink

A wall-hung sink is supported by a metal bracket mounted to a bracing board in the wall. If you're replacing an existing wall-hung sink, you may be able to use the old bracket and board.

To remove the old sink, turn off the water and disconnect the plumbing. Check under the sink for any bolts or mounting clips and remove them. Then simply lift the sink straight up.

For new installations, you'll need to remove a small section of the wall covering and install a new bracket. At the sink's proposed location, notch two studs to accommodate a 1 by 6 or 1 by 8 bracing board, as shown in **Fig. 30** on page 184. Nail or screw the bracing board to the studs and patch the wall covering (for help, see the chapter "Walls & Ceilings").

Countertop Sinks

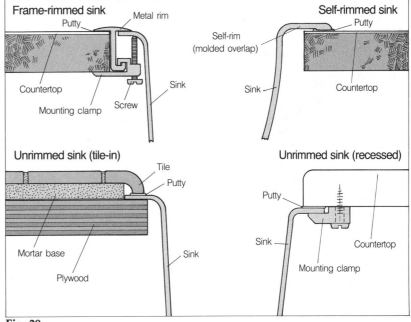

Frame-rimmed sink
Putty
Metal rim
Countertop
Mounting clamp
Screw
Sink

Self-rimmed sink
Putty
Self-rim (molded overlap)
Sink
Countertop

Unrimmed sink (tile-in)
Tile
Putty
Mortar base
Plywood
Sink

Unrimmed sink (recessed)
Putty
Sink
Countertop
Mounting clamp

Fig. 29

Next, using long woodscrews, fasten the mounting bracket to the bracing board at the desired height from the floor; check it with a carpenter's level. Refer to the manufacturer's instructions for attaching the sink to the bracket.

To help support the weight of the sink, you can insert adjustable legs into the holes under the front corners of the sink. Adjust the legs until the sink is level.

Seal the joint between the back of the sink and the wall with caulk.

Pedestal Sink

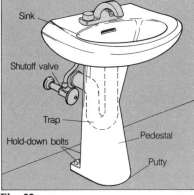

Fig. 33

Integral Sink & Countertop

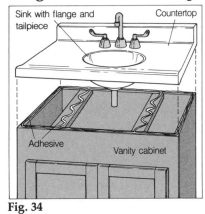

Fig. 34

Installing a pedestal sink

Most pedestal sinks are composed of two pieces—the sink and the pedestal, or base.

To remove an old sink and pedestal, turn off the water and disconnect the plumbing. If necessary, unbolt the pedestal from the floor (look for the hold-down bolts on the outside or inside of the pedestal). Unbolt the sink from the pedestal, if necessary, and then lift the sink free. Rock the pedestal to break any seal at the floor.

To install a new pedestal sink, position the pedestal with the sink on top in the desired location; check to be sure it's centered in front of the

drain stubout. Use the holes in the pedestal base to mark the locations of the hold-down bolts. Run a bead of plumber's putty or caulk around the bottom edge of the pedestal and bolt it in place.

Position the sink on the pedestal and, if required by the manufacturer, bolt the two together as directed.

Installing an integral sink & countertop

An integral sink and countertop unit is fastened with mounting clips and/or sealant to the top of a vanity.

To remove an old integral sink and countertop, first remove any mount-

ing clips or braces securing the unit from the bottom. Then lift off the entire unit. To break the seal between the countertop and the vanity, you may have to pry from the underside with a small pry bar or cut through the sealing material with a hot putty knife.

To install a new integral sink and countertop, cover the top edges of the vanity with an adhesive or sealant recommended by the manufacturer. Place the unit so it's centered on the vanity and flush with the back edge. Press along the edges to complete the seal and anchor the countertop with mounting clips, if provided. Caulk the joint between the wall and the countertop.

Installing a Wall-hung Sink

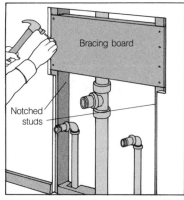

Fig. 30. Nail the bracing board *between two notched studs in the spot where you plan to mount the sink. Then patch the wall covering.*

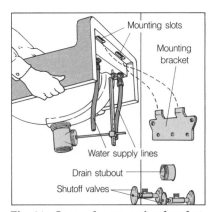

Fig. 31. Screw the mounting bracket *through the wall to the bracing board; then lower the sink onto the bracket and attach it as directed.*

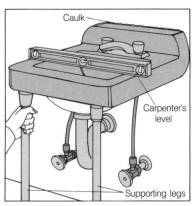

Fig. 32. Adjust the supporting legs, *if used, until the sink is level; then run a bead of caulk along the wall to seal the joint.*

Connecting the plumbing

Once you've installed your new sink and faucet, you're ready to connect the faucet to the water supply lines (see the instructions for faucet installation on page 186) and the sink to the drain lines.

Sink traps. The sink trap connects to the tailpiece on the flange or strainer body. At the other end, the trap connects to the drain stubout at the wall or floor (see **Fig. 35**). New traps are sold as complete units with all the necessary washers and threaded couplings to make the connections.

The two basic types are the S trap and the P trap, as shown in **Fig. 36.** The S trap is typically found in older homes. Since it exits through the floor, it can be a good remodeling choice where it's inconvenient to put the drain stubout in the wall. The P trap is more common. It comes in two forms—the one-piece fixed P trap and the swivel P trap, which can be adjusted from side to side. P traps may have a cleanout at the bottom of the curve.

Use a plastic sink trap where pipes are hidden; chrome-plated brass traps are for exposed pipes.

Connecting the trap. To attach a new swivel P trap, hand-tighten the coupling nuts that connect the elbow to the trap adapter and the trap to the sink tailpiece; use plumber's grease on the threads of the coupling nuts to ensure a watertight seal.

Sink Drain Elements

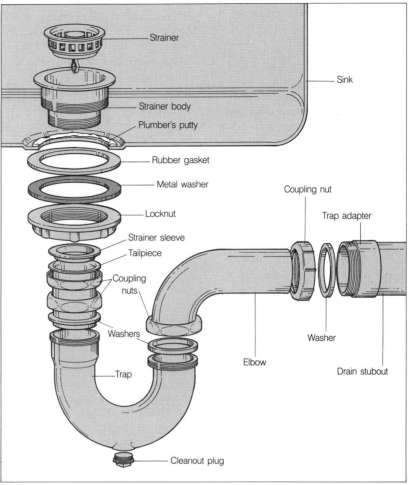

Fig. 35

Next, attach the trap to the elbow, aligning it carefully. Firmly tighten all the coupling nuts with a tape-wrapped wrench. Finally, attach the sink pop-up, if any (see page 186).

Testing your connections. Once the faucet is connected to the supply lines, turn on the shutoff valves, open the faucets, and check for leaks.

Types of Traps

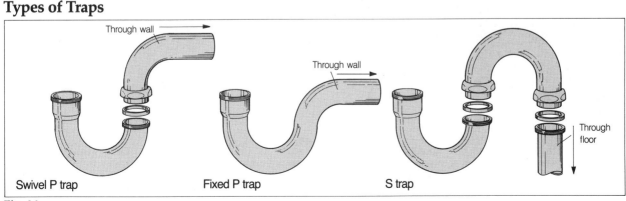

Fig. 36

Faucets

Whether you're replacing a worn-out faucet or selecting fittings for a new sink, shower, or bathtub, you'll have a wide choice of types and styles. This section explains how to remove and install deck-mounted faucets for sinks and wall-mounted fittings for bathtubs and showers.

Sink faucets

Most modern sink faucets are the deck-mounted type, seated at the back of the sink and secured from below. When shopping for a new faucet, you can choose between traditional compression faucets with separate hot and cold water handles (these use a washer) and an array of durable, single-handled washerless faucets, including valve, ball, disc, and cartridge types.

Faucet styles range from antique reproductions finished in gold or pewter to futuristic chrome compression models.

If possible, remove the old faucet and take it along with you when you buy a replacement. Choose a new unit that has clear installation instructions and readily available replacement parts. Make sure that the faucet's inlet shanks are spaced to fit the holes in your sink.

If you have an old wall-mounted faucet and are thinking of switching to a deck-mounted one, note that switching involves rerouting the supply pipes to shutoffs under the sink and then patching the wall. This may not be worth the effort unless you're already planning other remodeling changes.

Removing a deck-mounted faucet. First turn off the water at the shutoff valves under the sink and put a bucket under the water supply valves. If space under a sink is limited, use a basin wrench to remove both the coupling nuts attaching the flexible supply tubing to the valves and the locknuts on the faucet inlet shanks. Remove the sink spray, if any. Then lift the faucet out.

If you're working on a bathroom sink with a pop-up stopper assembly, disconnect it before removing the faucet. Disengage the pivot rod by unfastening the clevis screw and releasing the spring clip. Lift out the pop-up rod.

Installing a new faucet. It's often convenient to install the faucet before installing the sink itself. Most new faucets come with a rubber gasket on the bottom; if yours doesn't, apply plumber's putty to the base.

Set the faucet in position, inserting the inlet shanks and flexible supply tubing, if already attached, through the holes in the sink. Slip on washers, then tighten the locknuts onto the faucet inlet shanks with an adjustable wrench. (If you're working under an existing sink, use a basin wrench.) If your sink has a spray hose, attach it next.

For faucets without factory-installed flexible supply tubing, connect lengths of tubing to the inlet shanks of the faucet with coupling nuts, as shown in **Fig. 37**. Once the sink is installed, attach the tubing to the shutoff valves and install the sink and trap (see pages 181–185). Then turn on the shutoff valves and check for leaks. Connect a pop-up as shown in **Fig. 38**.

Bathtub & shower faucets

Faucets for bathtubs and showers are either compression models, usually

Installing a Deck-mounted Faucet

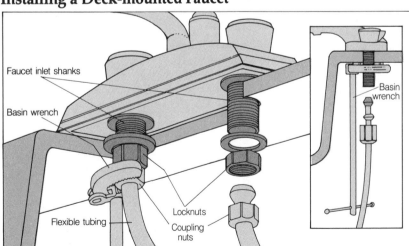

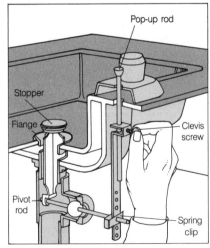

Fig. 37. To attach a deck-mounted faucet, *first use a wrench to tighten the locknuts on the faucet inlet shanks. A basin wrench (see inset) allows you to work in tight spaces. Flexible tubing connects the faucet inlet shanks to the water supply valves; make the connections with coupling nuts at both ends.*

Fig. 38. To attach a sink pop-up, *fasten the pop-up rod to the pop-up assembly, tightening the clevis screw so the stopper will seat properly in the drain.*

with separate hot and cold water handles, or washerless models, with a single lever or knob. Units for a tub-shower combination use a diverter valve to direct the water to either the shower head or the tub spout. Three common tub-shower faucet configurations are illustrated in **Fig. 39.**

Like sink faucets, tub-shower faucets come in a variety of decorative finishes. Choose one that's durable and easy to operate; it should also complement the decor of the bathroom. Regardless of the type, the body is mounted inside the wall, where it's connected directly to the water supply pipes.

You can either renovate an old faucet or replace it. If you just want to repair the faucet and it's in good condition, you may be able to buy new parts for it. But if the body is in poor condition or parts are unavailable,

you'll have to replace the entire faucet, which means tearing into the wall covering around the faucet.

The instructions below explain how to renovate or replace an old faucet, as well as how to add a new shower head.

Renovating a tub or shower faucet.
If you're basically satisfied with your present faucet, you can probably improve its looks and operation by replacing faucet parts, decorative trim, handles, or even the tub spout or shower head. To find the correct replacement parts, you may want to disassemble the old faucet and take the parts with you when you shop.

Before you start work, turn off the water at the main house valve or at the tub or shower shutoff valves, if there are any. (They may be hidden behind a panel on a wall or under the floor.)

Fig. 40 shows how typical compression and washerless faucets are assembled, but the methods vary with individual models. As you take your faucet apart, carefully note the parts and sequence of disassembly— you'll reverse your steps when you put it back together.

First remove faucet handles, trim, and stem parts; then remove the diverter (if necessary). Finally, take off the tub spout or shower head. Use a tape-wrapped pipe wrench to avoid marring finished surfaces.

Replacing a tub or shower faucet.
Replacing the complete faucet assembly usually involves cutting away the wall covering. You'll also have to remove the faucet body from the supply pipes with wrenches or a small propane torch.

Opening up the wall and then repairing the hole you've made can be

Tub & Shower Sets

Two Types of Tub & Shower Faucets

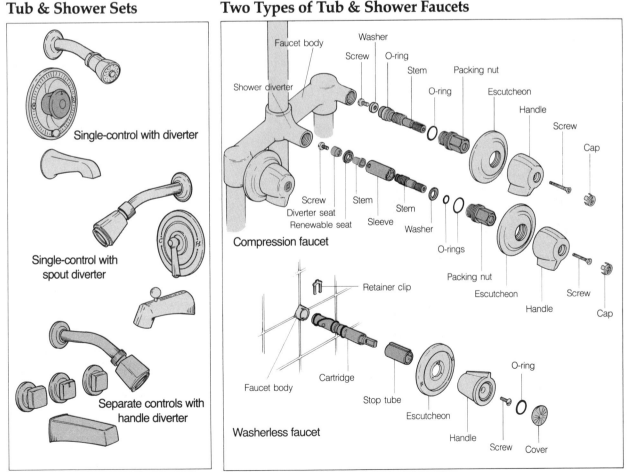

Fig. 39

Fig. 40

the biggest part of replacing a tub or shower faucet, especially if your wall is tiled. Look first to see if you have an access door on the back side of the faucet wall; if there is one, you won't need to open up the wall. Otherwise, consider cutting a hole behind the faucet in the wall of the adjacent room—it's a lot easier to patch wallboard than to replace tile.

If this isn't feasible or if you're planning to redo the walls anyway, you'll need to cut a hole in the wall around the faucet on the tub or shower side, as shown in **Fig. 41.** First, turn off the water supply at the tub shutoff valves or main shutoff valve. Plug the drain to avoid clogging it and use a drop cloth to protect the tub surface from scratches. Remove the handles, trim, spout, and shower head.

The faucet body is attached to the water supply lines with either threaded or soldered connections. Unscrew threaded connections by using one wrench on the supply pipe and another on the coupling nut, if any; unsolder (melt) copper connections with a propane torch.

If you're working from the back, cut through wall studs or blocks behind the faucet so you can pull the faucet out from behind, as shown in **Fig. 42.** Work carefully to avoid loosening tiles on the other side. Take the old faucet with you when you're shopping for a replacement so the new one will fit the existing holes.

If you can provide permanent access through a door or under the floor, you may want to add tub shutoff valves at this time.

To install a faucet body on threaded pipe fittings, apply pipe joint compound; then tighten the coupling nuts, if any, on the faucet bottom. If the faucet body must be soldered directly to copper pipes, remove the valve stems and diverter stems before soldering. (For soldering techniques, see pages 174–175.) Once you've made the connections, turn on the water and check for leaks.

The faucet body must be firmly anchored to the framing with plumber's tape or other hangers (see **Fig. 41**). If you've cut the framing to remove the old faucet from behind, reinforce the framing with a new 2 by 4, as shown in **Fig. 42.**

Make sure the body is the correct distance from the finished wall surface—check the manufacturer's specifications. Protect the faucet stems with tape as you repair the wall.

Removing a Tub or Shower Faucet

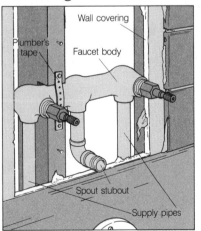

Fig. 41. To work from the tub side, *cut away the wall covering around the faucet body and unscrew or unsolder the connections to the supply pipes.*

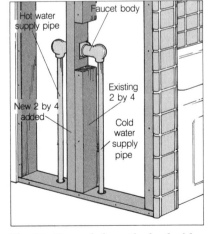

Fig. 42. To work from the back side, *cut away the wall covering and remove a section of the stud; later, add a 2 by 4 where framing was cut.*

A Tub & Shower Assembly

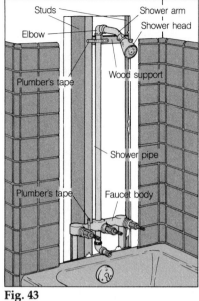

Fig. 43

Adding a shower head. To add a shower head above your old bathtub, you'll have to replace the old faucet with one equipped with a shower outlet and diverter valve. In addition, you'll have to install a shower pipe in the wall, as shown in **Fig. 43.**

If your tub surround is tiled, you'll have to remove the tile to add the shower pipe. (See page 99 for instructions.) Cut your access hole large enough to install the shower pipe. From the shower outlet on the faucet body, run a ½-inch pipe up the wall to the desired height and top it with an elbow. Nail a 2 by 4 wood support behind the elbow and anchor the pipe to it with plumber's tape.

To avoid scratching the shower arm while you're repairing the wall covering, thread a 6-inch galvanized nipple into the elbow in place of the shower arm. Finally, install the shower arm and shower head, using pipe joint compound on the male threads of the fittings.

Repairing the wall covering. To repair wallboard, see pages 92–94. If you need to replace ceramic tile, instructions for setting tile in adhesive appear on pages 99–101. Setting tile in mortar is a job for a professional.

DISHWASHER & GARBAGE DISPOSER HOOKUPS

In today's kitchens, dishwashers and garbage disposers have become almost standard equipment. To install them, you'll need to coordinate connections with your kitchen sink plumbing, as well as with your electrical system. Before installing either appliance, check your local codes for restrictions or special requirements.

Each manufacturer has specific installation instructions for these appliances. Here's a quick overview of general installation procedures.

Installing a dishwasher

Built-in dishwashers require a hot water supply connection, a drainpipe fitting, a venting hookup, and a 120-volt grounded receptacle or junction box. You may also need a separate 15- or 20-amp circuit; check the manufacturer's recommendations.

Supply pipe connections. To get hot water to the dishwasher, you can tap into the existing supply pipe under the sink by adding a tee, or you can replace the existing hot water shutoff with a special dual-outlet shutoff valve. (One outlet connects to the sink faucet, the other to the dishwasher.) The supply tubing for a dishwasher is normally ⅜-inch flexible copper tubing with compression fittings at each end (see page 181).

Drainpipe connections. The dishwasher drains through a flexible rubber drain hose into either the sink drain above the trap or the garbage disposer. For use with a sink drain, you'll need a special threaded waste tee fitting (see the inset drawing in **Fig. 44**).

Venting hookups. To prevent backup of waste water into the appliance, loop the drain hose up as high as the top of the dishwasher. Some codes may require an air gap to be installed at the sink or counter, as shown, to vent the drain line.

Installing a disposer

Disposers attach directly to the sink; their sink flange and mounting assembly replace the sink strainer. Normally, the drain elbow supplied with the disposer connects directly to the existing sink trap. In some cases, you may have to adjust an existing sink trap to fit the unit. For double sinks where there is only one drain stubout, some codes permit the sink drain and disposer outlet to be tied together with a one-directional flow tee (see **Fig. 44**).

Disposers require 120-volt, 20-amp electrical power. Depending on local codes, this can be provided by either direct wiring from a junction box or a plug-in receptacle operated by a switch on the countertop.

Plumbing for a Dishwasher & Disposer

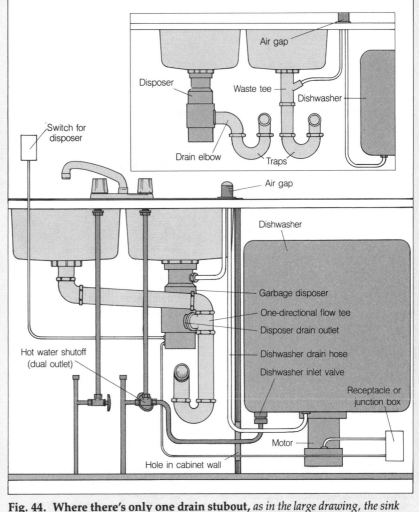

Fig. 44. Where there's only one drain stubout, *as in the large drawing, the sink drain and disposer can sometimes be tied together with a one-directional flow tee. The dishwasher drain hose either runs into the disposer or, as shown in the inset, is clamped to a waste tee below the sink drain.*

Showers

If you're installing a separate shower stall rather than a tub-shower combination, you have several choices of materials and installation techniques. Lightweight fiberglass units come either in panels, which can be easily set in place on top of a fiberglass or plastic base, or as a one-piece molded enclosure. The panel types are often easier to install inside existing walls; one-piece units may be too large to fit through doorways or windows.

Ceramic tile showers may be installed in one of two ways. Tiles set in a mortar bed are the most durable, but they usually require professional installation. To install ceramic tile yourself, you'll need to put in a fiberglass shower base, add a backing of water-resistant gypsum wallboard, and then apply the tile to the shower walls with adhesive.

A third type of shower stall—the metal type—is quickly fading from the plumbing scene. Though easy to install, such stalls are noisy when water splashes on them, and they may eventually rust out.

Replacing an old shower or adding a new one requires careful planning, as well as carpentry and plumbing skills. For information on extending supply and drain pipes and roughing-in new fixtures, see pages 177–180.

Removing a shower

Removing a shower is a three-step procedure: you disconnect the plumbing, then remove the wall covering, and finally remove the base. If you're altering the shower's dimensions, you may need to remove or relocate the plumbing and wall framing.

Disconnecting the plumbing.
Remove the shower door or rod and turn off the water supply at the fixture shutoff valves (sometimes accessible through an access door in an

adjoining hallway or closet) or at the main shutoff valve. Open the faucets to drain the pipes.

Remove the faucet handles and other trim parts, leaving the faucet stems. Remove the shower head with a tape-wrapped pipe wrench, as shown in **Fig. 45,** or an adjustable wrench. (If you're removing a one-piece unit or plan to install one, you'll also have to remove the faucet stems and shower arm.)

Unscrew and pry up the drain cover; then, with a pair of pliers and a small pry bar, unscrew the crosspiece (see **Fig. 46**). Plug the drain opening with a rag.

Removing the wall covering.
Most wall coverings can be removed with a pry bar. If the shower walls are metal or paneled, look for mounting screws or nails and pull

them out. For paneling, remove any molding or wallboard covering the panel flanges. Then pry off the panels, along with any backing. If you're removing a one-piece enclosure, you may have to cut it apart with a saber saw.

If your wall is made from tile that was set in mortar, it may have to be broken up with a sledgehammer. If the tile is set on wallboard with adhesive, use a cold chisel and soft-headed steel hammer to chip away small sections of tile and backing (protect your eyes with goggles); then insert a pry bar and remove the wall down to the framing, as shown in **Fig. 47**. Because tile may be difficult to remove, consider installing new tile over the old, providing it's in good condition.

Removing the base.
If the base is metal or fiberglass, simply remove

Removing a Shower

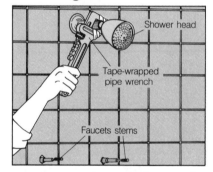

Fig. 45. Use a pipe wrench *wrapped with tape to remove the shower head after taking off the faucet parts.*

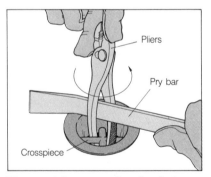

Fig. 46. After removing the drain cover, *use pliers and a pry bar to unscrew the crosspiece from the drain.*

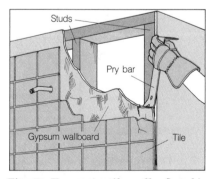

Fig. 47. To remove tile walls, *first chip away the tile; then pry off the tile and wallboard backing with a pry bar.*

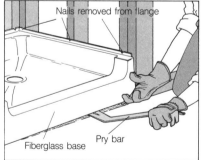

Fig. 48. To remove a fiberglass base, *take out any nails or screws holding the flange to the studs; then pry up the base.*

the nails or screws from the flange around the top and pry up the base with a pry bar (see **Fig. 48**).

If the base is tile on mortar, consider laying new tile over the old. Otherwise, the tile will have to be broken up with a sledgehammer.

Installing a shower

To install a shower in a new location or replace one with dimensions different from the old one, you'll first need to frame the walls. A typical installation is shown in **Fig. 49**.

Note that for comfort, showers should measure at least 32 inches square. If you're installing a one-piece fiberglass unit, you'll have to plan your wall framing and plumbing to match the manufacturer's dimensions. Using tile allows you more flexibility. (To frame a wall, see pages 86–87.)

Next, you'll need to rough-in supply and drain lines and install the faucet and pipe for the shower head (see pages 177–180). Some one-piece shower units and wall panels have preformed stubout holes. In this case, the plumbing must be carefully planned so that when the unit is tipped into place, the plumbing and holes will align.

Installing the base. Though it gives the most long-lasting results,

installing a watertight tiled base on a mortar bed is a complicated project best left to a professional. After plumbing in the drain and covering the wall with wallboard, the floor is waterproofed using hot tar, an elastomeric membrane, or a preformed metal or fiberglass pan. A wire-reinforced bed of mortar is then laid, followed by the tile.

A fiberglass or plastic base is the best choice for a do-it-yourselfer. To install one, position it over the drain outlet and connect the base to the drain by screwing in the crosspiece. Following the manufacturer's instructions, nail or screw the base to the wall framing (see **Fig. 50**).

Installing the wall covering. Getting precise alignment between the base and wall covering is crucial to a watertight shower.

To install water-resistant wallboard backing and tile, see pages 92–93 and 99–101. Note that the wallboard should be positioned ½ inch above the shower base; leave a ¼-inch gap between the tile and base for caulking, as shown in **Fig. 51**.

Fiberglass shower stalls, both panels and one-piece units, usually come with instructions. Some may require water-resistant wallboard backing. If you need to cut holes for the faucet stems and shower arm stubout, carefully mark their locations on one panel and, with the

Typical Shower Framing

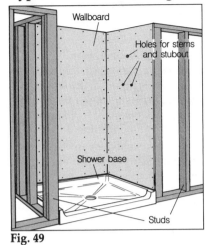

Fig. 49

panel on sawhorses, drill slightly oversized holes using a spade bit. Back the holes with scrap wood to prevent splintering.

If the base of your shower has grooves, fill the back one with caulking and install the back panel; repeat the procedure for the side panels (see **Fig. 52**), attaching them as recommended by the manufacturer.

Screw or nail the panel wall flanges to the wall framing and caulk between the flanges and wall covering. Install cover moldings over the nails or screws, if required.

With the wall covering or surround in place, attach the shower head, faucet handles, and trim.

Installing a Shower

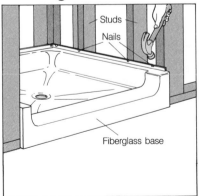

Fig. 50. To install a fiberglass base, *first attach the crosspiece; then nail or screw the flange to the studs.*

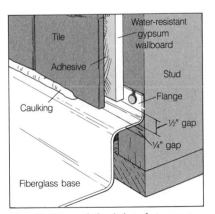

Fig. 51. To seal the joints *between a fiberglass base and tile walls, lay down a bead of caulking.*

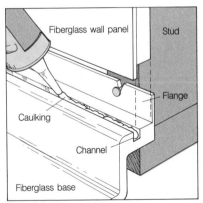

Fig. 52. To seal the joints *between a fiberglass base and fiberglass panels, fill the base's channel with caulking.*

Bathtubs

Tub choices range from heavy and durable porcelain-enameled cast iron or steel to lightweight fiberglass-reinforced plastic. Styles are diverse, including sunken, corner, soaking, and therapeutic whirlpool models.

Before you shop for any new tub, know the size of your existing fixture, if replacement is the issue. A standard tub is 5 feet long and 30 inches wide. Note that nonstandard tubs often have special framing, plumbing, and wall covering requirements.

The waterproof wall covering around a tub, often called a surround, can be made from ceramic tile or from fiberglass or ABS plastic panels. Also available are one-piece tub and surrounds made from fiberglass-reinforced plastic; however, these are not always a good choice for remodeling projects because they're often too large to fit through existing windows and doorways.

On these pages, you'll find instructions for removing an old bathtub and installing a new standard tub and its surrounding wall covering.

Removing a bathtub

There are three main steps to this job: disconnecting the plumbing, re-moving part or all of the wall covering, and removing the tub itself.

Disconnecting the plumbing. After turning off the water at the fixture shutoff valves (if accessible) or at the main shutoff, remove the faucet and diverter parts and the tub spout, as shown in **Fig. 53**. Next, unscrew the overflow cover and pull it and the pop-up stopper out (see **Fig. 54**).

If there's an access hole or access from the basement or crawlspace, use a pipe wrench to loosen the coupling nuts from behind the tub; disconnect the trap and waste tee, as shown in **Fig. 55**.

If you can't get access to the drain plumbing, you can work from inside the tub; disconnect the tub from the overflow pipe and drainpipe by unscrewing the overflow retainer flange and drain flange.

Removing the wall covering. You'll have to remove any wall covering that overlaps the tub flange or prevents the tub from being pried up and out. You may also have to remove some of the flooring in front of the tub, as shown in **Fig. 56**.

If the wall is tiled, you may only need to remove the bottom row of tiles and their backing; you can reinstall them (or new ones) after the new tub is in place. If the tile is set in mortar, it may have to be broken up with a sledgehammer. For tile set in adhesive on a backing of wallboard, use a cold chisel and soft-headed steel hammer to carefully remove each tile and the backing behind it. As you work, be sure to protect your eyes with safety goggles.

Since patching can be difficult, you may want to remove the entire wall surface; use a pry bar to pry the tile and its backing from the framing.

If the surround is fiberglass or plastic, pry the panel flanges off the studs with a pry bar; then pull the panels and any backing away.

If you plan to reuse the tub, protect its surface with plywood or a heavy drop cloth during demolition.

Removing the tub. Remove any nails or screws holding the lip, or flange, of the tub in place. If you're removing the tub in one piece, you'll need helpers and a doorway or window opening large enough to accommodate it. One method is to lift the tub up with a pry bar and slide two or three soaped wooden runners under it. Then you and your helpers can slide the tub out of the recess.

If you can't move a cast iron tub in one piece, you can break it up with a sledgehammer; be sure to protect your eyes.

To move a fiberglass tub, simply grasp it under the back of the flange and lift it up and out.

Installing a bathtub

Carefully inspect the subfloor for moisture damage or structural prob-

Disconnecting the Plumbing

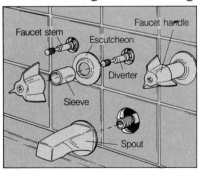

Fig. 53. **Remove the faucet** and di-verter parts and the tub spout, leaving the spout, faucet, and diverter stubouts.

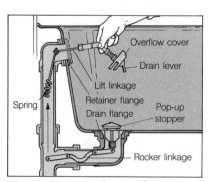

Fig. 54. **Unscrew the overflow cover** and pull out the drain. If necessary, remove the retainer and drain flanges.

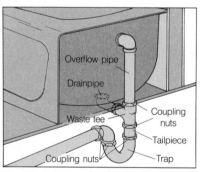

Fig. 55. **Loosen the coupling nuts** and remove the trap from underneath the tub; then disconnect the waste tee.

lems and correct them before installing the tub.

If you're replacing a tub with another of the exact same dimensions, it should fit the existing framing. But if you're installing a tub in a new location, you'll need to frame the space (see page 86) and extend the plumbing (see pages 177–180). To add a shower head, if required, turn to page 188.

Since a water-filled tub is very heavy, it may require additional floor framing—check your local building code.

Securing the tub. In order for the tub to drain properly and plumbing connections to be made easily, the tub must be carefully secured in a level position. To help support the edges, nail 1 by 4s or 2 by 4s to the studs at the exact height of the tub flange (see **Fig. 57**). Fiberglass and steel tub flanges may be anchored to the studs with nails or screws; cast iron tubs simply rest on the wood supports.

Before installing the tub, it's often a good idea to tip it on its side and attach the overflow pipe, drainpipe,

and waste tee. Then, with helpers, slide the tub near the wall and lift it so the flanges rest on the supports. Where access is limited and the trap is already plumbed in place, align the waste tee tailpiece so it will drop into the trap fitting when the tub is lowered into place.

Check the tub for level at both ends. If necessary, insert shims between the tub and the wall supports or floor to level it.

Note that if you're installing a one-piece tub and surround, you may have to remove protruding stubouts first.

Connecting the plumbing. Once the tub is secured, reconnect the trap to the overflow and drain assembly; then install the drain lever and stopper. Run water through the faucet and drain to check for leaks. If you find any, repair them now.

Install the faucet handles and trim, the tub spout, and, if required, the shower head only after you've installed the wall covering.

Replacing wall and floor coverings. The wall covering may be

ceramic tile, or fiberglass or plastic panels. Tile may be set in a mortar base or applied with adhesive. Though the former is the most durable choice, working with mortar is a job for a professional.

To install tile walls with adhesive, first apply a backing of water-resistant gypsum wallboard (see pages 92–93 for techniques); then you can lay the tile, following the instructions on pages 99–101. Be sure to protect the tub surface while you're working on the walls.

To install fiberglass or plastic panels, cover the wall studs with water-resistant wallboard, if required by the manufacturer. With the panels resting on sawhorses, mark and cut holes for the faucet stems and, if necessary, the shower arm stubout, using a spade bit and backing your holes with scrap wood to prevent splintering.

Install the panels according to the manufacturer's instructions. Seal the joint between the tub and the wall with tub and tile caulk.

For information on replacing the flooring, see the chapter "Floors & Stairs" beginning on page 114.

Removing & Installing a Bathtub

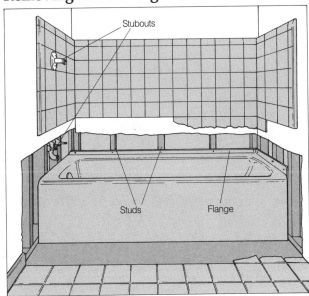

Fig. 56. To free the bathtub, *remove adjacent materials from the floor and bathtub surround, exposing the framing and subfloor. Then lift the tub out.*

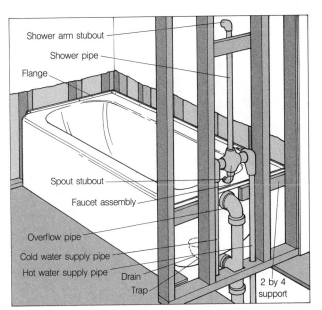

Fig. 57. Support the tub flanges *on horizontal supports nailed to studs. Check for level; then plumb the water supply and drain lines and add the necessary plumbing hardware.*

Toilets

Replacing an old toilet is a one-afternoon project you can tackle yourself. Installing a toilet in a new location, on the other hand, is more complicated because you have to extend drain-waste, vent, and supply lines to the new location.

When you plan where to place your new toilet, remember that compartments for toilets should be at least 30 inches wide; allow 21 inches of room in front of the toilet. In addition, the compartment or room in which the toilet is located must be ventilated by a window or fan. Note also that in any remodel involving the floor or walls, the toilet is the first fixture that's removed and the last that's installed.

Conventional toilets have a floor-mounted bowl with a tank mounted above. Older types may have the tank mounted on the wall. Models that reduce water use and noise are available as well.

Whatever your preference, choose a toilet that's ready to install. It should have the flush mechanism already in the tank and should come with mounting hardware for connecting the tank to the bowl.

The most crucial consideration is the toilet's roughing-in size—the distance from the finished wall to the center of the drainpipe. You can usually determine the roughing-in size of the old toilet without removing it—just measure from the wall to the center of the hold-down bolts at the rear of the toilet. The roughing-in size of the new toilet must not exceed this distance; if it does, the bowl won't fit.

Since local building codes may apply, you may want to check your code before you purchase a model.

Removing a toilet

Removing a toilet involves disconnecting the water supply and removing first the tank and then the bowl.

Disconnecting the water supply.
First, turn off the water at the toilet shutoff valve or at the main house shutoff. If the toilet doesn't have a shutoff valve, consider installing one (see page 181). Flush the toilet twice to drain the tank and bowl; then sponge out any remaining water. Unfasten the coupling nut on the supply line underneath the tank (see **Fig. 58**). Plan to replace the line if it's kinked or corroded.

Removing the tank.
On a floor-mounted toilet, loosen the mounting bolts that secure the tank to the rear of the bowl. Use a screwdriver to hold each mounting bolt inside the tank while you unscrew its nut with a wrench from below, as shown in **Fig. 59**.

If the tank is wall-mounted, use large slip-joint pliers or a spud wrench to disconnect the couplings on the pipe connecting the tank and bowl. Unscrew the hanger bolts holding the tank to the wall and pull the tank out.

Removing the bowl.
Pry the caps off the hold-down bolts and remove the nuts with a wrench. If they're rusted on, soak them with penetrating oil or cut them off with a hacksaw.

Gently rock the bowl to loosen it and lift it straight up (see **Fig. 60**). Stuff a rag into the drainpipe to keep noxious sewer gas out of the house and debris out of the opening.

Installing a toilet

Installing a replacement toilet involves preparing the floor flange and installing the wax gasket, setting the bowl and tank, and reconnecting the

Removing a Floor-mounted Toilet

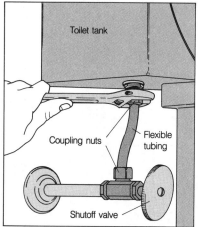

Fig. 58. Loosen the coupling nut *on the flexible tubing at the bottom of the tank.*

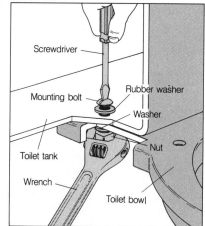

Fig. 59. Detach the tank *from the bowl by loosening the mounting bolts with a screwdriver and wrench.*

Fig. 60. Lift the bowl *straight up, keeping it level to avoid spilling any remaining water.*

plumbing. If you're adding a new toilet, you'll first have to extend and rough-in the plumbing (see pages 177–180).

Preparing the floor flange. This fitting connects the bowl to the floor and drainpipe. Using a putty knife, scrape off the wax gasket that formed the seal between the old bowl and the flange (see **Fig. 61**). Thoroughly scrape the flange so that the new ring will form a leakproof seal.

If the old flange is broken, replace it with a new one made from the same material as the existing drain-pipe. (Note: You may need to re-plumb the closet bend attached to the flange as well.) Remove the old hold-down bolts from the flange; then insert the new bolts through the flange, one on each side of the drainpipe.

Installing the wax gasket. Turn the toilet bowl over onto a cushioned surface. Slip the gasket over the horn (outlet) on the bottom of the bowl and apply plumber's putty around the bottom edge of the bowl, as shown in **Fig. 62**.

Note that if you're adding new flooring during your remodeling project, the floor level may be raised above the level of the existing floor flange. In this case, you can install an additional gasket over the first one to compensate for the built-up flooring.

Setting the toilet. Check that all rags have been removed from the drainpipe. Then gently lower the bowl over the hold-down bolts and flange. Press down firmly while twisting slightly to ensure a good seal. Check the bowl with a carpen-ter's level from side to side and from front to back (see **Fig. 63**); use copper or brass washers to shim underneath the bowl, if necessary. Be careful not to break the seal.

Hand-tighten the washers and nuts onto the hold-down bolts. You'll tighten them permanently after the tank is in place.

Attaching the tank. For a bowl-mounted tank, fit the rubber gasket over the end of the flush valve that projects through the bottom of the tank. Place the rubber tank cushion on the rear of the bowl. Position the tank on the bowl; then insert the mounting bolts through their holes in the bottom of the tank so they pass through the tank cushion and back of the bowl, as shown in **Fig. 64**. Gently and evenly tighten the nuts and washers.

Secure a wall-mounted tank to hanger brackets with bolts through the back of the tank. Assemble the large pipe that connects the bowl and tank and tighten the coupling nuts.

To secure the bowl to the floor, use a wrench to tighten the hold-down nuts; then cover the bolt ends with putty-filled caps.

Hooking up the water supply. If you're adding new flexible tubing, do so now. (For instructions, see page 181.) Tighten the coupling nut on the flexible tubing to the ball cock assembly on the tank. Turn on the water, flush the toilet, and check for leaks.

Installing a Floor-mounted Toilet

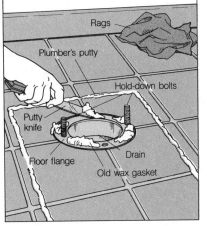

Fig. 61. Using a putty knife, *thor-oughly scrape the old wax gasket from the floor flange.*

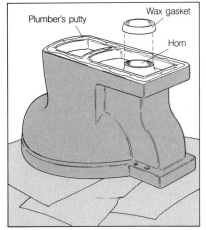

Fig. 62. Position the new wax gasket *over the toilet horn on the bottom of the bowl.*

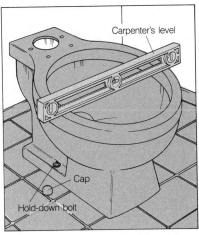

Fig. 63. Level the bowl, *shimming underneath with small copper or brass washers, if necessary.*

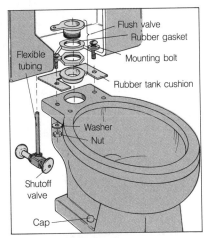

Fig. 64. Attach the tank *to the bowl with mounting bolts. Attach the tubing's coupling nut to the ball cock assembly.*

Gas Lines

Though the techniques for installing or extending gas lines are no more complicated than those for working with water supply lines, the flammability and explosiveness of gas require meticulous work. Some codes require all gas plumbing and venting to be done by a licensed professional.

This section describes the supply system, which brings gas to appliances, and the venting system, which exhausts the products of combustion from the house. Like plumbing pipes, gas pipes must be routed behind walls and under floors; for help, see pages 177–179.

The gas supply system

Normally, natural gas is supplied to your home by your gas company. In rural areas, propane, liquid propane, or butane may be supplied to a storage tank on your property. The gas is carried by supply pipes equipped with a series of shutoff valves (see **Fig. 65**).

Gas supply pipes. The most universally acceptable materials for gas lines are galvanized steel and black pipe (steel pipe without galvanizing). Either type is cut and joined in the same way as galvanized water supply pipe (see pages 175–176), though the pipe joint compound you use must be rated for your type of gas. In addition, all unions must be accessible, not enclosed inside walls or floors.

Local building codes specify pipe size according to type of gas, demand of appliances, and length of pipe.

Shutoff valves. You must install a shutoff valve at the gas meter or storage tank and at each gas-using appliance. Shutoffs must be rated for your type of gas and must be located in the same room as the appliance.

CAUTION: Before working on any gas line, you MUST be sure to shut off the gas supply upstream by turning the shutoff valve handle until it forms a right angle with the pipe.

An appliance is connected to the shutoff valve with either solid pipe or flexible tubing designed for gas. When using solid pipe connectors, add a union fitting (see page 178) that will allow you to disconnect the appliance. If you use corrugated flexible tubing, connect it to the shutoff valve with brass flare fittings.

Some gas shutoff valves come with a built-in flare fitting for the flexible appliance connector; others require you to thread the flare fitting to the valve or pipe. In either case, make sure the size of the fitting matches the coupling on the appliance connector.

Underground lines. To prevent corrosion, use only specially coated pipe rated for underground installation. Where the coating is removed for threading or fittings, you'll have to add a locally approved wrapping. Bury the pipe at least 12 inches deep on a solid base and don't run it underneath the house or under a concrete slab.

Testing. Before connecting any new gas-using appliances, you must inspect and test all gas lines before they're enclosed or connected to the meter.

To test extensive runs of new gas lines, cap off all the stubouts, screw on a pressure gauge, and pump up the line with 10 to 20 pounds of air pressure; maintain it for 15 minutes. Falling pressure indicates a leak. To find it, brush soapy water onto the fittings and look for telltale bubbles, as shown in **Fig. 66.** Try tightening the connection; disassemble and reconnect if necessary. Once your lines pass this rough inspection, connect them to the meter and to your appliances.

You can also use the soap suds technique to test your appliance connections and other small-scale alterations you've made to your gas lines, local codes permitting.

The venting system

To be safe, gas appliances must be carefully and correctly vented. Im-

The Gas Supply System

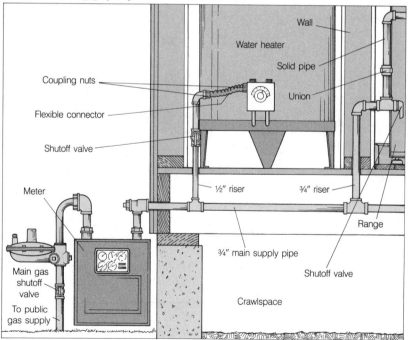

Fig. 65

Testing Gas Lines

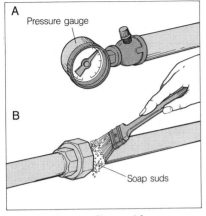

Fig. 66. Test gas lines *with a pressure gauge (A). If pressure falls, apply soapy water to fittings (B); bubbles indicate the leak.*

properly vented gas appliances can cause fires and deadly carbon monoxide poisoning. Below, you'll find general procedures for venting gas appliances. For specific appliances, follow the manufacturer's instructions.

What needs venting? All gas water heaters, space heaters, and furnaces require vent pipes, or flues, running directly from the appliance to the outside. Though it's desirable to vent the oven outlet of a gas range or to provide a vent hood, some codes may permit an unvented range if the kitchen is large and well ventilated. Clothes dryers are vented through a moisture vent, which should lead to an outside wall.

Types of flues. Flues come in two shapes: oval and round. Oval flues are designed to fit inside wall cavities, such as above wall heaters (see **Fig. 67**). Round flues are more difficult to conceal, but cheaper and easier to work with. (If you're adding a large flue, you may have to build a thickened wall or a special enclosure to hide it.)

When you're planning your venting system, make it as straight and vertical as possible to ensure a good draft. If you must angle or offset the flue, use adjustable elbows.

The flue typically connects directly to the flue collar or draft hood on the appliance. Water heaters and free-standing furnaces, however, can be vented through single-wall vent pipe running from the hood up to at least 6 inches from the wall or ceiling,

where it connects to the flue (see **Fig. 68**).

Normally, the flue must be kept at least 1 inch from any combustible material, and firestopping must be provided wherever a flue goes through a floor or ceiling. Check with your local building inspector for details. At the roof, the flue is flashed with a roof jack and topped with a vent cap.

Some gas heaters mounted on an exterior wall may be vented directly through the wall. The flue goes through a hole cut in the wall and attaches to a wall plate on the outside. The vent cap fits over the flue and attaches to the wall plate, as shown in **Fig. 69**.

Brick chimneys. Though common in older houses, unlined brick chimneys do not meet current standards for gas venting. You won't be allowed to vent new appliances into such a chimney.

If existing appliances are vented through the chimney, you may have to upgrade the old venting by adding new metal flues, or you may need to add a masonry liner inside your chimney.

Three Types of Venting

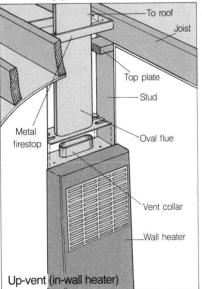

Fig. 67. Oval flue, *attached to a wall heater's flue collar, is designed to run inside a wall cavity.*

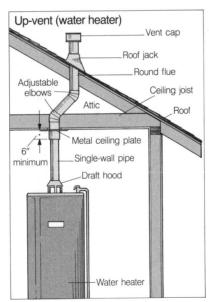

Fig. 68. Single-wall vent pipe *from a water heater connects to the flue at least 6 inches from the ceiling or wall.*

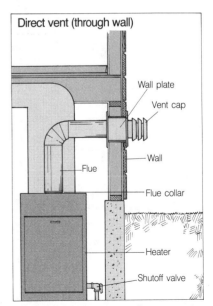

Fig. 69. Flue from a gas heater *vents directly to the outside; a vent cap fits over the end of the flue.*

Water Heaters

If your remodeling plans call for replacing a water heater, choose a model that's fuel-efficient (new units list their yearly cost rating) and just large enough to meet your household's hot water needs.

It's almost always preferable to stay with one that uses the same type of fuel as your old water heater. Though gas models are most efficient, the cost of running new gas supply lines may not be justified.

If you're relocating a heater, pick a location as close as possible to the main areas of hot water use in your house. Insulate the hot water supply lines and wrap the water heater with a fiberglass blanket for maximum efficiency.

In selecting the heater's new location, keep in mind that you must provide adequate clearance between a gas heater and any combustible materials, and you must have combustion air openings near the top and bottom of any enclosure. Heaters in a garage may have to be elevated. Check your local code for specific requirements.

Below you'll find instructions for removing an existing water heater and installing it or a new one in a different location.

Removing the old heater. Turn off the shutoff valve on the cold water supply line. Then disconnect the energy source: for an electric heater, turn off the power at the main panel and remove the electrical cable from the heater; for a gas unit, turn off the gas shutoff valve and unscrew the flexible connector or union. (If there is no union, cut the pipe with a hacksaw.)

Attach a garden hose to the drain outlet and drain the tank to the outside. Finally, disconnect the rest of the plumbing: temperature and pressure relief valve, hot and cold water lines, draft hood, and flue. Using a dolly or a helper, remove the tank.

Relocating a heater. To do this, you'll have to rough-in a cold water supply pipe and a hot water outlet, then add either a gas line or an electrical power cable. For help with the plumbing, see pages 177–179; for information on electrical wiring, see the chapter "Electrical Basics" beginning on page 142. You'll also have to add a new flue if you're installing a gas heater.

Install a shutoff valve on the cold water supply pipe. Then use flexible connectors or unions to hook up the water and gas lines. The water supply connectors simply thread onto the ¾-inch water pipe and bend as needed to make the hookup. To make any necessary gas connections, see page 196.

Screw a new temperature and pressure relief valve into its opening, if it's not already attached, and connect the overflow pipe to it. All water heaters need this safety valve; if there's no outlet for the relief valve, attach it to the hot water outlet (see the inset drawing in **Fig. 70**). Add the draft hood and flue, as shown in **Fig. 68** on page 197. If you live in an earthquake area, it's wise to strap the tank to the house framing with pipe straps.

With the plumbing connected, turn on the water and, if applicable, the gas and check for leaks. (To learn how to check for gas leaks, see page 196.) As the tank fills, open a hot water tap to bleed air out of the lines. Test the temperature and pressure relief valve by squeezing its lever.

Activating the heater. For electric heaters, connect the cable from the power source to the heater and turn on the power at the main panel. If yours is a gas heater, light the pilot, following the manufacturer's instructions. Adjust the temperature setting as desired.

A Typical Gas Water Heater

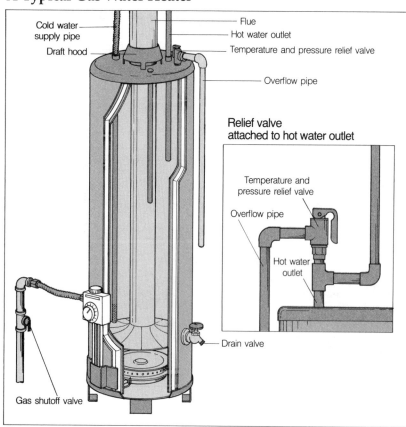

Cold water supply pipe
Draft hood
Flue
Hot water outlet
Temperature and pressure relief valve
Overflow pipe

Relief valve attached to hot water outlet

Temperature and pressure relief valve
Overflow pipe
Hot water outlet

Drain valve

Gas shutoff valve

Fig. 70

Warming Up with a Wood Stove

Adding a wood stove to your home has both aesthetic and practical advantages: a wood stove can create a cozy atmosphere as well as effectively supplement your home's main heating system. With proper planning, wood stoves can even heat an entire house.

On this page, we review the procedures for installing a stove and its hearth and chimney or flue; for more details, see the *Sunset* book *Homeowner's Guide to Wood Stoves*.

Though many styles are available, modern airtight stoves are generally the most efficient choices. Pick a model that's rated to heat your size living area—a stove that's too large will burn inefficiently. To heat several rooms, place the stove in a central location where openings between rooms allow the free flow of warm air. A stove located near a stairwell can help heat upstairs rooms, and ducts can help circulate air to remote areas of the house.

Installing the stove

Careful installation is essential for fire safety. The main consideration is the distance between the stove-chimney unit and any combustible building materials. Note the standard minimum clearances shown in **Fig. 71** and consult the manufacturer's installation recommendations, as well as your local building code.

The hearth and walls around the stove are exposed to the most direct radiant heat from the stove. By providing additional heat protection, you can move the stove closer to the walls and floor and still maintain adequate clearance.

Protective hearth materials are commonly 28-gauge steel over ¼-inch insulating stove board or 1½-inch-thick stone, concrete, brick, or ceramic tile. Bricks or tiles must have mortared joints to prevent hot embers from falling between them.

The walls can be protected with 28-gauge sheet metal or by mortared brick, separated from the wall by a 1-inch ventilation space.

Installing the flue

Typically, a single-wall stove pipe runs from the stove to where the flue first penetrates a wall or ceiling. From this point on, the flue must be a specially insulated metal pipe or a lined masonry chimney.

When planning flue location, remember that single-wall stove pipe must be at least 18 inches from any combustible materials. Insulated pipe will have a manufacturer-suggested clearance—usually 1 to 2 inches from combustibles.

At the ceiling, a metal ceiling support unit accepts the single-wall stove pipe and supports the rest of the flue. Blocking between ceiling joists boxes in the support unit. On the roof, the flue is flashed with a roof jack and topped with a vent cap. The chimney must extend at least 2 feet higher than any part of the house that comes within 10 feet of it.

You can also route a metal flue up an exterior wall, as shown in the inset in **Fig. 71.** Run the flue horizontally through a special metal wall thimble and into an insulated tee. Support the vertical pipe as shown.

Stoves can also be vented into masonry chimneys. The chimney must have a masonry liner and must be in good condition. The stove pipe can enter the chimney either through a fireclay or metal thimble inserted through the masonry, or through a sheet metal plate that replaces the fireplace damper.

A Typical Wood Stove & Flue

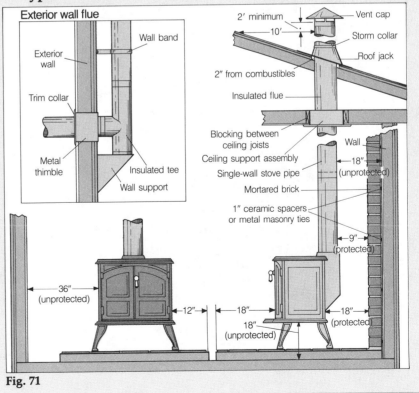

Exterior wall flue — Wall band — Exterior wall — Trim collar — Metal thimble — Insulated tee — Wall support

2' minimum — Vent cap — 10' — Storm collar — Roof jack — 2" from combustibles — Insulated flue — Blocking between ceiling joists — Ceiling support assembly — Single-wall stove pipe — Mortared brick — 1" ceramic spacers or metal masonry ties — Wall — 18" (unprotected) — 9" (protected) — 18" (protected) — 18" (unprotected)

36" (unprotected) — 12"

Fig. 71

Hydronic Heating Systems

Extending your hot water heating system can be an efficient way to heat new space created by remodeling. To determine whether expansion is right for your situation, you'll need to understand how your system operates, evaluate its capacity to heat the new space, and finally, decide how to do the work.

If you find that you need to add an entirely new system or make major changes, call in a professional heat-ing contractor. But installing or moving a few convectors or radiators is a relatively simple job that you can probably tackle yourself. Keep in mind, however, that in addition to doing the plumbing work, you may need to open up walls, floors, and/or ceilings to route pipes.

Before you can make any changes, you'll need to evaluate your present system. Because any alteration you make will affect the whole system's performance, you may want to get the advice of a professional.

If you find your system can handle the new convectors you want to add, proceed as outlined below. But if the heating demand for your new space is more than your current system can supply, you'll have to either add a higher capacity boiler or provide a new, separate heating system, such as a space heater or room heater.

Before you assume your old system isn't up to the job, make sure it's working to capacity—you may get increased performance by replacing radiators with more efficient modern convectors or by repairing existing problems. (For troubleshooting and maintenance tips, see the *Sunset* book *Home Repair Handbook.*)

Types of systems

Though there are several distinct types of hot water heating systems, all operate in the same general way: water heated in a boiler travels through a network of pipes to the heat distributors (usually old-style radiators or more modern convectors) where the heat is radiated into the rooms. The cooled water then returns to the boiler through a return pipe.

Gravity systems. In older homes, the movement of water in a hot water heating system may be controlled by gravity—warmer, lighter water rises and takes the place of heavier, cooler water. These systems are relatively inefficient, distributing heat slowly.

Hydronic systems. Modern systems, called forced hot water or hydronic systems, use a pump to force heated water through the pipes. The rapid distribution of hot water to the convectors makes these systems much more efficient than the gravity type.

Hydronic systems use either a single pipe or two pipes to circulate the water. In a *one-pipe* system, the hot water travels from the boiler and circulates through the convectors; then it re-enters the main pipe and returns to the boiler. The disadvantage of this system is that the water becomes progressively cooler at each convector; the last convector gets much cooler water than the first. This imbalance is even greater in *series loop* systems, where all the water flows sequentially through each convector.

A Two-pipe Hydronic System

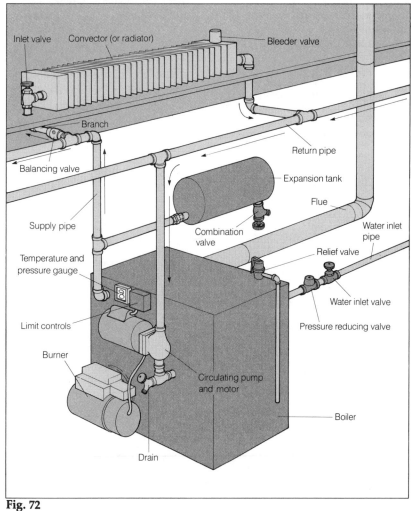

Inlet valve • Convector (or radiator) • Bleeder valve • Branch • Return pipe • Balancing valve • Expansion tank • Supply pipe • Flue • Combination valve • Water inlet pipe • Temperature and pressure gauge • Relief valve • Limit controls • Water inlet valve • Burner • Pressure reducing valve • Circulating pump and motor • Boiler • Drain

Fig. 72

In a *two-pipe* system, as shown in **Fig. 72**, the heat is more evenly distributed. One pipe, the supply pipe, always supplies hot water to the convectors, while the second pipe, the return pipe, sends the cooled water from each convector back to the boiler.

All systems have an expansion tank, usually mounted above the boiler, which contains air and water. The air acts as a cushion to maintain even water pressure in the system. A thermostat controls the pump and boiler.

Making changes

Adding a convector is a fairly straightforward plumbing project. To minimize the effect on your present system, choose a location for the convector that's close to the main hot water lines. You'll need to plumb and mount the new convector and then rebalance the system.

Adding a new convector. Most existing piping for hot water heating systems is galvanized, but most convector piping is copper. You can usually use either, though some local codes ban copper pipe because min-

eral deposits can clog it. To extend copper or galvanized pipe, see pages 174–176. If you must join copper pipe to galvanized, be sure to use a dielectric union, as described on page 178.

Before cutting into the lines, turn off the boiler, let the system cool, and drain the lines. Note the direction of the flow of water in the system—you'll put an inlet valve on the supply side of the convector and a bleeder valve on the return side, as shown in **Fig. 72** (except in series loop systems, which need no valves).

The plumbing for a new convector is simple—you tap into the existing supply line or lines by adding new tees or elbows; then you run pipes to the new location (see pages 177–179).

Depending on the type of system you have, you'll vary the procedure. For a one-pipe system, put a special venturi tee where the return riser meets the main line, as shown in **Fig. 73**. This tee keeps hot water moving through both the new convector loop and the main line. For a series loop, cut out the old pipe and route the water through the new convector (see **Fig. 74**).

Finally, for a two-pipe system, cut into both the supply and return

pipes and install tees and risers (see **Fig. 75**).

When the plumbing connections are completed, mount the convector to the wall or floor, turn on the water pressure (open the valve) to repressurize the system, and bleed out the excess air. Last, check for leaks.

Replacing a radiator with a new convector. Sometimes, you can connect a new convector to the risers of an old radiator you want to replace. If the size or placement of the risers is incompatible with the new convector, you'll need to replace or reposition the risers.

Balancing the system. Any alteration you make will change the system's balance. For example, if you replace a steel radiator with a copper convector, you may find that the convector is too hot and the rest of the radiators are too cool.

To re-establish the balance, gradually open or close the inlet valve on the affected convector or the balancing valve on the supply riser (see **Fig. 75**).

Another method is to install thermostatically controlled valves on loops supplying one or more convectors.

Three Hydronic Systems: Adding a Convector

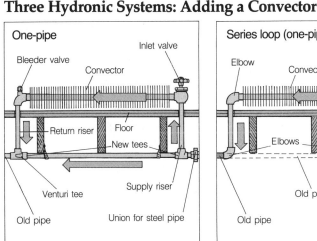

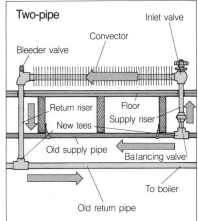

Fig. 73. For a one-pipe system, *cut the old pipe and connect the new convector with new risers, tees, and elbows. Use a venture tee on the return riser.*

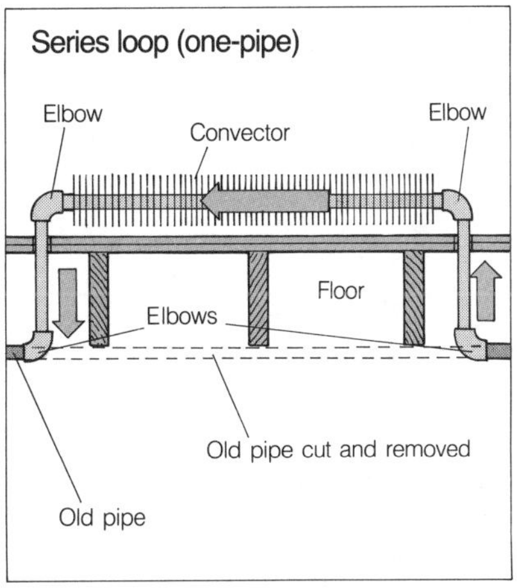

Fig. 74. For a series loop system, *cut out the old pipe, add risers and elbows, and route water through the new convector. No valves are needed.*

Fig. 75. For a two-pipe system, *cut both the supply and return pipes and connect the convector with new tees and risers.*

Forced Warm Air Heating Systems

Low installation cost, fast heat delivery, and reliability make forced warm air heating systems a popular choice. An extra advantage is that air conditioning can be added easily.

If your present system has enough reserve capacity and if the ductwork can be easily run to new areas, extending an existing forced warm air heating system can heat new space created by remodeling. Adding a new register and its branch duct requires only simple carpentry and sheet metal skills, as outlined on these pages. Consult a professional, however, if you think major changes are necessary.

You first need to analyze your present system to see if it can handle the additional heating load. Forced warm air systems are sized according to the total heated volume of the house and the total size and length of the ductwork. To heat large additional spaces, you may have to install a bigger furnace (a job for a professional); for smaller spaces, you may be able to get by with increasing the blower speed and keeping up a careful maintenance routine. (For maintenance procedures, see the *Sunset* book *Home Repair Handbook*.)

If you think your present system can handle new duct runs, remember that each alteration you make will affect the overall functioning and balance of your system. Because of this, you may want to call in a professional heating contractor to help you plan changes, even if you're going to do the work yourself.

To get the most out of your current system, plan to keep any new duct runs short—long runs put a greater demand on your furnace.

Types of systems

It's important to know what type of forced warm air system you have before you begin to plan an extension. In the *radial* system, illustrated in **Fig. 76,** all the duct runs begin at the warm air plenum and radiate out to the rooms of the house. *Extended plenum* systems (see inset drawing) have a large main duct from which the smaller branch ducts emerge. *Perimeter loop* systems run a continuous duct loop around the entire house.

Extending ductwork

Once you've evaluated your system, you'll have to decide how and where to run the new ducts. You must choose a convenient tie-in point, plan how to route the ducts through the house, and do the actual work of cutting and fitting the ductwork and installing the registers. Finally, you'll need to balance the system.

Tying in and routing the ducts. Where you tie in depends on the type of system you have. With a radial system, start new runs at the main warm air plenum. With extended plenum and perimeter loop systems, tie into the main duct as close as possible to where you want the new register.

Finding a path through your house for new ducts can be a challenge. If possible, run ducts through an attic or crawlspace, rather than opening up existing walls.

Ductwork materials. Duct parts, made from galvanized sheet metal, are standardized and designed to fit together easily. Bare, round ducts may come with open seams that need to be fitted together. Rectangular ducts are designed to fit between studs inside standard walls. Transition fittings allow you to change from round to square ducts,

A Typical Forced Warm Air System

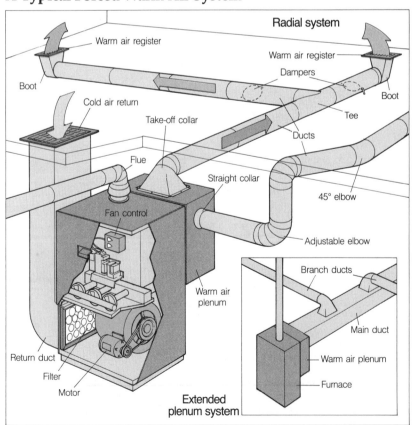

Radial system

Warm air register · Boot · Cold air return · Take-off collar · Flue · Fan control · Return duct · Filter · Motor · Warm air plenum

Warm air register · Dampers · Boot · Tee · Ducts · 45° elbow · Adjustable elbow · Straight collar

Branch ducts · Main duct · Warm air plenum · Furnace · Extended plenum system

Fig. 76

if necessary. To turn corners, use fixed-angle or adjustable elbows. If the planned route is particularly twisted, you can use special flexible round ducts.

Most duct runs begin with a fitting called a collar. A straight collar connects a duct directly to a plenum; a take-off collar has a flexible elbow that allows you to start a new run in almost any direction.

Each new branch duct should end in an outlet called a boot, which accepts a wall, ceiling, or floor register.

To work with duct parts, you'll need tin snips to cut the metal and duct tape for joining sections. An electric drill and screwdriver bit will enable you to connect ductwork and supports with sheet metal screws. Protect your hands with gloves as you work.

Doing the work. To install a collar, cut a hole the exact size of the collar in the plenum. Insert the collar, mounting tabs first, and then simply bend the tabs over inside the plenum, as shown in **Fig. 77.** Anchor the collar with sheet metal screws as necessary.

Once you've installed the collar, run the ducts, using any elbows or flexible sections necessary to follow your route. Join sections with sheet metal screws and duct tape. The section of duct that contains the damper (shown in **Fig. 78**) is usually—but not always—installed at the beginning of a duct run (see below).

On some systems, you may be able to add a short duct run by inserting a tee or wye fitting into an existing section of ductwork. To do so, you'll have to disconnect the existing ducts and insert the new fitting.

Cut a hole in the floor or wall for each new register, positioning the hole to avoid framing members. Insert the boot into the hole and fasten it to the subfloor or framing. Run the ductwork to the boot, supporting it with metal hangers, and install the register (see **Figs. 79** and **80**).

Balancing the system with dampers. At the beginning of each

new branch of your system, it's best to install a damper. This device can be adjusted to limit the flow of air and thus balance the flow of heat throughout the house. To install a damper inside a section of duct, punch holes in the sides of the duct, using a metal punch or electric drill. Then insert the pivot pins that come with the damper and position the damper in the duct.

If regular access to the dampers is difficult (such as in a cramped, dusty crawlspace), you can use register

dampers to balance the heating system; however, this is a less efficient method.

Individual branches, rooms, or even separate sections of a house can be automatically balanced by installing thermostats and thermostatically controlled dampers.

Once the dampers are installed, turn on the heat and adjust all the dampers room by room until temperatures are balanced. Wait half an hour after each adjustment before rechecking or readjusting.

Installing a New Branch Duct & Register

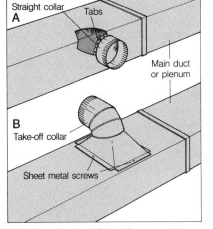

Fig. 77. **A straight collar** connects ductwork directly to the warm air plenum (A); a take-off collar allows for an immediate change in direction (B).

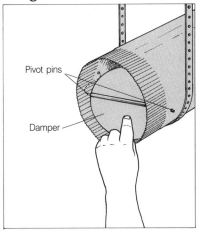

Fig. 78. **To install a damper** in a branch duct, punch holes in the duct section's sides, insert the pivot pins, and position the damper. Attach the adjacent duct.

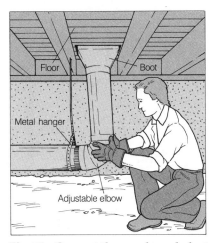

Fig. 79. **Connect the new branch duct** to a boot at the spot where you've cut the hole for the register. Support the ductwork with metal hangers.

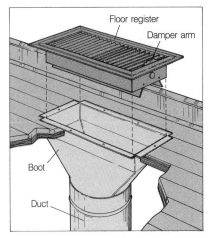

Fig. 80. **Insert the register** into the boot and screw it to the floor, if required. Use the damper arm to adjust and direct the flow of heat.

Incorporating solar design into your remodeling plans can help you reap substantial energy savings *and* create a pleasant, sun-warmed environment in your home. Solar remodeling options encompass everything from the simple addition of glazing on the house's sunny south side to a complete solar retrofit of your house.

On these pages, we explain solar space- and water-heating options and how they work. For more diverse solar heating strategies, see the *Sunset* book *Solar Remodeling*.

Solar heating

To work efficiently, a solar heating system must perform four distinct functions: *collection* of the sun's energy, *storage* of that energy as heat, *distribution* of the heat, and *retention* of the heat on cloudy days and at night.

Collection. Usually, the collection element is some sort of south-facing glazing that admits the sun's rays. As the sun's radiation penetrates the glazing, the surfaces inside absorb the radiation, become warm, and emit long-wave radiation, which doesn't easily escape back through the glass. This heat-trapping phenomenon is known as the *greenhouse effect*.

One way to make a solar collector part of your remodel is to simply add glazing area—windows, glass doors, and skylights—on the sunny sides of the house; in this case, the house itself becomes a solar collector. Another popular option is to add a glazed sunspace, such as the attached one shown in **Fig. 81.** More complex solutions involve putting specialized solar collectors on the roof or walls to heat air or water, which is then distributed throughout the house (see **Figs. 84** and **85**).

Remember that solar collectors must face the sun. If your house is on a shady site, you might consider building up or out to gain a sunny southern exposure.

Storage. Once captured, the heat from the sun must be absorbed and radiated back into the house during the cool hours, usually by means of a *thermal storage mass*—either a dense building material, such as masonry, or a "water wall."

Storage can be accomplished either by the "direct" or "indirect" gain approach. Sunlight directly warming the house's interior is called a direct gain system. When you're remodeling, it's often easiest to use the direct gain approach to take advantage of your home's existing features. For example, if you already have south-facing glazing, consider adding a thermal mass, such as a brick or ceramic tile floor or an extra-thick plaster wall, where the sun will shine on it (see **Fig. 82**).

Another approach to thermal mass is the thermal storage wall—an indirect gain system. One example, the Trombe wall (shown in **Fig. 83**), puts a masonry wall between south-facing windows and the interior of the house. The wall absorbs the sun's heat and then radiates it into the house's living space. Small vents in the top and bottom of the wall help circulate air.

Another variation of the thermal wall is the water wall, where containers of water are placed in the house

Three Passive Systems

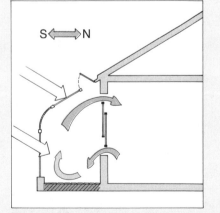

Fig. 81. In an attached sunspace, *sun heats the space directly. The adjacent area is heated by convection through openings in the house wall.*

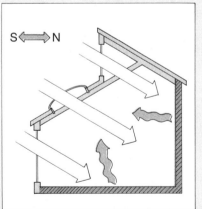

Fig. 82. South-facing space *is heated directly by the sun; the brick floor and wall serve as a thermal storage mass in this direct gain system.*

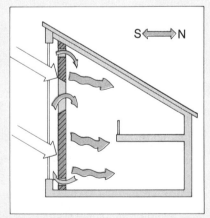

Fig. 83. Sun-heated Trombe wall *warms the air between the wall and the glazing; open vents allow the air to circulate.*

directly behind south-facing windows. Note that adding a heavy Trombe wall or water wall to a frame house may require structural reinforcement.

In some cases, the thermal mass can be located away from the sun. Here, a heat storage tank (for liquid systems) or a bin of rocks (for air systems) stores the heat. This approach requires an electrically powered heat-distribution system (see below).

Distribution. When the solar collector is adjacent to the room being heated or the room itself is a solar collector (as in a direct gain system), heat distribution is no problem. The thermal mass radiates heat directly into the room, and the room's air is heated as it flows around the thermal mass in small convection currents. This type of system, called passive, can be used to heat several rooms where the air flow between rooms is carefully planned.

Active systems, in contrast, use mechanical means to distribute the heat, often relying on extensive ductwork, fans, and pumps. In between fully passive and active systems is the hybrid system, which uses small fans and limited ductwork to improve the heat distribution of a basically passive system.

Retention. The heat that flows into a solar collector on a sunny day can flow out again at night all too easily. Some sort of insulation must be used to prevent heat loss.

In mild climates, installing double-glazed windows may be adequate protection against nighttime heat loss. In more severe climates, you may want to use triple glazing.

Other techniques include adding insulating curtains or shutters that close at night or, in the case of solar collectors mounted on the roof, shutting off the flow of water or air to them when temperatures drop. Any

solar remodeling plan should also include whole-house insulation and weather stripping.

Solar hot water
Domestic water heating is the most cost-efficient application of solar energy. Most systems will provide half to three-quarters of a family's need for hot water.

To add solar to your present hot water system, you'll have to add a collector (usually mounted on a south-facing roof) and find room for a larger water heater or additional water storage tank. Also, you'll need to run new insulated pipes through the house from the collector to the new tank. For active systems, you may have to add new electrical wiring to drive a pump and thermostatic controls.

Kits that supply a set of matched components are available; you may be able to install these yourself if you have plumbing and wiring skills.

Solar Heating: Two Active Systems

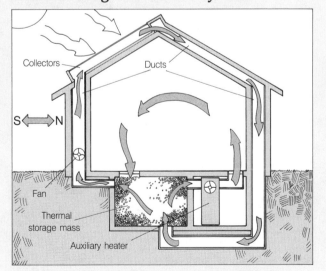

Fig. 84. In an active solar space-heating system, *fans circulate air heated in the collectors and stored in the thermal mass. An auxiliary heater warms the house if the heat in the storage mass becomes depleted.*

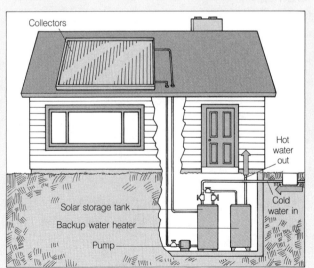

Fig. 85. In an active solar water-heating system, *a pump circulates the heat-transfer medium from the collectors to the storage tank and back. A thermostat turns the pump on when the collectors are warmer than the water in the tank.*

Index